Second Edition

COUNTDOWN TO A
New Library
MANAGING THE BUILDING PROJECT

Jeannette Woodward

AMERICAN LIBRARY ASSOCIATION

Chicago   2010

Jeannette Woodward is a principal of Wind River Library and Nonprofit Consulting. After a career in academic library administration, most recently as assistant director of the David Adamany Library at Wayne State University, she began a second career in public libraries as the director of the Fremont County Library System in the foothills of the Wind River Mountains of Wyoming. Woodward is the author of several books, including *Creating the Customer-Driven Academic Library* (2009), *What Every Librarian Should Know about Electronic Privacy* (2007), *Creating the Customer-Driven Library* (2005), *Nonprofit Essentials* (2006), and *Countdown to a New Library* (1st ed., 2000). She holds a master's degree in library and information science from Rutgers University, with doctoral study at the University of Texas at Austin.

While extensive effort has gone into ensuring the reliability of information appearing in this book, the publisher makes no warranty, express or implied, on the accuracy or reliability of the information, and does not assume and hereby disclaims any liability to any person for any loss or damage caused by errors or omissions in this publication.

The paper used in this publication meets the minimum requirements of American National Standard for Information Sciences—Permanence of Paper for Printed Library Materials, ANSI Z39.48-1992. ♾

Library of Congress Cataloging-in-Publication Data
  Woodward, Jeannette A.
    Countdown to a new library : managing the building project / Jeannette
  Woodward. — 2nd ed.
       p.   cm.
    Includes bibliographical references and index.
    ISBN 978-0-8389-1012-2 (alk. paper)
    1. Library buildings—United States—Design and construction. I. Title.
    Z679.2.U54W66 2010
    022'.3—dc22   2009045796

ISBN-13: 978-0-8389-1012-2

Printed in the United States of America

14   13   12   11   10   5   4   3   2   1

To my family, Laura, Chris,

Lowell, John, and Davey,

with all my love

Contents

Preface to the
Second Edition

In the decade following the publication of the first edition of *Countdown to a New Library*, some extraordinary changes have occurred both in society and in building design and construction. For example, the cost of heating fuels has risen far more rapidly than in the past, and it is now widely understood that petroleum and other fossil fuels are scarce commodities being rapidly depleted. Although conserving energy has been a concern among librarians for many years and was dealt with at some length in the first edition, it has now become a top priority in the design of a new or expanded library facility. Some alternative energy sources that were considered too expensive or too experimental are now practical options. Recycled materials once considered suitable only for "far-out" tree huggers are used in building construction every day.

Another major change that has occurred is the economic crisis crippling many libraries at this writing. The Chief Officers of State Library Agencies reported that 40 percent of existing library buildings are in fair or poor condition. The passage of an economic stimulus bill has raised hopes that some of these needs will be met, and plans are in place for about 16 million square feet of new library space and about 9 million square feet of renovated library space. Many libraries have health and safety issues that urgently need to be addressed. Within this challenging environment, I hope this book will provide support, encouragement, and sound advice to librarians coping with these issues. The world needs libraries, perhaps now more than ever.

Introduction

I began the first edition of this book with the wonderful quote from Elizabeth McCracken's *The Giant's House* that so resonated with librarians everywhere. "Do not trust an architect: he will always try to talk you into an atrium." Perhaps I am mellowing with age, but somehow an atrium doesn't seem quite as bad as it once did, and on cold winter days, I really enjoy a library atrium. Building professionals have learned how to prevent at least some of the leaks. But it's certainly true that library buildings seem to have more problems than they should. Again and again, brand-new buildings costing a king's ransom turn out to be terminally flawed. Before continuing, perhaps it's only fair that I bring my own prejudices out into the open and hazard some guesses as to how those flaws occurred.

For the most part, the fault does not lie with librarians. As researchers, we seek out information before launching into a building or remodeling project, and a substantial body of well-written, informative literature is available to help us. Most of this literature is concerned with those functions that are clearly the responsibility of librarians. For example, many sources provide excellent guidance for determining how many seats are needed or how much space should be allocated to book stacks. To a greater or lesser extent, the literature assumes that building professionals involved in the project, including architects, contractors, engineers, and designers, will translate the library's needs, as communicated to them by librarians, into successful, functional buildings. Such is not always the case.

THE LIBRARIAN'S PERSPECTIVE

The basic assumption that underlies this book is that the traditional division of responsibility between building professionals and librarians is no longer adequate. The modern library building has become so complex that it tends to grow of its own accord, figuratively reaching out in every direction without clear or consistent guidance from any single individual. If the library building is to serve the needs for which it was designed, there must be a key individual who monitors progress at every stage to be certain that the project has not taken an unexpected turn. Although at least one building professional is officially entrusted with this responsibility, most of your fellow librarians and archivists will testify that something always seems to go wrong.

We librarians are, of course, rank amateurs when it comes to building technologies, but we do know about libraries. With a little effort, we can acquire a bird's-eye view of the entire project, allowing us to see interrelationships and areas of potential misunderstanding. As you will discover from the comments of librarians included in the Tips and Tales sections, some vital piece of information may not be communicated. For example, the floor in the stack area is not built to withstand the weight of book stacks; the integrity of the vault is violated by punctures and cutouts; the complex security system allows thieves to leave the building unobserved; or the roof leaks on the library's most valuable collection. Such problems may require a degree in engineering to solve, but if someone had established effective channels of communication in the very beginning, they might never have occurred at all.

Naturally, it is impossible for the information professional to acquire the expertise of an architect or engineer, a plumber or electrician. It is possible, however, to understand how the components of a construction project knit together to create a completed building. No one knows better than members of our profession that the absence of information is at the root of many problems. Therefore, this book will outline the kinds of information needed to embark upon a building project. Reading *Countdown to a New Library* will not magically transform you into a building professional, but it will provide an overview of the entire process, not merely of the librarian's traditional role. Just as a classification schedule helps you see where a particular volume fits into the bibliographic universe, this book is intended to help you see how various specialties fit into the building project, where and when people are not making contact with each other, and where gaps in communication can be most damaging.

TIPS AND TALES FROM THE TRENCHES

Throughout the book you'll find Tips and Tales sections; that is, advice and stories from many of your fellow librarians and archivists who are veterans of a variety of building projects. In the past, an author could hope for input from only a relatively small number of colleagues; today's electronic discussion lists have made it possible to get input from many more. These tips or tales are a vital part of this book. Veterans of library building projects were extremely frank in their comments; therefore, I have tried to protect their privacy by changing small details in their stories if that seemed wise. However, I have not changed the tone of the comments. You'll discover that some librarians remain battle-scarred from their experiences, and it would be less than truthful to pretend that all stories have happy endings.

As I received each tale of triumph, woe, or something in between, I mentally applauded. Building a library is one of the most difficult construction projects.

Its extraordinary demands, which range from ultrasophisticated networking to environmental controls for archival materials, would challenge any builder or architect. Yet the information professionals, whose expertise lies in entirely different directions, put on their hard hats and taught themselves the basics of architecture, electrical engineering, disaster preparedness, and a dozen arcane specialties. Please think of them as members of your project team and take their advice to heart.

DECISIONS AREN'T EASY

Throughout the book, you will encounter seeming conflicts of opinion. One of the librarians in the Tips section may make a recommendation that another librarian contradicts. This is because today's library is expected to fill so many roles, some of them at odds with one another. Today's library is the community meeting place, the computer center, the book repository, the video store, the copy center, and even the theater and the children's day camp.

In addition, libraries have a historic tradition much cherished by librarians, older faculty members, and many community users. For example, my own mental image of the perfect library is the old Free Public Library of Madison, New Jersey, where I held my very first professional position. Though small, it was one of the oldest and most beautiful buildings in the area. Visitors first thought it was a miniature cathedral until they discovered that the subject matter of the Tiffany windows was the love of books and learning. Those gorgeous windows shed a soft, many-hued light that is impossible to describe. One really couldn't read by their mysterious glow, and the lovely chandeliers cast an equally misty light that was effective mainly for catching the gleam of the hand-stenciled, gold-leaf fleurs-de-lis covering the walls. It was, therefore, necessary to illuminate the long trestle tables with hand-tooled brass lamps. The painful memory of the treacherous metal stairs winding through stack levels floored with glass blocks has faded, but the glow of the Tiffany windows remains. There will always be a part of me that believes this is what a real library looks like.

The cost of renovating such libraries is often prohibitive. Not many communities can afford to restore their historic jewel boxes while providing for the vastly expanded needs of a modern library. Invariably, something has to go. Adequate funding to support the library depends on the support of a large segment of the taxpaying public or university community. Historic libraries may be too small and too limited in the services they can provide to attract this support, and no one understands this better than a librarian. In general, we library building planners usually come down on the side of common sense, but that does not mean that we have souls of Formica and polyurethane.

BEYOND THIS BOOK

A book of this length cannot cover everything you will need to know before embarking upon a building project. It cannot anticipate the needs of every type of library, the disaster potential of every working relationship, or the unique constraints of every situation. Therefore, you may want to refer to the lists of professional associations, organizations, and supplemental reading at the end of the chapters for helpful sources of additional information.

In general, *Countdown to a New Library* is more of a "hard hat" book than some others, occasionally emphasizing building technologies over library functions. This emphasis was chosen because of the numerous difficulties librarians in every type of library are currently experiencing with their new, high-tech buildings. Of course, in a book of this length, it is not possible to cover every aspect of construction from foundation to rooftop, so the emphasis is on those areas in which a library may differ from other building projects. For example, plumbing is given short shrift because it is not unique to a library setting, and telecommunications is emphasized because it is so integral to modern libraries. Roofs have been allotted a generous section because library horror stories about leaky ones destroying valuable collections are legion. Furthermore, depending on the library, climate control can be much more than simply a matter of heating and cooling, and security means more than a burglar alarm and a good book-detection system.

Libraries are changing rapidly, and designing spaces to meet the needs of tomorrow's library users can be quite a challenge. For excellent, on-target advice on specific library functions, I strongly recommend that you obtain a copy of the *Checklist of Library Building Design Considerations.*[1] You may find that by the end of your project, you've memorized substantial sections of it. In fact, you will discover that educating yourself for the work ahead is really a full-time job and will mean consuming a library of literature before your building is complete. I often wonder how those poor underprivileged souls in other professions, who don't have the resources of a library at their fingertips, can possibly survive a building ordeal.

WHO NEEDS THIS BOOK?

Although this book will be useful for many types of projects, it will be of greatest assistance to those of you who are designing a building from scratch or who are adding a wing or two to an existing structure. Renovation projects that involve no new construction are also covered. In addition, the book will be helpful for archivists and rare book librarians who manage collections housed within library buildings. However, although some special consideration has been given to archival collections, this book will be inadequate to meet the needs of those who are designing buildings intended specifically to house special collections.

WHEN YOU GET THE GREEN LIGHT

No two institutions share precisely the same set of priorities, personalities, and extenuating circumstances. The length of time from the first glimmerings of interest in a new library until its dedication varies from a year or two to as long as twenty years. A new building or addition is sometimes planned amid furious activity, and then the plans are put aside after a negative response from the legislature or city council. Years later, when the political climate is more favorable, the project may be resuscitated or shelved a second time.

Just to have a starting point, we'll suppose that the first semi-serious discussion of the new building, addition, or major renovation occurs about five years before the dedication ceremony. Your central administration, governing body, architects, and contractors will all have their own ideas about the order in which decisions and commitments are made, so the sequence is also somewhat arbitrary. Although this book is structured around the sequence of a typical library building project, in the real world, you may want to jump ahead to chapter 5 and come back later to chapter 3. However, every step is essential to the planning and construction of a new building, and most are necessary for an addition or renovation.

Countdown begins by discussing ways you can prepare yourself and your library staff to function effectively in the midst of a building project. In chapter 2 you will become familiar with the dramatis personae of a project: the architects, contractors, and engineers who will soon be your constant companions. The chapter also explains various project delivery systems and delves into contract and liability considerations.

Discussions of recent library developments and future prospects introduce chapter 3. The chapter also covers the important tasks of identifying a site and determining space needs. In addition, it examines the unique planning considerations of a renovation or remodeling project.

Chapter 4 gets into the "nuts and bolts" of a major construction project focusing on both functionality and sustainability. Although the topic of sustainable buildings was included in the first edition of this book, it has taken on a considerably larger role in the present volume as the true picture of the earth's limited resources has grown ever sharper.

Similarly, the topic of energy efficiency now occupies a larger part of chapter 5. Other sections in this chapter include the ways humans interact with their buildings and the conditions under which people are most comfortable and most productive. Technology gets a chapter of its very own since in some ways, it is possibly the most crucial and problem-riddled aspect of designing a twenty-first-century library.

In chapter 7 we consider all those ominous "what ifs" that could threaten the building as well as library users and staff. Such threats could come from a variety of sources such as vandals, fires, toxic fumes, and floods and other natural disasters. Next, chapter 8 looks at creating the kind of environment in which customers can feel both comfortable and productive. The considerations involved in selecting the floor materials, wall coverings, and furnishings are all discussed, as are cleaning and maintenance, custom furniture, ergonomics, computer workstations, and shelving issues. The chief task that remains is more difficult than it might seem: that all-important job of surviving and even prospering while everything around you is in chaos. Chapter 9 addresses these concerns and

TALE

Building a library is exciting, enervating, nerve-racking, and the best and the worst of everything.

some issues that are unique to libraries coping with a building renovation. In this "betwixt and between" period, you will be planning your signage system, using your old library as a laboratory to determine what information users need and where, and scheduling walk-throughs of the new building. Finally, in chapter 10, you're ready to bring order to the logistical nightmare of moving the staff, the network, the collection, and the library program. Is that all? 'Fraid not. You will be spending most of your first year on a "crisis-a-day" shakedown cruise.

NOTE

1. William Sannwald, ed., *Checklist of Library Building Design Considerations,* 5th ed. (Chicago: American Library Association, 2008).

Off to a Good Start

Many librarians, describing their first experience with "begetting" a new building, complain bitterly about their naïveté at the start of the project. If only they had known. . . . If only they had been prepared. . . . This book will provide some of that advance preparation. In a sense, however, you will always be playing the role of Columbus or Balboa, exploring uncharted seas. There is no way to anticipate all the crises that may await you. Nevertheless, you can have a game plan that will prepare you for the most frequently encountered possibilities. If you have a good, clear idea of your goals and how other librarians have achieved similar objectives, you're infinitely better off than if you approach the project unprepared.

PREPARING YOURSELF FOR WHAT'S AHEAD

At last, it's finally happened! You've received a tentative go-ahead to begin planning a new library or addition. You've been given permission to dream and to work harder than perhaps you've ever worked before. The wheels will soon be set in motion, but suddenly you've got cold feet. Where do you begin? What do you do first? What do you, a librarian, know about bricks and concrete and load-bearing walls? It may sound a bit simplistic, but you begin with yourself. Assuming that you're the library director or a member of the team that will be shepherding the project to completion, you've got an awesome job ahead. It will require all your intelligence, patience, humor, flexibility, interpersonal skills, strength of character, and intestinal fortitude to emerge triumphant from the experience with a functional building and most of your nerves intact.

You're the Expert

You will be spending the next few years with dozens of specialists in building design and construction. At times you will feel overwhelmed, even "cowed" by their technical knowledge, and you will cringe at your own inexperience. No matter what their specialty or however varied their skills and experience, you will find one subject on which most building professionals are ignorant: they will be as newborn babes when it comes to the nature and function of a library. Here, you alone are the expert. Perhaps you never thought of yourself that way, but now is the time to start. Without your expert guidance, the building that emerges from the rubble might be suitable for a factory, an office building, or a department store, but it won't work as a library.

Over the years, you've acquired an extraordinary amount of information about libraries from your library school classes and your work experiences. For example, you know roughly the number of staff members who will be working in the new building and the areas to which they will be assigned. One librarian in the Midwest could not convince her architect that a building of 80,000 square feet would be staffed by just a dozen people. Additional offices and service desks kept appearing mysteriously on floor plans because the architect was convinced the librarian must be mistaken about staff size. Libraries are indeed very different from other large buildings, and only you know precisely how they differ.

Libraries are not well understood by building professionals. Only infrequently does a contractor or architect arrive on the scene equipped with an intimate understanding of book stacks, learning commons, collaborative studies, teen gaming, or library traffic patterns. Look around. How many libraries do you see? Over the course of their careers, architects may design hundreds of apartment buildings, office complexes, and strip malls, but only rarely do architects ever plan a library. You're the one who must take responsibility for this part of their education. Don't allow an architect or contractor to make unilateral decisions that will determine how the library functions.

Your Sphere of Authority

It is your responsibility to encourage functional design and strenuously oppose design features that interfere with the library's effectiveness. This means clearly delineating the architect and contractor's sphere of authority and your own: the details best left to the judgment of a building professional, those on which you should at least be consulted, and those that you must approve. The items in the latter two categories are far more numerous than most building professionals believe, and you may have some heavy weather ahead until everyone settles down to a comfortable working relationship. Just remember that library considerations affect diverse issues such as hardware on the panic doors, wiring details, lighting requirements, and the desirability of design elements like balconies and atria.

TALES

I would emphasize knowing what you want, being able to articulate it, paying attention to all the details, and not assuming that someone else (like the professionals) will take care of something.

I found that my suggestions were often pooh-poohed. I wish I had stood my ground more often, though it might not have done any good—my position wasn't viewed as particularly authoritative or important.

DONNING YOUR LIBRARY HARD HAT

It won't be long before you discover that you have two full-time jobs. Unless you're starting a new library from scratch, you still have the job of taking care of the day-to-day needs of an existing library. In addition, you have the second and equally time-consuming full-time job of planning a new library building or expansion. As the song puts it, "Something's gotta give!"

If your library is large enough to enjoy the luxury of an assistant director, consider delegating one job or the other. It is usually best for the director to use whatever clout she has for dealing with trustees, deans, and other decision makers. This means that it is more usual for the assistant director to take on responsibility for the existing library while the director plans and oversees progress on the new one. It may be, however, that the skills and interests of the people involved make it preferable to assign the planning role to the assistant. Even if yours is a small library with a limited staff, delegate as many responsibilities as possible.

If you've always been the kind of supervisor who tends to micromanage, break yourself of the habit now before you drive yourself bonkers. Nothing is more important now than prioritizing your time. It's all a matter of deciding what comes first, what will eventually become a glaring problem, and what can safely be swept under the carpet. Lots of good and worthy projects can be swept under the carpet, and no one will be the wiser. When you delegate routine matters, don't insist on approving every little decision. You will send the message that you distrust the person to whom you delegated the responsibility, and you will still be doing two jobs.

> ### TIPS
>
> Anticipate that dealing with the architect and builder will use up most of your time on the project until the library is completed. Delegate your other responsibilities.
>
> Learn to translate architect-speak. When they say it can't be done, they mean that from their own personal perspective, the cost or sacrifice of other features would be prohibitive. When you know all the pros and cons, you may decide differently.
>
> Stick to your guns when you're told things like "you really don't need all those outlets." The few times that I had a chance to talk to anybody, I was treated like an eejit (as my Irish friends would say).
>
> I recommend Prozac, lots of it.
>
> Get into a frame of mind that lets you enjoy the project and, most important, have a generous budget for chocolate.

IDENTIFYING AND COMMUNICATING WITH KEY PLAYERS

You, of course, are not the only participant in the project. If you are working in a public library environment, your library board and numerous municipal or county administrators will be active participants in the building project, as will philanthropic individuals and foundations making financial contributions. In a university environment, the stakeholders include the board of trustees, benefactors, university president or provost, and an assortment of administrative staff members. Identifying these participants and determining how they will share in the decision-making process should be placed on your "to do" list as early as possible. Occasionally, a city council member, university president, or board chairperson views the new building as his own monument. Since these people have only a limited understanding of how the library functions, they are especially vulnerable to the extravagant enthusiasms of architects. Before your boss

TALES

Reality is different from theory. The architects made the plans. The treasurer approved them. The library director had limited input.

I was involved in a library building project several years ago in a New England state. I was hired about a month before bids were opened for a long-awaited addition to a 1905 building. The director, whose vision this was, had such a hard time with the trustees that she quit six months later. The trustees (who knew everything) micromanaged the building project, drove the architect crazy, asked the staff for input on colors and then ignored it (making them furious), and refused to hire an engineer or clerk of the works who could look out for the library's best interest.

or board ever gets near an architect, they need a crash course in libraries too. Don't assume that because they've approved or disapproved your annual budget requests and listened to your tales of woe, they know what happens in a library. Their impressions of day-to-day library activities may be as vague as those of your users. In fact, they probably view the library from the standpoint of users. That is, public services are all they see, and the only important materials are the ones they need.

MAKING GOOD DECISIONS

Who decides what? When can you resolve an issue without additional input, and when must you seek approval from someone at a higher level? Work together to agree upon procedures for communicating information, obtaining input, and making decisions. Reduce the number of people who must be regularly consulted to a manageable size. If you are in a public library, ask that your board appoint a subcommittee of no more than four people who will work directly with you. Encourage the board to choose people with the time, knowledge, and experience to contribute significantly to the process. What you don't need is deadwood, people whose egos demand that they be consulted but who have little or nothing to offer.

Flawed Group Process

In talking with many librarians, I've concluded that despite the talents and good intentions of the individuals involved in a building project, it's the group process that is often at fault when things go wrong. Groups have the advantage of bringing a wider variety of insights to bear on problems, but there is a downside to the group process as well. Some poor decisions seem to be the direct outcome of group dynamics rather than the bad judgment of any one person. Group decisions that initially seem brilliant get made on the spur of the moment. Looking back on them, however, it's hard to imagine why no one noticed their obvious flaws. Since groups are involved with the design of nearly all libraries and library additions, you had better confront the problem openly and honestly before it gets out of hand. If everyone involved in the project will agree to abide by the following rules and if the group accepts responsibility for seeing that the rules are followed, a lot of future wringing of hands will be avoided.

Rule 1

At the very beginning of the project it's important to make a pact with everyone involved, from board members to circulation clerks to academic deans to community members. There must be agreement in advance on the way group decisions will be made. Once that agreement is reached, participants will need to be reminded again and again and again.

Rule 2

One essential part of that agreement is a ban on spur-of-the-moment decisions. This is really a hard rule to follow and will require a lot of practice. Meetings are tiring. We begin our meetings with a clear focus and plenty of energy. Eventually, however, we become tired and cranky, anxious to go home or get back to that pile of work waiting on our desks. When meeting participants have arrived at this frazzled state, and are considering a knotty problem whose solution is eluding them, someone will inevitably make a loud, firm, and authoritative statement intended to put an end to fruitless discussion. Tired minds will grasp at it, wondering why they hadn't thought of it earlier. This decision is often the one that is recorded, and all too often, it is the one that should never have been made.

Perhaps the planning group works for months, exploring various alternatives before recommending a plan. Finally, their proposal comes before a board of trustees, a city manager, or a university dean. If those individuals are not parties to the agreement, they may become the victims of instant inspiration. They notice something that seems excessively expensive or inconveniently located. "We'll fix it," they say, and quicker than the blink of an eye they do.

Unfortunately, most decisions have a downside. If the circulation desk has a good clear view of the entrance, it won't have an equally clear view of the stacks. Most quick fixes will inevitably mean that something else "gets broke." The result will be arrangements and locations that are not quite right. Sometimes it is the less important problem that is solved while the essential function is sacrificed.

Administrators and oversight groups have a responsibility to critique and approve the work of their subordinates. The buck stops with them. However, they are no less vulnerable to the dangers of instant fixes. Since they cannot spend large amounts of time reviewing all the pros and cons involved in a decision, they should express their concerns and refer them back to the planning group. Individuals who are especially concerned may even wish to sit in on these deliberations. A building project is far too complex for any individual to understand at first glance, and no matter how perceptive one is, it will take time to see how one change affects other elements of the plan.

Rule 3

Observe the 80/20 rule. In every library, there are patterns that might be described as "business as usual." Staffing decisions are made based on past experience; collection development is guided by past circulation. Librarians try to call to mind their average patrons when they are making decisions about future needs. However, there are exceptions. The library may be adequately staffed most of the time but not at noon on Saturday, when the reduced staff must juggle lunch hours. Patrons normally request similar types of books, but every once in a while staff get that obscure question about cryogenic research in the Gobi Desert.

The same is true when planning a library. As you pore over floor plans, you should have a very good idea what your staff and users will be doing about 80 percent of the time. You can roughly predict the number of people using the Internet computers and anticipate the most heavily used traffic areas. However, there are always situations that don't fit the norm. The best decisions are the ones that serve the library and its customers 80 percent of the time. However, special needs, in other words, those that come up infrequently, must be addressed as well. As a librarian, you don't redirect your collection to meet the needs of that cryogenic researcher. You fill the request through interlibrary loan. In other words, you try to find a way to meet the unusual need without penalizing the many who have very different reading habits. The same is true in building planning.

Ask library staff members to describe their typical day. How many staff members are stationed in public services? How many customers are using the library at 10:00 a.m.? At 7:00 p.m.? Get out those statistics you've been collecting for so long. Which collections are the most heavily used and the most likely to expand? Which tables, lounge furniture, and study carrels are occupied first? Why are these popular? If an area doesn't get heavy use now, it's unlikely to attract users if you re-create it in the new library. Once you have this clear picture of an average "business as usual" day, you can design a library that can be staffed most efficiently and that meets most customer needs.

Now, what about the other 20 percent? The library has a responsibility to serve its customers with different needs. For example, a customer in a wheelchair has a right to a safe and successful library experience. A service desk may need to be left unattended for brief periods. Although the library must be prepared for such situations, a decision that interferes with its ability to function effectively 80 percent of the time or serve 80 percent of its patrons is a poor decision. Each time a decision is made about the location of an office or the positioning of an elevator, the 80 percent rule should be observed. Undoubtedly, there are situations in which you have no alternative, but every option must be explored before conceding defeat.

The "Libraries Will Be Extinct" Argument

As your construction project ascends from one approval body to the next, you will inevitably encounter a board member or bureaucrat who is convinced that there is no point in spending money to build or renovate a library since it will be obsolete in five to ten years. Naturally, academic and public officials prefer to save money wherever they can. The media's current fascination with the digital library provides an excellent excuse.

You will be tempted to become angry and defensive after you've heard the same argument for the twenty-third time. Anticipate your reaction and have a canned speech and written handout ready whenever the subject might

Medina County (Ohio) District Library, Medina Library, David Milling Architects, dmaa.com.
Photo: William H. Webb, Infinity Studio.

come up. Of course, it's true that librarians are worried about the future. No, we don't know exactly what the future holds in store, but we do know that the simplistic argument about the death of the book and universal delivery of electronic information is a smoke screen. Libraries are complex social institutions that provide a wide variety of services. You need not feel guilty or defensive; you are simply dealing with people who have a very limited picture of a library.

On some relatively calm and restful day when a new library is little more than a gleam in the library staff's collective eye, write a brief statement that speaks to the library doom-and-gloom argument. Limit your literary effort to a page and address the issue as simply and clearly as possible. Such esoteric points as the global information economy will not go down as well as local arguments illustrating how important the library is to your community. Make it clear that the book is unlikely to disappear anytime soon and that the library will be delivering both print and electronic information for the foreseeable future. Online access to the virtual library is a marvelous resource, but the library is far more than a website. Steer clear of arguments about whether books or computer equipment are more important. Collect statistics on library use, including civic groups using meeting spaces, educational programs, services for the unemployed, teen programs, and other functions that bureaucrats tend to forget when they see the library going the way of the dinosaur.

The "Hurry Up and Wait" Syndrome

Most librarians report that their building projects progressed not steadily but in a series of lurches. Long delays were followed by sudden bursts of activity when everything was due yesterday. Projects that have simmered on the back burner awaiting approval from a half dozen officials, government agencies, and advisory boards suddenly erupt into life and are given the all clear. It's full steam ahead and everyone is caught unprepared. Frequently, librarians find out about deadlines by accident or are forced to work around the clock to have their input ready for spur-of-the-moment meetings.

From the very first moment when your building project acquires some sort of tentative official status, start spending time on your own preparations. Many of the tasks described in the rest of this chapter can be done long before they are needed. Having a recommendation or request ready at a strategic moment can make all the difference between success and failure. It is also important to spend these quiet intervals bringing your building expertise up to speed. Use the time to take courses, read books and articles, and take frequent busman's holidays.

Create an Information Blitz

Many crises are avoidable if everyone is kept fully informed. Making use of her extensive experience with pathfinders and "quick bibs," one librarian got into the habit of creating one-page information sheets on every aspect of the planning and construction process. When the board and the architect were considering the best site, she gave all participants copies of her one-page bulleted list of the ten most important considerations. Then she explained her points quickly and clearly and relinquished the floor before she'd lost the attention of her listeners.

All through the design and construction phases, that librarian had small stacks of one-page handouts ready. One briefly and succinctly explained preservation issues; another dealt with library security requirements. She never distributed more than one handout at a time and never included more than the barest essentials on a sheet. Large type, lots of white space, and important points emphasized with bold print and bullets distinguished all her masterpieces. Best of all, the handouts were always ready ahead of time, so when the conversation turned unexpectedly to a new subject, the librarian was ready. When new team members arrived on the scene, she began the process all over again. Although I don't know it for a fact and she never talked down to anyone, I wouldn't be surprised if this librarian began her work life teaching third graders. She never argued, never became hysterical or irrational; she just kept plugging along distributing and interpreting her information sheets. The success of her new building speaks volumes for the efficacy of her method.

THE POLITICAL ENVIRONMENT

Every library is enmeshed in some sort of political environment. Of course, political considerations are a part of any human endeavor that involves large sums of money. However, in some libraries they may become such an overriding concern that they jeopardize the success of the project. How can you cope? Well, first of all, take a good look at your community. Think back on the role of politics in past library decisions. You will know the extent to which library issues have been seized upon by competing political factions. You can probably predict many of the challenges that lie ahead even without the help of a crystal ball.

Your People Resources

Making effective use of the skills and resources of your board, boss, and library users is always necessary, even in the calmest of times. If the library is going to be at the center of a political firestorm, these supporters will be absolutely essential to the success of the project. As soon as you see the new library or addition looming on your horizon—in fact, long before any official approval is obtained—begin mustering your library's political strength. If you have some influence over the appointment of your board, seek out good politicians who have connections with decision makers in your community. Look for articulate people who will speak out and help communicate the library's needs to local government representatives and other citizens. Make them stakeholders in the project by keeping them informed and going to them for advice.

Even if you have little or no influence on the election or appointment of the board, never see your board as the enemy. Though you might willingly wring a few necks, you have far more influence over this group than you do over the other powers that be. Make allies on the board; work with them, inform them, and finally make them participants rather than spectators. Academic libraries also operate in highly charged political environments. Of course, you're familiar with your usual chain of command, but you may find that the real decision makers are people you've never worked with before. Set yourself the task of identifying these unknown players. Consider how your needs and insights can be communicated to them without appearing to go over your boss's head.

You Gotta Have Friends

In addition to developing support on your board or among your administration, you should nurture the same kind of "people resources" in your Friends group, library foundation, and other sympathetic community organizations. Most libraries already have some group that raises money and advocates for the library. Take a good look at yours. If it's been inactive, what can you do to bring it back to life? Begin identifying regular library users who have the kind of political skills you are seeking. Personally invite them to participate. Use some of your precious staff time to plan activities that will reinvigorate Friends meetings. Then, as the building project begins in earnest, make regular reports to the group, encouraging them to attend hearings and lobby for the new library.

Start New Library Groups

Occasionally, a library has a Friends group that is, you might say, "on its last legs." Most of the members joined in 1976, and it has gradually become stagnant and fusty. You know deep down that the articulate, politically savvy newcomers you're looking for would never want to join, and anyway the old guard would discourage their advances. If this is a good description of your Friends group, all is not lost. Start one or more new groups that can coexist side by side with the old one. Book discussion groups work well for this purpose, or you could develop a special fund-raising group for the new library. The point is that you will want to hand-select as many of the members as possible. Once they're hooked, you must keep them involved with activities and responsibilities. One way or another, nurture a sizable group of people who are both involved in the community and possess the kind of political skills the library so badly needs.

Steer Clear of Dissension

Remember that building projects cause tempers to flare and nerves to fray. It is not even unusual for heads to roll in such a highly charged environment, and you certainly do not want to place your own head in danger. You will have to balance your determination to build the perfect library with your instincts for self-preservation. When the last carpenter has taken his lunch box and departed, you can also bid adieu to the architect and contractor. If your superior diplomatic skills failed you and you nearly came to blows, you need never speak to them again. Your job, however, should be just as secure as the day you took on the project. In fact, you should have established such a good working relationship with your superiors that they now understand far more about the library and its needs.

Get Support

It is an unfortunate fact of human nature that we want someone else to take the blame when things go wrong. Depend on it: many things will go wrong during a building project. Hours will be spent arguing over who is at fault. Even when you are working with the nicest and best-intentioned people, you will want to protect yourself from such recriminations. It happens all too frequently that the individual who has done the least is the most critical of the work of others. The best way to avoid problems is to provide ample opportunity for input from all the important stakeholders.

Be sure you have plenty of support before going out on a potentially controversial "limb." If you don't have support and believe strongly that you are in the right and your colleagues in the wrong, tread carefully. If it's important enough, launch an educational campaign to clarify the situation. Assemble and present factual information to support your point of view. If, however, you begin to see yourself as a kind of Joan of Arc who alone understands what's really needed, or you feel like a suffering martyr buffeted on all sides by ignorance, stop! Pull yourself together. You're not going to survive this project unless you can calm down, back off, and acquire a more detached attitude.

TIP

Our project supervisor (hired by us to oversee the work of the contractors) advised me to leave the decisions on shingle, exterior trim, and brick color entirely to the board. I think he was wise. It is a very big decision. If it is a wrong decision it is very obvious, and we will have to live with it for a long time. It is better if the board has no one to point a finger at!

TALES

The building was designed by committee—we had a community group of thirty-five people involved in the planning stages and still ended up with a beautiful, functional building.

As the saying goes, "For God so loved the world he did not form a committee." That goes double for construction projects.

The president decreed that the campus store will be in the new learning center building. No one has been able to overturn that directive to this point. Why not bring in Kinko's? It would be cool if it were a big building, but it's only 22,000 square feet.

ESTABLISHING LINES OF COMMUNICATION

Several years ago, I worked in a library that had a gaping hole in the floor in front of the circulation desk. Patrons joked that anyone not returning books on time would be hurled into the chasm. It seems that a special (and very expensive) type of flooring material had been used. It was intended for easy removal when, at some time in the future, the library would expand to the floor below and a staircase would be erected. Unfortunately, the floor chose to remove itself much earlier than planned. The architect had passed on an instruction booklet to the builder describing how the flooring material was to be installed. Unfortunately, one vital page was missing.

There was probably nothing the librarian could have done about this particular instance of miscommunication, but many other tragedies are easily avoided if the efficient flow of information becomes a priority for all concerned. The basic problem is that information often gets lost or buried before it gets to the right person. Changes requested by the librarian may have to go through so many different intermediaries that when they finally reach the contractor or subcontractor who can execute them, it is too late to make the alterations. Changes that once might have cost nothing to implement may later require extensive retrofitting at a cost of many thousands of dollars.

The Owner's Representative

As you read the tips and tales recounted in this book, as well as the recommendations in the text, you may find yourself confused. Who is doing what? Who reports to whom? This is partly a problem with terminology and partly a result of different local practices. The terms *commissioner of work, project manager,* and *clerk of the works* usually refer to the person hired by the owner (either the library board, university, or local government unit) to make sure everything is done correctly. *Commissioning* is a term that's used increasingly for the process of making sure that building systems work as planned, so the term *commissioner of works* is similarly becoming popular. In the tip below, the county engineer is acting as the owner's representative.

Ideally, such a person possesses both loyalty to the owner and expertise in building design and construction. A city or large university may have a permanent department assigned to this task. On the other hand, library decision makers may be unwilling to hire another highly paid professional. They may assign the job to the library's own facilities manager or to the library director. In fact, they may not even consider such a role necessary. To make matters more complicated, the architectural firm may appoint a project manager. This is usually an architect who is responsible not to the library but to the firm.

In the best of all worlds, the library board or university administration hires a highly qualified professional who possesses extensive experience in building design and construction. This paragon works closely with the librarian, clearly understands the library's needs and priorities, and makes sure that contractors and subcontractors comply with them. In reality, there are probably as many chains of command as there are libraries. This makes it difficult in a book such as this to precisely define the role of the library director and staff. However, the project will not be a success unless those relationships are defined and widely understood. The biblical exhortation that you cannot serve two masters is appropriate here.

In some situations, librarians are prevented from communicating directly with building professionals by administrators who fear their "add-ons" will drive up the cost of the project. This understandable concern can be alleviated if a clear procedure is established for approving financial commitments. Work out a system whereby key players involved in the building project routinely "copy" one another on important memos, making it clear that this is for information only.

Help Building Professionals Communicate

Although you don't have a lot of say in the matter, it's vitally important that your contractor, architect, and other building professionals communicate well with one another. Any time you can bring them together, do so. They are all extremely busy, and unless they get together frequently, they may not take the extra time to make sure they're really "on the same page." The term *charrette* is often used for a collaborative session attended by all major players involved in a building project. Architects, engineers, contractors, and owners' representatives get together to brainstorm, identify design problems, and discuss solutions. They usually require multiple work sessions. You can get a good idea of how much communication is taking place among your team by asking about a charrette. If the term seems foreign, it may simply be a matter of terminology or you may have a problem.

Based on personal experience and the comments of other librarians, it seems as if far more time is spent passing around the blame for a mistake than is spent fixing it. When problems are identified early, they are usually easy to fix. Simple, inexpensive solutions are often the best ones. This means that success depends on a librarian who stays abreast of what's happening and on a contractor who checks back with the architect when something just doesn't feel right.

Write It Down

Get used to putting things in writing. In the classic Japanese film *Rashomon*, several people describe their memories of the same incident. Each is being honest, but each appears to have witnessed an entirely different event. This is often true of meetings with the various participants in a building project. Each will take away a different understanding of what occurred.

Follow up on meetings with messages or memos outlining the decisions and commitments made. If a decision cannot be made without more information, identify the person responsible for providing that information and the time frame in which the decision must be made. Mention anyone who has volunteered to perform a task or who has been asked to take on a responsibility. Although no one enjoys taking minutes, appoint yourself as official or unofficial reporter of the discussions in which you participate. Distribute photocopies of the minutes to everyone involved. If other members of the group understood matters differently, now is the time to discover their differing interpretations while the meeting is fresh in everyone's memory. Some people, of course, will consign your

TALE

I met on-site with the county engineer, the construction foreman, and the architect every other week. It was tremendously helpful to know the building from the ground up.

memos and minutes to the trash can, but at least you've provided an opportunity for them to express their views. When an argument arises months later, you will be able to produce written evidence to support your position.

At this point, it is important to include a few additional words about the whole business of taking minutes. How many meetings have you attended at which everyone spent the first part trying to get out of taking minutes? Few chores are so unpopular. Nevertheless, the page or two of notes you take during a meeting or discussion can pay astounding dividends. First, you are establishing your interpretation of what happened as the official one. If minutes are distributed and group members are asked to submit corrections, you have provided an opportunity for the expression of other interpretations. Even though people rarely avail themselves of this opportunity, your minutes will usually be taken as the official version of an event in a court of law or in an arbitration hearing.

Human Relations 101

Make it a point in the minutes to present participants in their best light. Of course, you must not distort what actually happened, but the difference of just a few words can make a comment sound wise or foolish. Be sure everyone sounds wise, because they will be more likely to actually read what you have to say. We enjoy nothing more than reading complimentary things about ourselves. It's all very well to have the minutes available for ammunition in some future dispute, but it's much better for project participants to understand one another right now.

Never use your minutes to make yourself look like the only intelligent member of the discussion. Never use them to give voice to all your grievances or get revenge on an adversary. You'll simply initiate a spate of angry memos accompanied by hurt feelings and embittered reprisals. Focus your efforts on the building, not on the personalities. If you don't, by the end of the project you may be seething with hostility, and others may be feeling exactly the same way. The last thing you want to do at this point is to set off a tinderbox of explosive feelings.

TIP

At building progress meetings, have a staff person who takes minutes along with the architect. Make sure the staff person records the stated concerns of contractors and the answers of the architects as part of the meeting minutes. (This procedure would have helped us later on when architects and contractors fought to establish the blame for problems.)

YOU CAN'T DO IT ALL ALONE

If you imagine that the entire library staff will be doing their usual jobs while you drive yourself to a nervous breakdown with added responsibilities, better think again. Take off that halo. You're all in this together. Your staff's library lives are going to have to change almost as much as yours. Review the library's priorities. What functions can be compressed or postponed? How can you free staff time for the many tasks that a construction project involves? You're going to need someone who is in charge of public relations, whether this is an official position or is incorporated into an existing job description. Look around at your staff. Don't stop at the professional staff. It doesn't take an MLS degree to be a charming and effective publicist and event organizer. Your library probably has some highly competent staff members who are active in the community and would do an excellent job.

Get Staff Involved

In most cases, you are enlarging your present library or designing a new building to replace an existing structure. This means that you already have a laboratory in which to experiment with new ideas and a staff of experienced professionals and paraprofessionals who together possess many years of library experience. Bring everyone in the library into the planning process. Not only will working together as a team improve their morale and job performance, but it

---

TIPS

Insist on staff involvement; they have to work there every day!

Staff members are heavily stressed during a building project. If they are also heavily involved and have bought into the project, they take the added stress with courage and good humor. At least ours did.

We had an incredible battle rearranging the interior to make sense, but the staff finally won that one. The staff and I kept each other going.

---

will improve the quality of your own library work life as well. Involve them in creating your checklist of needed features and functions. Work together to weigh the importance of individual items. The staff can help you separate the "absolutely essential" from the merely desirable.

Don't forget that there are other employees who should be involved in the project as well. Custodians can provide expert suggestions on which materials wear well and which are especially difficult to clean. Maintenance staff and all-purpose handy people can also troubleshoot plans, identifying problems in their particular areas of expertise.

Library directors who have suffered through a building project often relate that they felt like martyrs, abandoned by people who didn't understand how hard they'd worked and how much frustration they'd experienced. It is sometimes hard to avoid such a neurotic outlook when board members demand the sacrifice of stack space for a reception area or the president cuts the construction budget by another million dollars. We do sometimes feel that we alone are holding up the bloodstained banner, and such an attitude can seriously interfere with our judgment. Involving the library staff provides a support group on which you can depend for informed advice and encouragement. These are people who understand both the mission and the practical reality of a library. Although opinions will differ sharply, they will tend to see the project in much the same way you do.

Nevertheless, be careful that you do not unload all your frustrations on the library staff. Naturally, you will feel the need for a sounding board when the board chairman has done something really dastardly, but your staff should not be used as confidantes. It is especially unwise, in a moment of anger, to utter insults or make wild accusations that you will long regret. You might instead develop a network of librarians outside your own library with whom you can let down your hair—colleagues who will understand what you're going through but who will regard your verbal torrents as confidential.

Tap the Staff's Institutional Memory

Pooling the experience of staff members can result in some unexpected bonuses. One staff member may remember a crisis that occurred because of a badly designed circulation desk; another will recall an error that made it impossible to use a service elevator or work space as originally envisioned. Such memories can keep you from making many costly mistakes. Invite staff members to walk through a typical workday using the preliminary floor plans. Looking through their eyes, you will discover a gaggle of traffic problems, unsupervised niches, poorly organized work spaces, and noisy reading areas. You will wonder how you could possibly have missed such obvious problems, but you are in no way at fault. We each view the world from our own unique perspective. Your role is not to be omniscient but to integrate the many views into one coherent whole. Staff are probably the ones who will catch the details while you are focusing on the big picture. Although some initial brainstorming sessions will be useful, staff must also be attuned to the project schedule so they don't identify problems after it's too late to do anything about them.

DEVELOP YOUR SKILLS

Although you are an expert on libraries, you still have a lot of homework to do before you're ready to launch a building project. For example, you have a new vocabulary to learn. Although you certainly have every right to insist that the architect and other building specialists speak English and avoid jargon, you must meet them halfway. Describing the fittings for a large, complex building requires an understanding of hundreds of new terms. (They are not gizmos or thingamajigs.) Small details like locking mechanisms that you may never have noticed come in endless varieties. A certain minimal understanding is needed to reinterpret technical details in terms of the library's needs.

Continuing Education

Your local technical college offers a wide assortment of courses designed to introduce students to the building trades. You might audit a course in architectural drawing and learn to read a blueprint. Electrical connections, data lines, load-bearing walls, and plumbing lines are clearly indicated on a floor plan and obvious to a building professional. They are easily overlooked, however, unless you acquaint yourself with the symbols in standard use.

Branch out, if you have time, to other introductory classes dealing with electricity or heating, ventilation, and air-conditioning (HVAC) systems. The point is simply to acquire enough vocabulary and basic information to communicate effectively. If you haven't the time for a course, take a look at your own library shelves. Public library collections are especially rich in basic architecture and construction texts. Even "do-it-yourself" homeowner books can be helpful.

TIPS

Read all you can. You can't learn too much!

When it was evident that we would add on to our building, I was sent to participate in a very good workshop. It covered everything from planning and blueprints to how to deal with the architects. I can't recommend workshops and focused conference sessions enough!

Know how to read a blueprint. There will be construction mistakes, and only by knowing what the blueprints include will you be able to have change orders written at no cost to you. (This is very important because change orders add up quickly.)

Architects, project managers, contractors, and so on were all surprised to learn that I knew how to read a blueprint. They're much more careful when they know you can keep tabs on them.

We had 30-inch shelves installed as 18-inch shelves and outlets installed 6 feet apart when they were supposed to be 4 feet apart. These are examples of mistakes that were corrected at no cost to my project, since I could go through the blueprints and point out the mistakes. I really recommend staying on top of these details.

Fixing mistakes will cost money, but it's better than living with a gross error for years afterward.

Learning Where the Money Comes From

How much do you know about your library building budget? How is it divided? Will you have any freedom to move funds around if some bids come in lower and others higher than expected? Resolving these questions is crucial to any successful project and absolutely essential to maintaining positive relationships with the library's parent body, whether it be a university or a county government. Plan to meet individually with key staff members in your county or university business office or purchasing department. Become familiar with their procedures. Ask about other building projects in which they've been involved and find out how they expect your project to proceed based on their past experience. It is extremely important to develop a good working relationship with individuals in these offices. It is not usually difficult to follow their rules and submit the right paperwork at the right time. In exchange, they will be your friends for life.

The people who pay the bills often have an undeservedly negative reputation. They're the ones who must satisfy the auditors and whose jobs are on the line if any financial irregularities should be discovered. It is only natural that they lose their cool when their procedures are ignored. If you spend the time to get to know these people as human beings, you will be amazed at how they can expedite your requests and keep you informed of progress on bids and contracts.

Become a Building Connoisseur

As soon as a building project appears on the horizon, start looking at other buildings. When vacation time rolls around, take a busman's holiday. Learn what it feels like to enter a new building, to look for a particular office, to ride the elevator, or

New York Public Library,
Francis Martin Library,
1100 Architect P.C.,
1100architect.com.
Photo: Timothy Furzer.

to find the restrooms. Watch what other visitors do. Although you'll want to take care that security officers don't identify you as a stalker, take notes on what tends to confuse people and where visitors look for assistance. Look at older buildings as well. Which materials look old and worn? Where does dirt collect?

Make a Scrapbook

When you visit these buildings, take your camera along. Start a scrapbook illustrating the features you like and want to incorporate into the new library. Just describing these features to the architect isn't enough; there is simply no way to transmit the picture in your mind to someone who doesn't have the same frame of reference. When trying to communicate your vision of the library, you may be tempted to couch your specifications in vague terms such as "family-friendly," "public image," "library philosophy," or other subjective phrases. This is a sure way to derail your project. You will believe that you and your architects are in perfect agreement until that fateful day when you look with horror at the way they have interpreted your suggestions.

Look at All Types of Buildings

Don't just look at libraries. In fact, it is sometimes even more helpful to look at other buildings because you won't be distracted by library functions, and you will be more likely to focus on architectural details and building materials. Visit museums, hotels, office buildings, and theaters. Take pictures of flooring materials, stairways, doors, windows, signage, counters, and all the other details that go into a modern building.

For example, during a summer vacation I visited a friend in Reno, Nevada. Not being much of a gambler, I found the casinos rather boring until I began looking at them as if they were libraries. In that tawdry world of excess, I discovered samples of almost every conceivable building material. Some casinos had opened only recently while others were showing their age, so I could see how wall treatments, carpeting, and restroom fixtures held up over time.

In addition, I discovered that designers rarely think about the people who will be cleaning the new building, especially its complicated surfaces that get dirtier as the years go by. Designers may not notice that light fixtures are positioned in such a way as to make them unreachable when bulbs inevitably burn out. It was interesting to compare older casinos with older libraries. Because the profits for some older casinos had declined, they no longer had the money to spend on expensive equipment like lifts or "cherry pickers" to reach those hard-to-get-to places, and so they got grimier and more tattered. It was clear that the more elaborate the decoration, the more rapidly the casino aged.

Become a Catalog Junkie

It's helpful to put your name on the mailing list for as many building-supply catalogs as possible. Don't stop at library catalogs. There are many construction-trade catalogs that are free for the asking. Of course, you should begin with the buyers' guide issue of *Library Journal,* but go on to explore the world of restroom equipment, door and window manufacturers, and lighting fixture distributors; the list goes on and on. ConstructionNet on the World Wide Web is a good port of entry into this unfamiliar world. In fact, the Web in general is full of good ideas. However, you will want to obtain printed catalogs so that you can cut them up, adding pictures of desirable features to your scrapbook.

Take care, however, that the materials and equipment you find in catalogs are in the moderate price range. A friend found herself accused of driving up building costs with her demands when the real reason for cost overruns was the architect's patrician taste. Architects may not mean to be extravagant, but they do not share your priorities. As a catalog junkie, you'll gradually come to know what things cost and will be alert to wasteful spending. If you can buy an item "off the shelf"—in other words, if it is made in huge quantities on an assembly line—it will be much cheaper than one made in small, buyer-initiated production runs. It is amazing how "plain vanilla" materials in the hands of an accomplished architect can be used to create a unique and imaginative structure.

COMPLEX MODERN BUILDINGS

Libraries are very big buildings. Not big enough, maybe, when you're trying to squeeze in a few thousand more books, but big nonetheless. Think of the number of fluorescent tubes that burn out at the exact hour and minute the custodian announces he's run out of replacements. Remember how many yards of carpet you discovered you would need to replace the library's frayed acreage? In addition, think about the thousands of bits and pieces of shelving hardware, and the panes of glass whose life expectancy is directly proportional to the number of skateboards and softballs in the immediate area. The complexity of a building gets overwhelming, to say the least. Occasionally, the library seems even larger, as when the climate ranges from arctic levels in the basement through a somewhat temperate zone on the street floor to equatorial heat at the top. There's no getting around it. Library buildings are fraught with endless peril; ultimately, you're the one who must get the roof patched. (I know you told them flat roofs leak, and they said it wasn't really flat.) As you begin a building project, bear in mind the many experiences you've had as a librarian. Some problems are inevitable, and no architect and no builder can save you or your staff from grim reality. On the other hand, some problems were caused by building professionals who failed to understand how libraries really work.

Intelligent Buildings

Later in this book we'll be discussing what are called "intelligent buildings," structures designed around technologies that allow building systems including lighting, HVAC, security, and communications to be controlled centrally from a website. Such buildings can be more functional, more earth-friendly, and more energy-efficient. The smart or intelligent building of today contains an abundance of microprocessors that operate these internal systems and allow them to work in sync with one another. In addition, they support sophisticated telecommunications systems for voice, data, and video transmission.

Soon you will find yourself surrounded by building professionals who are bubbling over with enthusiasm for these innovations, and certainly your new building should be technically sophisticated. The problem is that apostles of modern technology sometimes seem to work in a world that is entirely divorced from the realities of library management. They are always planning and constructing buildings, never maintaining existing ones. Before you allow yourself to be carried away by their rosy visions of the future, take a moment to think about your own library environment. The last time the temperature rose or plummeted to unacceptable levels, how difficult was it to have the problem remedied? How computer-literate are your maintenance supervisor and staff? How responsive is your central administration when it comes to calling in outside technical expertise? How generous has funding been for library preventive maintenance? Is "deferred maintenance" the option of choice when budgets are tight? Have new electrical circuits been installed when you needed them, or are wires strung haphazardly around the library? Has your roof been repaired and replaced on schedule, or must you cope with leaks and buckets for months before something is finally done?

Next, look beyond your own library building. If you are in an academic library, how well maintained are the other buildings on your campus? Public librarians might select other county or municipal buildings for comparison. Ask the facilities manager or building occupants about climate control, maintenance, and repairs.

Money spent on new building materials that reduce the need for routine maintenance is usually well spent—as long as the materials have been thoroughly tested. You don't want to incorporate them into your building and then discover unanticipated problems. What might work fine in a laboratory can be a disaster in real day-to-day situations. New computer-controlled HVAC and other systems can be great choices, but they require service and maintenance staff members who understand them. They depend on computer software and hardware that is subject to all the same tragedies you encounter daily with the library network. Therefore, people who work on the system must not only be able to cope with mechanical problems, but they must possess computer skills as well. If your library is located far from a large metropolitan area, they may not be up to the job.

No matter what you discover in library literature about a new building in Denver or San Francisco or Oshkosh, remember that your situation is not quite like any other. What may work in one environment may be a disaster in another. It may be your grasp on the realities of everyday library existence that best qualifies you for the work ahead. Don't let your unique perspective be eclipsed by what can sometimes be the uninformed enthusiasms of those around you. Continually draw from your past experience to inform your decisions, but make sure you're not stuck in a rut. New technologies can greatly enhance the library; they just can't alter or transform the environment in which the library operates.

RESOURCES

Bennett, Scott. *Libraries Designed for Learning.* Washington, DC: Council on Library and Information Resources, 2003.

Bolan, Kimberly. "Library Design Tips for the 21st Century." LYP Marketplace Resource Center (2006). www.lyponline.com/LLP_home/guides_art/library_design_tips.aspx.

Carlson, Scott. "Thoughtful Design Keeps New Libraries Relevant." Library Supplement, *Chronicle of Higher Education* 52, no. 6 (2005): b1–b5.

Forrest, Charles, and Lisa J. Hinchliffe. "Beyond Classroom Construction and Design: Formulating a Vision for Learning Spaces in Libraries." *Reference and User Services Quarterly* 44, no. 4 (2005): 296–300.

Freeman, Geoffrey T., Scott Bennett, Sam Demas, Bernard Frischer, Christina A. Peterson, and Kathleen B. Oliver. *Library as Place: Rethinking Roles, Rethinking Space.* Washington, DC: Council on Library and Information Resources, 2005.

Gardner, Susan, and Susanna Eng. "What Students Want: Generation Y and the Changing Function of the Academic Library." *Portal: Libraries and the Academy* 5, no. 3 (2005): 405ff.

Kenney, Brian. "After Seattle: By Discarding Every Preconception about a Public Library Building, They Created the First 21st-Century Library." *Library Journal* 130, no. 13 (2005): 34–37.

The Library as Place: Symposium on Building and Revitalizing Health Sciences Libraries in the Digital Age. National Library of Medicine, Association of Academic Health Science Libraries. DVD. National Library of Medicine, 2003.

The World of Architects and Contractors

As you will discover from the Tips and Tales sections, building or renovating a library is a lot of fun, but there's no denying that there will be days when you want to tear your hair out. If there is such a thing as a key to success, it may be found in establishing productive working relationships with the building professionals who will be involved in your project. A good place to begin, therefore, is with a basic understanding of who these people are and how they are selected.

HOW NEW BUILDINGS HAPPEN

Unless you've recently been involved in designing your own home, you may feel that you're totally in the dark about the way buildings come into being. Even if you've worked with an architect or contractor on your own home, you may still find the sort of wheeling and dealing that goes into a large building project rather overwhelming. So how does it all happen? The following is a brief description of the three basic project delivery systems currently in use in the United States.

The Traditional Building Project

Design-bid-build has long been the most common project delivery system in the U.S. construction industry. As owner, your library or its parent organization contracts separately with an architecture/design firm and with a builder/contractor. Your organization as owner contracts with a design firm to provide complete design documents that will allow the library to solicit fixed-price bids from contractors for the performance of the work. The contractors enter into an agreement with your library to construct a building in accordance with the plans and specifications. This system ensures, for better or worse, that design and construction functions are totally separate. Thus, the contractor is only chosen after the design has been completed.

In most situations, the library works with a general contractor who in turn hires subcontractors; in some places, however, libraries must contract directly with several prime contractors like those providing general, mechanical, and electrical services.

Construction Management at Risk Project Delivery System

The construction management at risk project delivery system also involves the owner's contracting with the design firm and contractor separately, but the contractor is selected early in the project before plans are completed. The contractor performs construction management services and construction work, in accordance with the plans and specifications, for an agreed-upon fee. Because contractors enter the picture much earlier, they are able to have considerably more input into the design process. In fact, this is essential because the cost of the building has already been agreed upon, so it must be possible to construct the structure designed by the architect for the agreed-upon price. Since both building professionals are on board earlier, this method allows the project to progress at a much faster pace than with the design-bid-build project delivery system.

The Design-Build Project Delivery System

In recent years, however, a third type of project delivery system has been gaining in popularity. In the case of the design-build project delivery system, the library or its parent organization contracts with just one entity that performs both design and construction as part of a single design-build contract. With this system there is a single point of responsibility for both design and construction services. Specific work may be contracted out to other companies, but only the design-build firm is responsible directly to the owner. Discussions in this book will devote considerably more attention to this option than to the other two, since it is a recent innovation that is sweeping the world of publicly funded construction. It is important that you be prepared if your parent organization is moving in this direction.

THE WORLD OF ARCHITECTS

As the library building planning process becomes increasingly stressful, take comfort in the fact that librarians have been coping with building crises for hundreds, even thousands, of years. Assurbanipal's librarian in ancient Assyria endured many of the same headaches. Leaky roofs are nothing new; think how much more vulnerable (as well as heavy and breakable) those clay tablets must have been. In theory at least, we should have an easier time of it with all our modern conveniences, but sometimes I wonder. For instance, did those ancient Babylonian librarians have to contend with architects?

Probably the ancients had someone comparable (names of some of the architects who designed the pyramids were actually recorded), but I doubt that any ancient architect ever designed a balcony on an upper level overlooking a fountain in the lobby. Few modern architects have ever paused to think of how a ten-year-old child will use such a golden opportunity. The splashing you hear represents a sizable portion of the book collection being hurled joyously into the fountain. The graciously curving central stairway with which I was once burdened served a similar function, but the books were aimed at the crania of friends below (not by children but by college students who also enjoyed sliding down the spiraling banister).

The Lure of the Library

I think that such errors in judgment may be the result of the delight architects experience when commissioned to plan a library building. Rarely do they have so much scope for their imaginations. Think of all that open space! What an impressive opportunity to exercise their talents! Office buildings are boring with their endless halls and small cubbyholes. Classroom buildings offer few opportunities to really let go. But a library! Think of all those imposing edifices from the old Carnegies to modern chrome-and-glass extravaganzas. Each looks magnificent until you have a chat with the librarian. As you enter one of those newer libraries, you may encounter a mystic maze of electric cords strung from wall to wall dipping precariously between computer workstations and book stacks. Apparently, the architects were picturing a nineteenth-century library.

Despite the librarian's input, the architects somehow failed to comprehend the plethora of computers, photocopy machines, printer stations, microfilm readers, and videoconferencing equipment that have become standard in a modern library. If you were to continue your progress through the building, you might encounter temperatures ranging from arctic to tropical. That might be due to the charming atrium at the center of the building. The architects apparently failed to consider the resulting heat gain in summer and heat loss in winter when designing the climate control system. The smell of decaying vegetation comes from the atrium's tropical jungle that overburdened staff members are too busy to care for properly.

Librarians spend a great deal of time finding fault with their buildings. Sometimes they ascribe the fault to their predecessors or to changes in technology. More often, they lay the blame at the feet of their architects. Regard such ravings with caution, but do listen. Some architects are flexible enough to respond to the library's requirements; others are not. It is not possible

TALES

From the start, everything suggested a good working relationship with the architects. We spent a lot of time poring over blueprints and pinpointing the location of every outlet and window, but somewhere along the line we neglected to make sure the architects knew what they were doing.

The stairs only go to the third of five floors. We also have another staircase that doesn't go anywhere but can be clearly seen from the outside of the building.

The marble counters retain the cold, which means you can freeze meat most of the year.

The clocks are so high that it requires maintenance to change them with the tallest ladders they have.

to know what really transpired during the planning and construction phases of any given library, but patterns do emerge. Look at the architect's work as a whole rather than judging her by any one building.

CHOOSING LIBRARY ARCHITECTS

Considering how important the architects are to your building project, how do you choose the best ones available? Of course, you will not have a free hand in the choice, but you can at least make sure the decision makers are prepared with the right information. Begin with a list of architectural firms that have demonstrated experience in projects similar to yours. Since library commissions are few, also look at firms that have designed other public and commercial buildings in your area. Analyze the buildings' good and bad features as you might a library. Does form follow function, or does it seem to be the other way around? Try to identify and interview the individuals who were involved in the projects. Ask how receptive the architects were to their suggestions. Did the architects appear to have a separate agenda, or did plans emerge from the expressed needs of the owners and users?

The American Institute of Architects can provide project-specific lists for your area. Begin with as long a list as possible and compare the architects' past work with your own project. Compare project size, project scope, time line, experience with nonprofit organizations, and reported interactions with clients. Invite the architects under consideration to make presentations so you can discover how they perceive the library's role. Did the architects do most of the talking, or did they listen more than talk? Did they ask the right questions? Did they come to the presentation prepared with knowledge about libraries in general and your project in particular? Did they communicate in jargon or in understandable terms? Are they accustomed to working with groups of people such as committees and boards? Do they understand and accept your budget limitations and the tight budget constraints that libraries must work under?

It Takes Time and Talent

You and your planning group will want to be wary of free services or the offer of a substantially reduced fee structure. No matter how large or small, your library will require many hours of highly individualized and highly professional labor. It is usually not possible to adapt the design of another building to the library's needs. Neither should you take a chance on a fledgling architectural firm that is looking for a large project to make a name for itself. The money saved in architectural services will not outweigh the problems that will ensue if the building is not properly designed.

Why are the architects under consideration interested in your particular project? Can you detect any particular enthusiasm or commitment, or are they simply casting their nets for any business that presents itself? Ask them about the specific expertise that makes them the best choice for your project. Inevitably, the discussion will generate ideas, and it is important to note whether those ideas are focused on form or function. Are the architects describing what the building will look like, or are they focusing on what activities will be taking place within it? During these first contacts they will, of course, know little about libraries, but beware the architect who enthusiastically discusses the granite countertops or the dramatic staircase.

If you have a chance, take a look at the San Francisco, Denver, or Chicago main libraries. All three are amazing buildings, and all three say loudly and clearly that libraries are cool, trendy, and ready for the twenty-first century. After early encounters with architects, I thought that all I wanted was a vast warehouse or supermarket that tempted no architect's creativity. Now, after years of ranting, I have come to realize that the public's image of the library depends to a considerable extent on its architecture. We do, indeed, want a building that shouts "I'm an important place; I'm the focus of my community." I no longer begrudge the architects their awards as long as they do not turn a deaf ear to my service-oriented pleas and those of my colleagues.

Other Important Services

Seek out architects who are willing to participate fully in fund-raising. This means that they are willing to include deliverables in the contract such as presentation-quality visual materials, floor plans, material boards, renderings, and even computer model walk-through imaging. Ask about a presentation-quality site plan as well as exterior and interior perspectives and models. These can be extremely useful tools for increasing enthusiasm among your patrons and donors. It is not uncommon for the library capital campaign to be offered in-kind gifts from local businesses. These are sometimes welcomed with open arms, but they may also create problems. Deciding not only what is acceptable but what gifts will be sought out should be part of the contract. Since the architects' fees may be tied to the total cost of the project, it is especially important that they not artificially inflate costs by discouraging gifts.

TIPS

Take some time and find a design firm you can trust and that has experience in designing a library, a museum, or an archive. We spent over six months looking for our architect, and the result has been well worth the effort. Be sure you're comfortable working with the firm you select because things get pretty intense in the latter stages of the project.

I'd say that one of the requirements for a good architect, apart from experience and ability in designing libraries, is flexibility and willingness to present alternatives.

The architect should have the diplomatic skills to deal with college presidents, librarians, donors, and others and in some cases to negotiate compromises among them.

Try to make your building a community showplace without being the architect's monument to himself.

WHAT TO EXPECT FROM YOUR ARCHITECT

Before entering into an agreement with a firm of architects, you should obtain the American Institute of Architects (AIA) publication *You and Your Architect.*[1] This sixteen-page booklet was developed by a group of architects, owners, lawyers, and insurance risk managers. It presents the AIA's interpretation of the architect's role and responsibilities, and it is important that you be acquainted with this perspective. Since it is brief and simply written, you can provide it as suggested reading for other members of your project team. Included is a four-page removable instruction sheet addressed to the architect. It provides an opportunity to go over basic information so you can be sure you and your architect are both literally "reading from the same page." Becoming familiar with this pre-agreement checklist can alert you to issues and problem areas that may come up in your relationship. Discussing these items with any potential architects can help you make a final decision about whether this is the firm you want to design your building.

AIA forms have regulated transactions within the building trades since 1888 and have provided an important service by establishing standards to guide business transactions. The institute's publications constitute a coordinated system that spells out the legal relationships among owners, architects, contractors, subcontractors, and others. Since AIA documents have been around for so long, they have usually been tested in the courts, and legal interpretations have been amassed.[2] If your parent institution or its lawyers have a question about a provision, there is a whole body of literature available for review. Because the AIA documents will serve to clarify the roles and relationships of all of the parties involved in your construction project, they should be part of your professional reading (even though most are far less lucid than the pamphlet just cited).

Expanding Your Reading

Other organizations in the industry like the Engineers' Joint Contract Documents Committee also publish contract forms, and some of these are more likely to protect the owner. It may be in your library's interest to familiarize yourself with the different forms available because the competition among industry associations may work in your favor. The Associated General Contractors and the Construction Management Association of America are yet additional sources of standard documents.[3] You will quickly find yourself overwhelmed by unfamiliar terminology, but you will at least be able to talk intelligently with your library's legal counsel about expectations of your architects. If you believe that your library has insufficient access to legal assistance, be wary of highly customized contracts, since they must be scrutinized very carefully.

Cyburbia, an interesting website sponsored by the State University of New York at Buffalo's School of Architecture and Planning, is a directory of about 7,000 links to sites about planning, architecture, and related professions. In addition, it includes information about 130 architecture and planning-related mailing lists. Checking this site from time to time will familiarize you with many architectural issues and, in some ways even more important, with the perspectives of architects themselves.[4]

The Architect's Contract

Before much more time passes, find out about B141, the Owner-Architect Agreement, otherwise known as the architect's contract recommended by the AIA. You might also browse through *The Architect's Handbook of Professional Practice,* which contains very useful explanatory material entitled "B141 Commentary."[5] Take a look at the Annotated B141, which is a provision-by-provision discussion of the Owner-Architect Agreement.[6] It explains the purpose of key provisions and provides a series of "practice pointers" intended to guide architects. In addition, it includes a number of liability alerts regarding the dangers that can arise from making changes in the standard document.

Another AIA publication, *Compromise Contract Language Alternatives,* illustrates a series of hypothetical owner-suggested modifications to the architect's contract and comments on the problems these create for both the architect and the owner.[7] Possible alternative compromise language is suggested. Of course, you will discover that many of these modifications in the contract serve to protect the architect and increase the owner's responsibility. If forewarned is forearmed, then this is the publication for you.

Does it really matter, you may ask, what is included in the architect's contract? Most emphatically yes, and the most important part may not be what you actually read in the contract. Since much of the contract consists of references to other sources, documents outside the body of the written contract may make all the difference in holding architects responsible

TALE

Due to a budget freeze on travel, my enrollment in an excellent seminar on building project planning was delayed by a year. When I finally got to take it, I learned about the elements of a standard architect's contract on such projects as mine. My own campus folks, despite having several other projects under their belts, never bothered to tell me what I did and did not have a right to expect from the architect under the terms of his contract. That might have saved some confusion and misunderstanding and also might have given me more info and confidence as the project got under way. Taking the seminar in time might also have schooled me in what kinds of questions to ask and saved me some time and effort. . . . We saved the taxpayers several hundred dollars by not sending me that first year. But then . . . we spent the same amount next year—a year too late.

for their mistakes. The phrase "attached hereto and made a part hereof" can mean much to the success or failure of your project. The terms of whatever documents are referenced are just as binding as the terms and conditions in the body of the contract. Even if the document referenced is not physically attached, it is probably a binding part of the agreement. Not only inexperienced owners but professional contractors with many years' experience may overlook these potential land mines. The specifics relating to a particular project are often quite brief, simply naming the parties; the name and location of the project; and the terms of the price, payment, and schedule. Referenced items, on the other hand, are often so numerous that few people are willing to spend the time looking each up separately to be sure the references mean what readers think those items mean. If you have the opportunity, make sure the library's attorney does not simply give her perfunctory approval but actually spends time with the contract.

Architect's Liability

Let us assume that due to the architects' error some dreadful problem arises, jeopardizing the success of your building project. Are your architects responsible? Can you sue them? Though it pains a librarian to be as equivocal as a lawyer, the answer is unfortunately "maybe yes and maybe no." If architects fail to exercise reasonable care in the performance of their duties, they can be held liable to persons who are injured as a result of their failure. These persons can include the contractor, the owner, and any others involved in the project who, as a result of the architects' acts or omissions on a project, have incurred financial losses.

This does not mean, however, that architects are automatically liable if something goes wrong. As long as they can demonstrate that they have exercised reasonable care, it is extremely difficult to hold architects responsible for many problems. The courts have interpreted this obligation as nothing more than exercising the ordinary skill and competence expected of members of the profession. The owner is merely purchasing the architects' services, not insurance that everything will be done correctly. Nevertheless, architects have usually been held liable for obvious carelessness or other situations in which it is fairly clear that they "should have known better."

In complicated legal battles, architects sometimes succeed in avoiding liability by providing experts who will testify that they did, in fact, exercise reasonable care under the circumstances. In such cases, the owner or contractor will have to prove by a preponderance of evidence provided by their own expert-witness testimony that the architect did not exercise reasonable care. With more traditional project delivery systems, much time and energy is often spent passing blame back and forth between architect and contractor. One of the reasons many people feel positively toward the recent growth of the design-build industry (discussed later in this chapter) is that it brings the architect and contractor under one umbrella. Although this is a recent development and case law is inconclusive, there has been a tendency to hold the architect to the higher standard required of the contractor.

Meeting Your Architects

At some point after the "go" decision has been made, you will be asked to meet the architects. Ideally, your involvement should have begun much earlier, when you met all the architects being considered for your project. One way or another, however, a first encounter is looming on your horizon. How should you handle it?

This first meeting is a momentous one because it will set a pattern for future encounters. Most architects begin a project with enthusiasm and with a sincere desire to design a building that will please the people who will be using it. They also, however, begin with a picture in their minds of what a library should look like. It will be up to you to gradually change and fashion that picture until it reflects the realities of a modern library facility. Not only do the architects have a picture of a library embedded in their subconscious, but they have a picture of librarians as well. Unless they have been involved in other library building projects, that librarian picture may be a fluffy older woman in orthopedic oxfords, immersed in her books, who could never understand the basics of architecture or construction. This image must be dispelled immediately if you are to exert any influence on the project. Therefore, careful preparation for this first meeting is essential. The following is an action plan to prepare you for the first meeting:

1. Go first to your library shelves and find a glossary of architectural terms. Although you will find a number of these terms sprinkled throughout this book, you will need many more to describe the library that is taking shape in your mind. It is wise to get the vocabulary under control before you begin the project. If you are familiar with widely used terminology, you will be able to conduct this first meeting on a much more professional plane. This should be a conference between colleagues, not the more typical "doctor-patient" consultation.

2. Make a very short written list of the things the architects should know about the library before proceeding further. Go over this list again and again, whittling it down to the items you are absolutely sure you can cover in the time available. Remove or explain any library jargon. Be sure that you are not assuming knowledge that the architects may not possess. In other words, begin at a very basic level and don't digress. You want to be certain that they leave the meeting with list in hand, knowing more about your vision of a library than they did when they arrived. The point is that you are beginning their library education. The next time you meet, refer to the information you provided and distribute part 2 of your library primer. Make the architects feel just a little guilty if they have not read their homework assignment. If necessary, provide another copy and make it clear that you will be discussing it later.

3. Try to arrange the meeting so that you are alone with the architects. This is not always possible, and you may be one of a group meeting together. The more people present, the less control you have over the meeting. You probably can't dislodge the principal, president, board chairperson, or county commissioner, but you may be able to schedule other occasions when you can meet with the architects more privately.

4. Be sure the architects take away an image of you that is friendly and competent. Welcome them enthusiastically to the team, but keep the ball in your own court.

The Architects and the Library Staff

At one time, I thought it was a very good idea for the architects to meet with the library staff early on to better understand their needs; now I am not so sure. I happened to come upon an article written by an architect for a professional architecture journal; the architect discussed a major public library project in which he had been involved and emphasized how sensitive he had been to the needs of the library staff. It was immediately clear that he had missed the boat

Lycoming County (Pa.) Library System, James V. Brown Library, Larson Design Group, larsondesigngroup.com. Photo: Eric Stashak Photography.

entirely. He had listened while several dozen people expressed their frustrations with the old building and their hopes and dreams for the new library. Out of this mishmash, he seemed to pull the most irrelevant points and miss the really important ones. This was probably not entirely his fault, because he lacked the body of knowledge needed to evaluate the relative importance of the diverse contributions.

The library staff will naturally want to be involved as much as possible, but their contributions should be honed and shaped in just the way you prepared for your first meeting with the architects. Work with the staff to prepare for any meetings. Make a list of priorities and help staff understand the importance of hammering away at important points. When they do meet with the architects, staff should have their agenda and talking points prepared and be ready to redirect the discussion if it veers away from these key issues.

WHAT ARCHITECTS NEED TO KNOW

Because libraries are such an integral part of your life, you may forget to communicate simple, basic information. Before any architects begin sketching floor plans, they will need a crash course in libraries. By this I do not mean anything remotely resembling the introduction to library science you remember from library school. Although it may be obvious to you, the architect must be told who will use the library. How will they use it? Children have very different needs from elderly adults, and college students use a facility in still different ways. What do staff do when they're working in the processing area? How are their needs different when they're working in public services? How many patrons will use the public computers, collaborative studies, restrooms, or meeting rooms at one time?

Architects need to know, for example, that your customers will enter through only one door and that all other doors will be emergency exits. They need to know that there will be a security system at this door and a service desk nearby so that customers setting off the alarm can be asked to return. They need to know how much space should be devoted to book stacks and how much to computer use. One would also think that, with all the stereotypes of the dowdy librarian shushing noisy patrons, they would know that a library should be a relatively quiet place, but this is often not the case.

The Two-Step Process

It is common on some projects to divide negotiations with an architectural firm into two phases. Phase one may involve contracting with the firm to produce only a conceptual design of the new library. Public libraries, especially, may need to have a detailed plan to present to their local government agencies and ultimately to the voters. Such a plan shows most of the building's important features but does not show detail. It may cost from $20,000 to $100,000, depending on the size of the project. The conceptual plan is needed as part of the library's capital campaign strategy, and architects may assist with the campaign by attending public meetings, providing the services of a public relations consultant, and producing attractive drawings and models that will help the library "sell" the project. Only when full funding has been obtained are architects hired to draw up the detailed sets of plans needed by a contractor.

The Case Statement

Before getting into the nitty-gritty of space requirements and load-bearing walls, get together with your planning group and take some time to hammer out a statement describing just what you expect from the new or renovated library. What will make it different from other libraries, from other public buildings? From the environment your patrons have come to expect? Why is it needed? Why is it worth the millions of dollars that will be spent on it? This will become, in a sense, your marching song. Often called a case statement, it will provide the foundation for negotiations with county commissioners and city planners and discussions with your architects, as well as the basis for newspaper interviews and presentations to community groups.

We often find it more difficult to write a brief case statement than a long laundry list of all the things we want to include in the new building. So I thought it might be helpful to include a fairly typical statement that covers important points clearly and succinctly.

SAMPLE CASE STATEMENT

It is the consensus opinion of the Bozeman Public Library Board of Trustees that the design for the new Library should strive to create a building and a place that

Responds to the wants and needs of the citizens of our community for lifelong learning.

Becomes a highly active, multiuse, family-centered learning environment for the twenty-first century.

Is responsive to the built, natural, cultural, and historic context of the site.

Demonstrates good stewardship of public funds by exploring alternative site developments that are cost-effective (affordable), provide the greatest cultural return to the community for the invested dollars, and allow for all foreseeable expansions of the Library.

Functions in an efficient and effective manner while being sufficiently flexible to meet the evolving technological and educational requirements of a contemporary library.

Has integrated interior and exterior learning environments.

Has a significant central organizing interior space with a sense of life (through plants, sunlight, people, etc.) within which, and about which, the Library functions are organized.

Is inspiring, provoking community pride and involvement on a continuing basis.

Responds to, and clearly integrates, the various modes of transportation serving the site.

Will be described as beautiful, exciting, inviting, and appropriate for Bozeman.

Addresses and engages both Main Street and Lindley Park through building and site design elements.

Demonstrates, and teaches, concern and respect for the preservation of our natural environment through the utilization of sustainable design principles, materials, and systems.

Minimizes the cost of construction and maintenance through life-cycle cost estimation.

Demonstrates a sense of history through an appropriate incorporation of the old depot building into the new site development.[8]

YOUR PRESENT AND FUTURE NEEDS

I sometimes think that architects fall victim to a sort of "Sleeping Beauty" complex. Since you entered the library profession, you've seen constant change. Almost every year of your professional career, you and your colleagues have made substantial alterations to the library. You've knocked down stacks and moved them to areas experiencing rapid collection growth; you've added phone lines; you've wired study carrels to provide media access and upgraded the electrical system to accommodate all the new equipment. An architect, however, works with a snapshot of a building frozen in time.

Wendell Wickerham of the architectural firm of Shepley Bulfinch Richardson and Abbott expressed frustration that architects work very closely with a building until it opens, but then they lose contact with both the staff and the activities that take place in the building. It is, therefore, difficult for the architect to determine exactly which of his ideas worked well and which should not be repeated. One of Wickerham's firm's major projects was the Leavey Undergraduate Library at the University of California. Overall, Leavey was an extremely successful library project, but Wickerham, not fully understanding library security problems, was disappointed that the patio he designed, complete with pleasantly situated tables and chairs, went unused.[9]

An architect soon moves on to another project and fails to see how the building changes over the years. On one project, our library architect tried to cut the carpet around the stacks so that they would rest more securely on the cement floor. It did not occur to him that those very stacks would be moved twice in the next ten years. This is information that only you can communicate.

If you are going to have a successful relationship with your architects, begin by clarifying which decisions you must make (or at least exert considerable influence over) and which offer more opportunity for the architects' imaginative design features. I don't know how you feel about working in an enchilada-red building like the San Antonio Public Library, but it's not your issue. Of course, you're free to express an opinion, but make it clear that it is not the same as your opinion on the load-bearing capacity of the floors. Let the trustees, the general public, the media, and anybody else so inclined debate the peripheral issues. Just be sure you don't get caught in the cross fire.

Establishing Priorities

Begin making a very precise list of just what your issues are. Let it evolve gradually over time as you delve into library literature, visit other libraries, talk with your staff, and analyze concerns about your present library building. It will soon become quite a long list, so be careful to prioritize. Just because you happen to come across an attractive design feature or hate the color green, you should recognize that these are very minor points. Your list should be focused on function, and including peripheral issues may serve to confuse your architects. Of course, you can't possibly cover everything. The point is to train your architects on the kinds of issues you consider important. At the same time, understand that the architects' values are important too. Try hard to be encouraging and supportive of their creative input when it does not have a negative impact on function.

Library Spaces

In addition to basic information about library functions, begin describing specific library spaces. Will you need technically sophisticated classrooms for library literacy instruction? Meeting rooms that can be used when the library is closed? What about a twenty-four-hour study area in an academic library? This may be the appropriate time for an impassioned plea for adequate restrooms if your library's only conveniences are located off a dark hall or in the basement.

Consult published standards for your type of library to estimate the space requirements for collections and reading areas. Be sure you make it clear that a space or area does not usually mean a room. Walls in a library should be kept to a minimum, since they reduce flexibility and make supervision difficult. They also impede traffic flow and cause both customers and staff to waste time and energy taking the "long way around."

Once you have a general description of the spaces you'll be using, the architect will need to understand the relationships among them. Which ones should adjoin one another? Which can be widely separated? Make it clear that libraries, though spacious, are short-staffed and that staff time is valuable. Staff need to be able to do their work efficiently with the fewest number of steps. Customers also resent having to walk long distances unnecessarily. Don't attempt to draw a floor plan. Architects are far more knowledgeable about the technical and aesthetic considerations that go into such a plan. Be clear from the start about your roles, respecting their professional expertise but also demanding respect in your own professional sphere.

Other useful additions to your "magnum opus" are statistical summaries showing the way space has been used in other libraries similar to your own. Information included might cover collection and staff size; numbers of study carrels, tables, collaborative study rooms, and computer workstations; and floor space allotted to circulation, periodicals, acquisitions, and cataloging functions. Although you don't want to tell your architects how to do their job, obtain a variety of floor plans from other libraries so you can point out both the positives and the negatives.

Libraries Are Not Affluent

Since long before Andrew Carnegie financed the building of thousands of libraries, new library construction has depended on special or outside funding. The result may be generous or meager, but it bears little relation to the library's operating budget. Your university development office may solicit foundation grants or the voters in your municipality may approve a bond issue, but any funds obtained are earmarked specifically for the building project. They cannot be expected to support your everyday operations. It is a sad fact of library life that a new library will further tax your resources, forcing you to do even more with less. Any increases in your operating budget will inevitably be swallowed up by the increased workload of a larger, more popular library.

Save Now, Suffer Later

If your institution chooses a traditional project delivery system, a universal law of nature states that the building the architects initially design will cost far more money than has been budgeted. Of course, everyone concerned had a wish list, and the architects brought their own visions that substantially inflated the cost. Now it is clear that the proposed building must be trimmed down to an affordable package, and a group is given the task of cutting enough fluff to allow the project to come in under budget. Unfortunately, what you consider necessities and what others, especially architects, consider necessities may be poles apart.

Another law of nature states that early in the paring-down process, it will be suggested that the library can do without a central light control panel, half the planned temperature zones, and windows that open. Well, it can't! Neither your staff nor your patrons should be asked to make such sacrifices to preserve the cherished atrium or spiral staircase that your design professionals hope will win architectural awards. The library is not just a showcase for their talents.

There are many ways that features incorporated into the plans now can result in lower utility bills and fewer maintenance expenses later. On the other hand, design features can considerably increase the cost of operating a library. For example, in buildings with atria, it is very difficult to balance airflow; therefore, service calls to repair malfunctioning circulators, pumps, blowers, and other HVAC components are more frequent. You needn't overdo your impassioned speeches about library poverty, but be sure your architect understands that your operating budget is not generous.

Maximizing Staff Effectiveness

As mentioned earlier, library staff size inevitably surprises architects. That such a large and expensive building can be staffed by such a small number of people continually confounds them. Stress the fact that libraries are unlike many other buildings in that funding is often more readily available for capital outlay than for ongoing expenses. In contrast, when a corporation decides to construct a new office building, expenditures for the building are in line with the overall corporate budget. If the corporation is doing well, one might expect more generous funding for construction, staffing, and other corporate needs. Hard times would result in across-the-board cuts.

What all this means is that architects should design the most efficient library possible, one that requires the smallest staff to operate it and one that uses staff time most efficiently. For example, unnecessary walls make it impossible to keep disruptive or possibly dangerous patrons under observation. A centrally located light switch panel that allows one staff member to turn off all the lights in the building is not the luxury it might be in an office building where staff are assigned to all floors. Security cameras are far less expensive than staff members personally monitoring the same spaces. Be sure the architect understands that you want to operate your new building efficiently with the number of staff currently employed. Considering the present uncertain state of libraries, it might even be desirable to plan for a reduced staff.

THE WORLD OF CONTRACTORS

As you've probably noticed in the Tips and Tales sections, librarians involved in a construction project may eventually find themselves at war with their architects. Contractors, however, seem to escape much of our venom. I used to think the basis of the conflict with architects was sexism, since librarianship is a female-dominated profession and architects were usually men. However, in recent years, more and more women are becoming architects, and yet I see no movement toward reconciliation.

Lately, however, I have adopted a new hypothesis (probably no sounder than the old one). We usually begin our relationship with our architects when we are filled with excitement and enthusiasm. The architects appear to share that enthusiasm and weave verbal visions of the ideal library. It is probably inevitable that we blame the architects when the fluffy pink clouds part and we behold our less-than-perfect library building. On the other hand, we usually begin our relationship with the contractor at a low point. He probably does not want us to set foot on the site and throws a first-class temper tantrum if we forget our hard hat or step in the wrong spot. The contractor makes us feel like naughty children, and we complain loudly that this is our building.

Two against One

As the project progresses, we gradually get used to one another. We discover that we're more welcome if we heap praise on the contractor's latest efforts. Since we really are delighted to see the building take shape before our eyes, the atmosphere starts to thaw. At about the same time, however, we begin noticing little problems. The cabinets we were promised in the processing area have disappeared from the plans. The contractor has a more recent set of blueprints, and somehow the conference room has shrunk by four feet. This means the custom-built conference table that's already been ordered no longer fits.

"That's just like an architect," the sympathetic contractor assures you. Contractors have had years to hone their resentment of architects (in fact, the two professions have probably been at odds with one another since the building of the pyramids), and you're more than willing to join the lynch mob. As the project progresses, you encounter more and more unpleasant surprises, many of which have to do with the design of the building, and your most understanding confidant is inevitably your contractor. Of course, the contractor is creating his share of problems, but it will probably be months or even years before you discover some of them.

Choosing a Contractor

Depending on your own unique library environment and the individuals involved in the building project, you may or may not be consulted in the selection of a general contractor. In some organizations, it may be considered none of your business and will be handled entirely through a purchasing or facilities department that sends out requests for proposals (RFPs) and selects the low bidder. Nevertheless, a few words of caution are in order in hopes that you can use your influence to avoid potential catastrophes.

Obtain bids from a number of qualified contractors using a detailed RFP that specifies what information is required and how it should be presented. That way, you can compare prices accurately. Ask the contractors for references from banks, suppliers, and insurance companies and review those responses carefully. Be suspicious of estimates that are not accompanied by "backup detail," including the names of sources for materials and subcontractors. You should also be suspicious of estimates based on a printout from a computer program or a boilerplate estimate that was really prepared for someone else's project. Then make sure you have read and understood all terms and conditions. Remember that this is a language unfamiliar to you, so obtain legal advice when necessary.

Large institutions and governmental units have usually had experience with other building projects and know the ropes. Small public and college libraries, however, may not have access to this kind of expertise. Board members may imagine that they can select a library contractor in much the same way they chose one when they built their own homes. This is not the case. To begin with, libraries are large, sophisticated, and expensive buildings. Any contractor under consideration must have had experience constructing other buildings at least as large and expensive as yours—preferably larger and more complicated. Of course, every building project is different and requires a new approach, but you do not want to be an experiment or a practice exercise for your contractor. You want someone who's already a pro.

Financial Stability Is Essential

Be sure that you consider only large, stable firms. Although Board Member Smith's brother-in-law may be in construction, this is not the place for a small business person. Be sure that decision makers have obtained excellent bank references before signing any contract. One of the worst things that could possibly happen is to have your contractor go bankrupt before the project is completed. In addition to these words of warning, be sure that your project team is considering only contractors who are licensed in your state. Insist on documentary evidence of this status. Find out how long the contractor has been in business and avoid any contractor who moves often or who hasn't been in your area long enough to provide local references.

It is a good idea to call previous customers, so you'll need to request names and other information from the contractor. Be sure, however, to request a list of all recent projects, not just the ones the contractor is most proud of. Check into the other types of buildings the contractor has experience with (residential, commercial, etc.) and visit former customers at their building locations. While you're there, find out whether the contractor has kept to the established schedule and ask about the contract terms. Ask how problems were resolved on previous jobs and how willing the contractor was to make any necessary corrections. In addition, here are some other important ways to protect yourself and your project:

> Ask for a bid bond that guarantees that the party bidding for the contract will, if the bid is accepted, enter into the contract and furnish performance and payment bonds for carrying out the work. Be sure that the cost of bonds is paid by the contractor and included in the bid.

> Check that the contractor is a member of recognized local and preferably national professional organizations.

> Insist that the contractor carry workers' compensation and liability insurance coverage. Insurance companies can provide evidence of coverage by issuing a certificate of insurance. They can also notify you in case of policy cancellation.

The Contract for Construction

Contracts and warranties, especially their sticky, tricky little clauses, define the legal obligations of all the participants in a building project. These documents are vitally important when it comes to clarifying who does what and who is responsible to whom. Conflict is an inevitable part of many building projects, and it's best to be fully prepared.

The most important document in any legal dispute, the Contract for Construction, is an agreement between the owner and the general contractor. Often referred to as the general contract, it establishes the rights and obligations of each party. In addition, it provides the framework of the whole project as well as the basis for most courtroom litigation. Insist that the contractor provide a contract bond for the project. This will guarantee the fulfillment of contract obligations.

General Conditions

Incorporated within the Contract for Construction are a number of "general conditions." For example, you might insist on a maintenance bond that requires that the contractor redo any unsatisfactory work or replace any materials at his own cost within a specified time after completion of the work. Also be sure that any contracts include the time frame in which the work must be completed. Check that contracts include a description of what constitutes substantial commencement of work and a notice that failure to substantially commence work within twenty days from the specified date without lawful excuse constitutes a violation of the contract. Be certain that the schedule of payments showing the amount of each payment is included and that any down payment does not exceed 10 percent of the contract price. To help keep track of payments, consider engaging a funding-control service (also called builder's construction-control, fund-disbursement, or cost-disbursement service).

Although some of these conditions and bonds will be explained in full, most will simply make reference to AIA Document A201. It is extremely important to have a copy of this publication handy, and since you work in a library, this should not pose a problem. A201 includes many of the specific requirements that define the obligations of the owner and the contractor. If you are in a law library or have relatively easy access to one, investigate the AIA Citator Service. You should at least know that this service exists, because if and when a conflict arises, it is the best source of information on the ways in which specific clauses found in AIA documents have been construed by the courts.

Special Conditions

In addition to "general conditions," the Contract for Construction contains several "special conditions." These may address any topic related to the project. For the most part, they concern technical requirements, and naturally they tend to be difficult to understand and extremely important. Most of the plans and specifications pertaining to the project are not actually physically included within the contract. (They're too big and bulky.) However, they are referred to throughout the document. Of course, this means they are very easy to miss because you probably don't have all these materials on hand. Check the general contract's "incorporation clause" carefully to clarify which additional documents may affect your rights and obligations.

Warranty Clause

This is one of the sections that should be read very, very carefully. Although we might automatically assume that a warranty is intended to protect the owner, it is, to a large extent, intended to protect the contractor. It may, for example, state that the owner must notify the contractor of any nonconforming work within one year of substantial completion to trigger the contractor's obligation to make repairs without additional cost to the owner. The law, however, may hold the contractor legally liable at any time within the applicable statute of limitations for negligent, nonconforming, or defective construction or for cost overruns. Some librarians believe that the warranty clause is nothing more than a wordy attempt to weasel out of this obligation.

Bonds and warranties are usually quite narrowly defined. If the basement leaks six months after you move into the new building, you need to know who will pay for it. How long is the contractor obligated to fix things? Most contractors provide a warranty or guarantee, but what's included varies with the individual contractor. It is inevitable that there will be situations that are not covered, but try to get the most inclusive language possible. Request specific wording that lists only what is not covered and includes a clear statement that everything else comes under the warranty. Discuss these issues as early as possible, preferably before the construction contract has been awarded.

Performance and Payment Bonds

The contractor is usually required to provide performance and payment bonds as part of the Contract for Construction. A performance bond is a separate contract that promises the owner that the work will be performed either by the original contractor or a substitute contractor. Be sure to require an additional payment bond if it is not included in the performance bond. Often referred to as a labor-and-materials bond, it guarantees that bills for subcontractors' labor and vendors' materials used in the work project will be paid. A surety company issues the bonds, and it is in that company's interests that the contractor meet his obligations. The contractor may be more likely to listen to the surety company than to the owner or the architect. Insist that an insurance or surety company stand behind the bond if the contractor fails to perform.

Arbitration

In case of a dispute between owner and contractor, arbitration is the usual method of resolving conflict. Therefore, most construction contracts contain an arbitration clause. Either the actual clause will be included within the contract or it will be incorporated by a reference such as "Paragraph 4.5 of A201." References to standard AIA documents have the advantage of being widely accepted and therefore reasonably open and aboveboard. However, you should know what you are getting into, so at least make sure you have A201 on hand. If it is incorporated by reference into the arbitration clause, you are usually agreeing to arbitrate any dispute arising out of the contract by submitting the dispute to binding arbitration conducted in conformity with the Construction Industry Rules of the American Arbitration Association (AAA). You can obtain a copy of the rules from an AAA office, which can be found in most major cities. Cases are categorized by the amount of money in dispute. If the amount is under $50,000, your case qualifies for fast-track procedures. Next comes the regular track, and for very large amounts there is a large, complex track. A fee ranging from $500 to $7,000 is paid to the AAA at the time the demand for arbitration is filed.

THE DESIGN-BUILD DELIVERY SYSTEM

One of the big changes in the building industry in recent years is the emergence of the design-build project delivery option. Although it is currently the subject of many books and articles in the building trade, the term *design-build* is only gradually appearing in library literature. If you will have a role in contracting for the design and construction of your building, you should be aware of the advantages and disadvantages of design-build. It is also important to have a grasp of the basics if you will be working with a design-build firm on a day-to-day basis.

One Entity

Traditionally, the owner hires an architect or engineer to design the facility and produce plans to send to several contractors for competitive bidding. When an owner chooses the design-build option, the same corporate entity both designs and constructs the facility. The designer and contractor are, in a sense, partners representing the same firm. They may both actually work for the same firm, or they may be from two or more companies working together as a joint venture. Still another configuration involves one of the firms serving as the prime contractor and the others as subcontractors. No matter what the specific arrangement, the owner contracts with only one entity that will be responsible for both designing and constructing the facility. This provides the library with greater fiscal control of the project—an important point when safeguarding taxpayers' money.

An excellent example of the design-build approach is the experience of the Harold Washington Library Center in Chicago. The dramatic building was the creation of the SEBUS group, an acronym taken from the names of the four major team members involved in the project. (Schal Associates was the construction services firm involved. A. Epstein and Sons International was an engineering/architecture firm that provided the engineering expertise, but another group of architects, Hammond Beeby and Babka, was primarily responsible for the design of the building. The final team member was the developer U.S. Equities Realty, Inc.) Working together in a joint venture, they guaranteed to provide the 765,000-square-foot building for $144 million. The group was chosen from a field of five contenders in a hotly contested design-build competition.

On a somewhat smaller scale, the Utah Valley University Library, a facility of nearly 200,000 square feet, received the Design-Build Institute of America's 2008 Design-Build Award of Excellence. A number of successful public library projects like the Ramsey County Library in the Minneapolis-St. Paul suburb of Maplewood, which received an AIA Minnesota Honor Award for design excellence, have also been designed and built using this delivery system.

Advantages of Design-Build

It is becoming obvious that a great many owners believe there are significant advantages to choosing this option compared with more traditional project delivery methods. Among these advantages is a shortened project delivery time. The planning phase need not be complete before construction begins, and there is no waiting for contractor bids to be submitted. In addition, the last months of the design phase can overlap the first months of the construction phase, saving both time and money.

Fixing Responsibility

Another big advantage of the design-build system is a single point of responsibility. In traditional construction, architect and contractor spend a great deal of time pointing fingers at one another, blaming each other for every problem that arises. Warranties may not be honored, and protracted litigation may become necessary to fix responsibility. The design-builder, on the other hand, takes full responsibility for the outcome of the project.

In chapter 1 you read about the defective floor installation that resulted in a large hole in front of the circulation desk. Litigation went on for years while the participants argued the seemingly arcane question of whether the architect had provided every page of an instruction booklet needed to install the flooring material properly. When the designer and builder are the same entity, that entity is responsible for everything. As mentioned earlier, architects do not guarantee the outcome of their work but agree only to exercise reasonable care. With the combined system, the design of the building is usually subsumed within the designer-builder's warranty. This is usually a big advantage, although, as will become evident later, the owner must be ever vigilant.

In traditional construction projects, the contractor is ordinarily entitled to additional compensation if he must deal with errors, omissions, or ambiguities in the architect's plans. In other words, with traditional construction models, the contractor stands to make money when the architect makes mistakes. Since the design-build model unites designer and builder into the same entity, that entity must assume full responsibility for its work. However, change orders that arise from the owner's requests still cost money, unless it can be established that the change is needed to rectify an error.

Design-build agreements allow performance warranties to be much more comprehensive. Again, this is possible because it is so much easier to fix responsibility for problems. However, even in design-build projects, the performance warranty will generally have exclusions in areas for which the owner is responsible. Designer-builders often take on more responsibilities than traditional contractors, sometimes providing turnkey services. This means that certain responsibilities that the owner normally assumes may be included within the design-build contract.

Improved Communication

When architect and contractor work for different companies, they have few opportunities to meet with one another. If your building is being planned and built by two or more traditional firms, you are going to have to assume some responsibility for communication or risk major misunderstandings. Of course, the whole point of plans and specifications is to communicate the design and construction details, but specifications can't transfer expertise from one professional to another. With design-build projects, expertise can be better shared. A single organization allows for improved communication and continuity between designer and builder. The adversarial approach to the project, frequently encountered among building professionals, can also result in mistakes and added expense. In theory, at least, everyone on a design-build project is working toward the same goals and is part of the team.

Of course, you know very well that communication, even among your library staff, is not necessarily improved by working under the same roof, so a unified organizational structure does not guarantee good communication. With all the new technologies involved in a library, architect, engineer, and contractor should all be knowledgeable about the entire range of materials, equipment, and systems processes that will be incorporated into the new building.

Disadvantages of Design-Build

Unfortunately, attractive as it may be, there is a downside to the design-build option. Although many libraries have good experiences to recount, you do lose some of the safeguards associated with multiple entities. For example, you lose the system of checks and balances that is characteristic of traditional construction. In the past, the architect or engineer, to some extent, played the role of watchdog, helping to ensure that the facility was built as designed. Designers, at least in theory, owed their loyalties to the owner. Since designer and contractor were not members of the same team, they were to some extent adversaries and might be willing to blow the whistle on one another when they discovered irregularities.

Team Members or Adversaries

Because the architect and contractor are part of the same corporate organization in design-build agreements, the old assumptions may no longer be valid. For example, the design professionals or architects are not your consultants; they are on the contractor's team. Traditionally, the owner has a right to see the architect as an advocate or a partner when it comes to conflict with the contractor. Association with the contractor may cause architects to place such factors as ease of construction over other criteria that you consider important. Although it is always a good idea to hire someone specifically assigned to the job of watchdog or owner's representative, this becomes absolutely essential when dealing with a design-build firm.

You and the others on the project team may also be provided with less information than would otherwise be the case. You will no longer have access to the sort of candid appraisals that an independent architect can provide. Problems may be glossed over or hidden. (However, the outside consultant or watchdog is really a better solution anyway, since even with traditional delivery systems, architects have their own agendas.) Less information can result in less control, but it is possible to specify the kinds of information and the degree of detail that the designer-builder must provide to the owner.

Absence of Competitive Bidding

Another disadvantage of this system is that it is difficult to select a design-build firm through competitive bidding. A company must be chosen at the beginning of the project, when little information is available about cost. With traditional projects, the architect's fee is firm, and construction RFPs do not go out until the building has been designed. That way, contractors know what they are bidding on. When the services of architect and contractor are lumped together, separate bids are no longer possible. (It is possible, however, to specify that subcontractors be chosen through competitive bidding.)

Because the usual bidding process may be eliminated, the library must be extremely clear about its requirements. You will need to work with facilities experts to determine how large a building can reasonably be built with the funds available. Be specific about your most important technical requirements, such as electrical load and data capability or sophisticated environmental controls for a special collection, but leave some room for negotiation. You don't want to find yourself burdened with a designer-builder who, after having been selected for the project, tells you that the funds available are not sufficient to provide for the library's most important needs.

Using the design-build system may have legal repercussions. It may be that your state or municipality has laws that severely restrict the use of designer-builders. Furthermore, licensing restrictions for design professionals and contractors may limit the permissible types of design-build structures. Insurance and bonding may also be more complicated to arrange. This situation is changing rapidly, however, as the delivery system becomes ever more popular.

Holding All Participants to a Higher Standard

Special care must be taken with the design-build contract so that the owner gets more protection rather than less. Standard contracts favor the designer-builder, and many provisions may be intended to transfer liability from the designer-builder to the owner when construction in accordance with the plans does not achieve the results intended.

You will want contract provisions to resemble the standard AIA Contract for Construction, not a standard architect's contract. Architects are usually held responsible only for exercising a reasonable degree of skill or care, and they do not normally warrant or guarantee a successful outcome for services. Since the contractor does warrant that the result of his services will be a successful project, the designer-builder should assume the obligations of the contractor, not those of the architect.

If you are entering into a design-build agreement, be extra careful, in reading over the provisions, that the standard of care is not changed by contractual agreement. The phrase "appropriate levels of skill and care" should set off alarm bells because it is an attempt to hold both architect and contractor to the lower standard. Instead of gaining greater accountability from the architect, you would be losing the level of accountability that has come to be expected of the contractor.

Tread carefully. This is certainly a matter that should be discussed with a lawyer. Your lawyer should go over the contract carefully and probably propose substitutes for a number of its provisions. If at all possible, use the services of a lawyer who is familiar with the design-build system and who can craft sections clarifying the parties' rights and remedies to reflect your institution's assumptions and understandings about the project. Boilerplate provisions might work with traditional construction, but they are not adequate for this new environment. Although the design-build option may provide additional protection for the owner, it is quite a new development, and the courts have not really established clear guidelines.

Who's the Boss?

Another potential disadvantage of the design-build system is the possible confusion about who is in charge of the work. Who is the prime contactor with the owner, and who is serving in the role of subcontractor? This may not be an issue if the two are really one entity. However, all sorts of business arrangements such as joint ventures and limited liability companies complicate the problem. Nevertheless, libraries across the country are embracing this new delivery system.

If you've ever felt like a Ping-Pong ball being batted back and forth between an architect and a contractor who are blaming each other for a problem, you'll see that working with them as one entity has some real advantages. The majority of court cases have held that a designer-builder is more nearly like a contractor than like an architect or other design professional, and the same warranty standards may apply to the architect's work as to contractors.

Other Difficulties

There are also potential licensing, insurance, and bonding problems when dealing with design-build firms. The insurance carried by architects and other design professionals ordinarily excludes construction services, and contractors' general liability policies exclude professional services. This could create a sticky wicket if it becomes necessary to make any claims. General liability policies also have little or no deductible, whereas professional liability policies have large deductibles. Surety bonds create similar problems. Be sure that your lawyer checks into the matter of adequate and appropriate insurance and bonding if you are considering a design-build firm. These are problems that can be fairly easily solved, but the time to solve such issues is before you're irrevocably committed.

CHOOSING A TEAM TO RENOVATE OR REMODEL

If you are about to embark upon a renovation project, the decision was probably made for any or all of the following reasons:

- ◆ inadequate space
- ◆ inflexible interior design
- ◆ outdated electrical and telecommunications systems

Medina County (Ohio) District Library, Medina Library, David Milling Architects, dmaa.com. Photo: William H. Webb, Infinity Studio.

- inadequate access for people with special needs
- inability to develop the collections and services you need

In addition, you may be forced to renovate instead of build because of political, fiscal, or historical factors. You may have hoped to start fresh with a whole new building, but funds were not available. Possibly, your county or city lacks the tax base to fund major new construction. Because of its historic or architectural importance, your institution or local government may also have a commitment to your existing library building. You will be seeking ways to improve access, create additional space, and accommodate new technology while at the same time preserving what is most valuable in the old building. How will you bring the library into the twenty-first century and still preserve the flavor of the past?

Experienced Building Professionals

If your project is a renovation rather than all-new construction, be sure the builder has experience in this area. If your library plans to remain open while construction work is in progress, your contractor should be accustomed to working with other people such as staff and visitors on the premises. Keeping the two operations—renovation and the library's ongoing services—separate and on track requires a great deal of planning and organization. Such skills are not learned easily. If the contractor has never had to consider how routine activities will continue side by side with construction, you probably don't want to be the one to educate him.

When you ask for a contractor's references, be sure that other projects similar to your own are included in them. Talk to the references who remained on-site while their building was being renovated or remodeled. Ask how cooperative the contractor was and how much advance warning staff were given when an area had to be vacated. You might even ask for specific examples of how disruption was avoided. If you have the opportunity to interview contractors who are being considered, ask what techniques they have developed for minimizing noise and debris.

Special Requirements

In many ways, planning for renovation and remodeling is not so very different from planning a new building, so most of the recommendations contained in this book will be relevant. You will be defining future needs, anticipating growth, and considering how technology will affect library services in the future. However, working with an existing structure adds new challenges. For example, modification of a historic building may be subject to review and oversight by federal or local historical commissions. You may find that you will need a more diverse team of building professionals if historic preservation is an issue with your building. For example, you may need an architect who understands how older buildings were constructed and what should be preserved.

The National Park Service publishes an extensive collection of guidelines and documents on the preservation, rehabilitation, and restoration of historic buildings. If you are contemplating rehabilitation and expansion of a historic building, you should become familiar with what's happening in the field. In a guide to library restoration and expansion published by the Illinois Historic Preservation Agency, Lonn Frye writes: "With each project, architects learn new techniques and easier ways of integrating historic preservation and contemporary design."[10] If your building is not already listed on the National Register of Historic Places, there should be a clear consensus on whether this is a goal. Once historically significant features have been altered, there's usually no turning back.

HIRING A WATCHDOG

One of the best ways to ensure that you get what you pay for is to hire an owner's representative. Also called a watchdog, quantity surveyor, project manager, or construction inspector, this individual is hired to keep an eagle eye on your project. No matter what the title (and it differs widely from one region to another), the job is similar. The watchdog remains at the construction site looking after the interests of the owner. Larger academic institutions and governmental units usually have some office or department for overseeing building projects. However, such departments frequently lack the time and expertise to effectively look after a building while it is under construction. Although this can be a very sensitive subject, use your persuasive skill (and tact) to obtain the services of a qualified, professionally trained overseer. She will

- ensure that the building is in compliance with regulations
- prevent unnecessary and expensive change orders
- ensure that the building is safe from hazards
- ensure that the building can pass state and federal inspections
- prepare samples for laboratory testing
- interpret blueprints and specifications
- maintain a construction and inspection log
- measure distances and verify the accuracy of structural layouts

Watchdogs come with a variety of qualifications and expertise. Among their many roles, they estimate and monitor construction costs and serve as consultants to the property owner. Some of them are faculty members who teach in the building and construction disciplines. Others may work for financial institutions. Watchdogs, whatever their name, use their knowledge of construction methods and costs to advise the owner on the most effective and economical way of achieving the construction requirements. Some of them are trained in cost planning, estimating, and cost analysis.

TIPS AND TALES

For any building project, you need to have what we call a quantity surveyor on-site all the time. A quantity surveyor is usually someone trained as an architect and/or engineer who acts as a building inspector for the client and checks to make sure everything is built as designed, according to the plans, before the work is signed off. This can result in saving several thousands of dollars of work.

The first recommendation I have is to find a project manager who is able and willing to do the work and give him the authority to get the job done. Many a project has run into problems when folks decide to manage it with a committee.

Another issue is construction management. If you are talking about a project over $15–20 million, which most libraries would be, then you're going to have a mob at the door wanting to manage your project and save you money. If you have a fast-track project or multiple prime contractors, then you do need a firm specializing in construction management to help you out. Get them in place early. These folks can do as much or more in the design process as they do in managing the contractor.

We contracted with our architect to place someone on-site for the entire construction phase. This allowed me to have expert technical advice immediately while getting much faster response on submittals, RFPs, and other questions.

Choose one person as the main contact with contractors and subcontractors. Our contact would call me to answer a question someone else had asked. I had no idea what he was talking about, and he would tell me one thing and give someone the exact opposite answer. It got very confusing.

Commissioning

In recent years, the concept of a "commissioning agent" has taken hold, especially in commercial real estate. Commissioning may be defined as "a process that ensures that a building conforms to the original intent of the owner." The commissioning agent can be involved in the early design phases; through installation and start-up; and during the installation of lighting systems, HVAC systems and controls, elevators, and structural elements. The commissioning agent represents the owner throughout the planning and construction period, seeking to ensure that design objectives are met, that all systems are functional, and that all equipment is installed properly. Seeing that all needed support documentation is available is another important role.

Buildings have become so much more complicated in recent years that most professionals may lack the breadth to understand the project as a whole. For example, advances in technology, improved materials, new methods, and other factors have meant that centralized integration and coordination of the project may be lacking. This integration is an important role of the commissioning agent. New materials, such as extra-strong concrete and super-plasticizers, make it possible to build flatter floors and smaller columns for more available floor space. In steel construction, the old standard of 36,000 pounds per square inch (psi) has now been replaced with 50,000 psi, meaning that buildings require less steel. This can mean a savings of thousands of dollars in construction materials and labor costs if your building professionals are well informed. If they're not, it's up to your own expert to bring such matters to their attention.

Medina County (Ohio) District Library, Highland Library Branch, David Milling Architects, dmaa.com. Photo: William H. Webb, Infinity Studio.

KEEPING YOUR PROJECT ON TRACK

As plans change from day to day, you may lose track of how the new design will affect the library's function. As you solve one problem, you may be creating another. Thus, you will need some way of measuring each round of changes against a set of basic requirements. As the building evolves, it becomes increasingly complex. You will need a procedure for regularly reviewing plans to be sure that the features you've requested are still present and located in appropriate places.

Checklist of Basic Requirements

At the end of the preliminary information you provide to the architect, add a checklist of basic, nonnegotiable requirements. Although the items on the checklist will be more specific and concrete than the other information, they should, as much as possible, proceed from the information you have already provided. If the architect understands why you want extensive electrical capacity in the stack areas or a sight line to computer equipment, such considerations are much more likely to appear in the floor plans. Over time, the checklist will be amended and may become very long, but it is essential that you continue to go over it again and again. New players appear onstage almost daily, and your concerns may not be communicated to later arrivals such as subcontractors.

The Contractor's Schedule

If this is your first building project, you will discover that it is all unbelievably complicated. There are literally thousands of tasks that must be accomplished, thousands of items to be ordered, and thousands of decisions to be made.

All these elements must be integrated into a very structured, rigid schedule. In many instances one subcontractor cannot begin work until another has finished. The electrical contractor, for example, cannot install wiring until after the framing for the partitions is in place but must complete most of the work before the drywall installers arrive.

Your contractor's project schedule may be the most critical element in your project plan. Not only is it important for scheduling your actual move, but it will clarify which decisions must be made first. The project schedule allows you to plan ahead and avoid those high-stress moments such as when the contractor tells you he needs a decision on locks for all the doors in the building immediately. Be sure you get a copy every time the schedule is revised. The final schedule may be very different from the one initially proposed. Such a schedule is long and elaborate.

Occasionally, you may encounter a contractor who has only a vague idea of what will be happening when. The resulting project schedule is incomplete, and it is clear that the contractor has not thought through the sequence of activities very carefully. This is an indication that you are dealing with the type who "flies by the seat of his pants" or who is not accustomed to working on large projects. By the time you discover this, the papers have been signed, and there is little you can do. It will probably be difficult to pin the contractor down without alienating him, but do your best. Remain enthusiastic and supportive, but ask lots of questions. Then create your own schedule based on your contractor's responses and go over it with him. It may serve to jog your contractor's memory and help ensure that the plumbers are planning to arrive at the right time or that the electricians will be free when needed.

The Library's Project Schedule

In addition, you will need to make yourself a separate internal project schedule from the library's perspective. Such a project schedule is a list of the tasks that must be accomplished, the length of time each task will take, and the order in which they must be completed. You will need to break down your preparations into small, definable units that can be given probable beginning and end dates as well as absolute deadlines, so you and the staff will know where you are on your project—what activities are on track, what is running behind, and what lies ahead.

The business world has given us some excellent ways of dealing with such complexity, but you don't have to become an expert. Lots of excellent computer software is available to keep track of a simple project or a very complex one. Most are quite easy to use. The best known is probably Microsoft Project. Most of the larger construction companies use professional project software to stay on schedule. If this is the case with your contractor, you might ask for periodic printouts. If your library and your general contractor use compatible software, you might ask instead for a copy of the project file.

Preserving the Paper Trail

Yours may be one of those lucky projects that moves along steadily to completion with few detours along the way. Just because there is a flurry of interest, however, your new building or addition may not be just around the corner. The economy may plummet. Legislators and board members may change. Even after plans are drawn and land is purchased, your new building can be put on hold indefinitely. Multiyear delays can mean a succession of library directors and architects who know little about the planning that took place before their arrival. Gradually, information can disappear, and changes can get lost or never be recorded. The plumbing contractor may end up working with outdated blueprints that show incorrect restroom locations, and the millwork subcontractor may be sizing a circulation desk for a space that's been cut in half.

Begin collecting information about the project, whether it's your own research, minutes of meetings you attend, consultants' reports, or notes taken during conferences with the architects. Label materials as carefully as possible and file everything. Imagine the years passing. A new architect is hired; your own memory dims. You've put a lot of hard work into the project, and it could all go down the drain unless you can bring the new team members up to speed. Once the project is back on track, continue to collect materials.

Libraries are repositories of information. You as a librarian are an information specialist, an expert on collecting and organizing resources. While your building is under construction, vast quantities of written instructions, wiring diagrams, blueprints, service manuals, and installation guides are floating about. Copy every one of them and file the copies in a safe place. Obviously, this is a lot easier when you're on the premises, as is the case with a remodeling project or a new addition. Ask to copy any brochures or installation instructions that accompany equipment. Copy guarantees and warranty information.

This is especially important with HVAC and other high-tech equipment that changes often and will soon be out of production. When systems break down, as they inevitably will, information about model numbers, replacement parts, and liability will all be vital. If such materials tend to get lost at the job site, you may want to routinely request them from manufacturers. Implementing these procedures may be a true test of your relationship with your architects and contractors. However difficult it may be, be sure you make it clear that you simply want to do what librarians do best—preserve vital information. Explain that you are not trying to second-guess your building professionals, and you have no plans to do anything with the materials you collect except to preserve them. They will object loudly the first time you remove a sheaf of papers from their office or the construction site (a battery-operated scanner can prevent bloodshed), but if you're back in ten minutes, they will come to accept you as a harmless lunatic. The first time they themselves lose a manual or booklet and discover they can come to you for a copy, your relationship will improve considerably.

High Turnover

Don't depend on some other department in your organization to retain this kind of information or to pass it down through the years. Whether you rely on the maintenance staff of your city, county, or academic institution to maintain your equipment, you're talking about positions that have extraordinarily high turnover rates. Physical plant supervisors will take their institutional memories with them when they move on to other jobs. One of the most helpful things you can do is see to it that each new generation of staff members involved with maintaining equipment is provided with copies of the printed instructions. Never, however, lend your only copy—within hours the information may be trodden underfoot or smeared with a gooey black lubricant.

This chapter has emphasized the preparations that will be needed for the journey ahead. You have a long way to travel, so your preparations must be extensive. A building project should never be started casually. It will take up most of your time for several years and may have a profound impact upon your career. You now know whom you will be dealing with and the sort of interactions you can expect. Even more important, you now have an idea where you fit into the process and the kind of unique expertise you can provide. Recognizing the contributions that only you can make to the project will give you confidence to express your ideas freely. It should not, however, encourage you to be bossy or opinionated, telling other professionals how to do their jobs.

NOTES

1. American Institute of Architects, *You and Your Architect* (New York: American Institute of Architects), available at www.e-architect.com/consumer/yarch.asp and at www.aiapvc.org/yourarch.htm.
2. Werner Sabo, *Legal Guide to AIA Documents,* 5th ed. (New York: Wiley, 1988). This guide provides coverage of key AIA documents such as A101 Owner-General Contractor Agreement, A201 General Conditions, B141 Owner-Architect Agreement, and C141 Architect-Consultant Agreement. The guide also has annual supplements.
3. See the list of resource organizations below for addresses and telephone numbers of these organizations.
4. State University of New York at Buffalo, School of Architecture and Planning, Cyburbia, http://cyburbia.ap.buffalo.edu/pairc/.
5. *The Architect's Handbook of Professional Practice* (Hoboken, NJ: D. C. Wiley and Sons, 2008).
6. American Institute of Architects, Annotated B141: Standard Form of Agreement between Owner and Architect with Standard Form of Architects' Services (Washington, DC: American Institute of Architects, 1997).
7. American Institute of Architects, *Compromise Contract Language Alternatives* (Washington, DC: American Institute of Architects, 1997).
8. Bozeman Public Library, www.bozemanlibrary.org/newlibrary.html.
9. Wendell Wickerham, "Designing and Building Leading Edge Libraries" (paper presented at the 9th annual conference of the Association of College and Research Libraries, Detroit, April 8–11, 1999).

10. Lonn Frye, *Older Library Buildings: Special Building and Design Problems* (Springfield: Illinois Historic Preservation Agency, 1999), available at www.uic .edu/~build1.htm.

RESOURCE ORGANIZATIONS

American Institute of Architects
1735 New York Ave. NW
Washington, DC 20006-7918
(202) 626-7300

Associated General Contractors
333 John Carlyle St., Ste. 200
Alexandria, VA 22314
(703) 548-3118
E-mail: info@agc.org

Construction Management Association of America
7918 Jones Branch Dr., #540
McLean, VA 33102-3307
(703) 356-2622

Engineers' Joint Contract Documents Committee
American Institute of Architects
1735 New York Ave. NW
Washington, DC 20006-5292
(202) 626-7300

The Emerging Library Design

By this point, you've established the procedures, working relationships, and lines of communication that will see you through the project. Therefore, it's time to begin planning your new or renovated building. If all is going well, you're beginning to have an idea of what lies ahead. You've been introduced to your architects and, hopefully, you've had time for a few heart-to-heart chats. You now have some idea of how much money buys how many square feet of library space, but those numbers will change as plans evolve. The new library will probably expand and contract in concept several times before the first brick is laid. Whatever its eventual size and shape, the completed building must be able to function as a well-designed, technically sophisticated library that meets the needs of its users.

This will be a very busy time for you, and you're going to feel as if you're juggling dozens of decisions with too little information and too many conflicting opinions. You'll need plenty of information on recent library trends and a clear idea of how far you can stretch the definition of a library. The new building must serve future needs as well, so you'll also have to become a fortune-teller or at least an informed amateur prognosticator who can predict probable future directions. You can expect both good and bad times ahead, so the new building must be designed to weather years of low budgets and even civic neglect.

Once you have a clear idea of how the new library will function under these diverse conditions, you're almost ready to begin thinking about bricks and mortar—the physical elements of your particular building. Little can be done, however, until a site is chosen. The site will affect the size of the building, its orientation, the location of public spaces and windows, and many equally vital considerations. If your library will be sharing facilities with other units, such as a recreation center or county offices, the site must accommodate other functions and other priorities. Space needs must always be determined early in any planning process or you risk creating a dysfunctional building that will need immediate reorganization.

However, not all projects begin with a new site and a new building. If you're renovating or remodeling an existing structure, you'll need to add still more complex matters to your list, for example, asbestos removal or coping with a structure that was not designed for use as a library. If all this sounds daunting, take comfort in the fact that your new or renovated building is on its way to becoming a reality. It's all starting to happen, and you have a front-row seat.

RECENT LIBRARY TRENDS

Have you seen any vaulted reading rooms lately? Probably not, unless you're still coping with an old Carnegie building. Today's customers seek out personal places to read and study. If you watch them selecting a study carrel or table, notice how they try to keep their distance from one another. We need not be antisocial to want a little personal space in the library. Most of us try to avoid directly facing another customer, and we seek out nooks where we feel we have a space to ourselves. This, of course, presents a conundrum for librarians who worry about the safety of their users and of their materials. However, we are not about to return to the Carnegies or the big, open boxes of the 1960s and 1970s, so we must find ways of creating spaces that are both safe and enticing. Security considerations may make real privacy undesirable, but it is possible to give the appearance of quiet nooks even when they are readily visible. As you plan different spaces for different functions, give some consideration to the way customers use libraries. For example, with computers finding their way into so many library spaces, consider whether you need some "click-free" zones far from the clatter of computer keyboards.

Collaborative Study

If you're like many librarians, you're so aware of changes linked to computerization that you may have overlooked other recent developments. Have you thought about collaborative spaces, for instance? Whether you are building a public, academic, or some other type of library building, recent educational and management theories stress working together in teams. Naturally, teams need spaces where they can get together. Have you planned group spaces in which four to eight people can get together to discuss a project? Have you planned spaces for one-on-one literacy training or GED tutoring?

Be sure that you provide informal spaces for people to meet and talk with one another as well. This social function of a library is one we may rarely consider, but it is an important one nonetheless. No matter whether it's a public, school, or academic library, each serves as a community center. Students profit from studying together, and community groups can combine their research and

Norfolk (Va.) Public Library, Mary D. Pretlow Anchor Branch, The Design Collaborative, designcollaborative.cc. Photo: The Design Collaborative and Alexandra R. Fenton.

their deliberations. Computers, too, encourage collaboration and so should be included in the planning of group spaces. A modern library should

- accommodate collaboration between individuals
- support learning as a social enterprise
- serve as a primary meeting ground for a campus with a large nonresident population
- accommodate team information seeking and decision making

Media Integration

Another recent development has been the gradual disappearance of the lines separating different media. This merging of media makes separate, specialized areas where one can listen to audiotapes or watch videos all but obsolete. Media equipment is increasingly computerized and multifunctional. This means that service points should also be multifunctional for "one-stop shopping." This increasingly tiresome phrase when applied to a library means that patrons should never be sent from desk to desk. It also means that equipment to use a variety of media formats should be available throughout the library.

Service Consolidation

If the old model of separate and specialized departments is firmly entrenched in your present library, consider how you can make the transition to the new model as painless as possible. Not only do customers profit from clustering services, but you may be able to keep more services available during evening and weekend hours when staffing is at low ebb. Such integration may create problems if staff, who must serve as trainers, are unfamiliar with different types of equipment. Increasingly, librarians and support staff are becoming jacks-of-all-trades, and your new library may hasten the trend toward consolidating services. Be sure your staff are ready for it. As you've already discovered, your staff are doing a lot of computer training as well. It's no longer possible to teach customers to use reference sources without including the web-based databases and computer equipment needed to access those sources. How can you organize and position your staff in such a way that they can provide needed help wherever computers are available?

In some libraries, however, the clustering of services has resulted in making fewer staff members available to the public. The natural tendency of staff to closet themselves in offices works against the library's best interests. Customers need more, not less, contact with staff to become loyal library users. When the clustering of services results in reducing interpersonal contact and staff members have less time to devote to individual customers, the result will be a weakening of the library bond and a loss of support.

Planning for Change

Libraries are changing rapidly, so leave your options open. Build as much flexibility as possible into your floor plan. For example, stay away from built-in desks, counters, and other furnishings that may have to be relocated in the future. Small rooms with load-bearing walls will also stand in the way of change, as will walls shaped to fit around a piece of furniture. Think of all those old card catalog units that were recessed into walls. Fixed task lighting also inhibits change. Lighting installed for one floor plan may be useless when you begin moving things around. Also avoid permanent partitions, since you may want to reconfigure spaces as needs change.

Expanding Technology Needs

Changes in the delivery of information in modern libraries affect every aspect of the planning process. For example, how much use are you getting out of your expensive, specially designed index tables? With the advent of online indexing and abstracting services, the use of printed indexes has dropped precipitously.

Your library has canceled many of its printed indexes, and the ones remaining can probably be shelved in the reference stacks.

Study carrels should be chosen with future computer purchases in mind. The type of carrel with a shelf above the work surface may not accommodate tomorrow's computer equipment or even today's large monitors. In fact, you might compare product catalogs to find out whether you pay a premium for units designated as library carrels as opposed to office workstations. Analyze differences both in cost and in functionality before making your selections.

Avoid low ceilings if you can. Someday you may need to use ceiling space for electrical and telecommunications lines. Low ceilings also make it difficult to light an area effectively or to install hanging signs. Make sure your architect understands that there must be room to accommodate future technology. It's often impossible to tell where you are going to want to hook up a computer or some other piece of equipment. If the past few years are any indicator, some of your stack areas will probably be redesigned to accommodate computer workstations. Be sure power outlets are sufficient for this purpose and request considerably more electrical capacity than you'll need immediately. It's much less expensive to do it now.

TIPS AND TALES

Every library needs a well-defined delivery area with a door wide enough to move large pieces of furniture through it.

Halls and doorways, all types of passageways, need to be wide enough. No bad corners. All sorts of book trucks and other "hauling mechanisms" must be used to get books, furniture, and other equipment from place to place.

Our biggest problem is not enough space (we think) to do all we wish. Size is driven by a strict budget.

Round buildings don't use square footage wisely. They also make for lots of funny-shaped rooms that don't work well.

PLANNING FOR THE FUTURE

What does the future hold for your library? All kinds of social institutions are changing rapidly, but libraries are going through an especially rapid metamorphosis. Since we don't really know what next year will bring, how can we possibly plan a library that will continue to serve our public's needs for the next fifty years?

As you work with your board, dean, or committee, you will discover that the news media have convinced some of these people that the book is dead. Will Manley, in his article "The Manley Arts: Clean, Well-Lighted Stacks," writes that several years ago he interviewed a famous architect about a library building project. The architect challenged Manley to be innovative and daring. It turned out that the architect's view of the "millennium-three library" had no books at all. Instead, the architect exclaimed, "We can create an ambiance of reflection and research by stressing the concept of books rather than the books themselves."[1] Of course, this view is a bit extreme, but you are bound to encounter some who believe that libraries no longer need to spend money housing books, since all information of importance will soon be converted to an electronic format. In fact, some believe that the library need not accommodate large numbers of users because most will soon be able to access the library electronically.

On the other hand, you may be working with a computer-phobic administrator or board member who thinks money spent on technology is wasted: "All this computer stuff is just a flash in the pan and takes precious dollars away from the book budget." Unfortunately, there's rarely enough money available to satisfy everyone, and arguments can become heated. Ideally, yours should be the sweet voice of reason advocating compromise, but you will probably find this to be one of the most treacherous shoals of dissension you are forced to navigate.

We have a task ahead of us that's fraught with peril, but a little crystal-ball gazing is possible. Will the digital library totally eliminate the need for printed materials? Most authorities believe it's best to assume that book collections will remain but will begin to shrink. The book is a wonderfully successful technology in and of itself, and its funeral is not scheduled for anytime soon. However, recent developments like Amazon's Kindle and free access to over a million Google e-books in the public domain will mean that there are few reasons to retain large collections of older titles. Printed journals are disappearing even faster. The brief length of most articles, coupled with the computer's aptitude for searching vast quantities of text, give electronic formats a big edge over their print counterparts. Full-text services like ProQuest are proving to be enormously successful in libraries, and infrequently used print subscriptions are routinely canceled in favor of online access. In general, academic libraries will be affected more by electronic media than public libraries, and so their print collections will shrink more rapidly. Legal materials are also more useful in electronic formats, and users applaud the powerful search engines that can pinpoint relevant information where they once searched weighty volume after weighty volume. The jury hasn't quite reached its decision about popular magazines. Although many titles have ceased publication and there's probably no reason for libraries to continue binding most titles, the public continues to enjoy their ready availability, glossy photos, and portable format.

Safe Assumptions

How will all this affect the design of a new library? No one can be sure of the future, but here are some suggestions:

- Assume some decrease in book purchases in the near future, but don't do anything drastic.
- Assume that most bound periodical volumes will eventually be discarded or relegated to a low-use storage area.
- Be sure your building can handle a much higher power load than is presently needed.
- Install electrical outlets at frequent intervals even in the stacks.
- Imagine what would happen if you took down the stacks in an area and substituted computer-equipped carrels.
- When you begin economizing, try not to make cuts in power or network access till the bitter end.

One maxim upon which everyone agrees is that you will need more computers more quickly than you anticipate. One new library after another has found that it underestimated the speed of change and the demand for computers. For example, the Scholarly Communication Center at Rutgers University, which is a part of the Alexander Library, included one unfinished area that was eventually intended to be used for additional stacks and offices. Instead, it quickly became necessary to spend $3 million to convert the area into a computer and media center and other high-tech facilities.

Harold Hawkins, in his article on "The Uncertain Future of High School Library Design," cautions that "there appears to be less need for expansion of square footage within the library" since, increasingly, the library is no longer the only repository of academic resources. He also concludes that

the humanities will continue to need print materials

science and technology are more dependent upon electronic resources

high school libraries will become more decentralized, since electronic libraries can be accessible throughout the building from individual workstations

the learning process is becoming increasingly based on collaborative experiences, thus requiring spaces for group discussion

libraries can expect continued funding for technology

the look of the library will not change radically, but librarians should plan for a gradual decrease in table seating space and an increase in computer workstations[2]

Listen to Users

Libraries must be what our customers want us to be. Amid the uncertainty and confusion we're feeling about the future, we are gradually coming to realize that we must listen to them when they tell us what they want. Of course, there must be limits, and we cannot be all things to all people, but be sure you listen with a receptive ear. When you find yourself defensively muttering something like "This is a library, not a computer lab," or "This is a library, not a community center," think a moment. Your users probably already see you in that role or the issue wouldn't have come up. One of the librarians quoted in several Tips sections was asked to accommodate a Kinko's copy service. In the 22,000-square-foot building he was planning, it would have taken precious space from more important library functions. However, in my own 300,000-square-foot library, there's plenty of room for a copy center, and we love having one close at hand.

This brings up the whole issue of balancing practical needs with customer preferences. For example, customers like a comfortable, relaxed environment, and they want to sip a cup of coffee or enjoy a snack while they're working. Older, more traditional libraries are steadily losing support, and we are all actively seeking ways of making our libraries more relevant to the public of the twenty-first century. We can readily see from the enormous popularity of bookstores with

New Castle County (Del.) Public Library, Hockessin Public Library, ikon.5 architects, ikon5architects.com.
Photo: James D'Addio.

coffee bars that people enjoy sipping a latte, drinking a Coke, or even munching on a sandwich as they read. In fact, new libraries around the country are being built to accommodate some sort of eating facility. We all know perfectly well that visitors will want to take their coffee with them to the stacks or OPAC computers, and then what do we do? It's a puzzlement that we're all facing. We'll talk more about this issue later in the book, but like so many issues confronting today's library, the need for flexibility and openness is greater than ever before.

Beyond Traditional Services

Conference and meeting room facilities are also important. You may ask, "Why should we be the one to provide them?" When you're short on space, there may be some justification for a negative response. However, meeting spaces make the library an integral part of the community, even if the people they attract do not normally use other library services. As Anya Breitenbach, public relations manager for the Denver Public Library, says: "You build this beautiful public landmark and you expect people to be excited about it and drawn to it, but you don't necessarily realize all the ways in which they will want to use it."[3] There is a lot of evidence that the "real" users—the ones who check out library materials and spend time in the reading rooms—are a fairly small percentage of the taxpaying public or student body. If, however, you add the people who come in just to use your copy machine, check their e-mail, or type a paper on the library computers, you may be serving far more people than your funding agency realizes.

We Need Friends

As I write these words, I feel rebellion growing in the back of my brain. Don't we librarians think of ourselves as being above the role of social director or computer technician? We also think of our book-toting users as very special people—the intellectual elite. Isn't it those people we're there to serve, not the hoi polloi who use our meeting rooms? If the little voice in the back of your brain is uttering similar complaints, you'd better remind it that this "elite" segment is shrinking. In fact, it was probably never large enough to win a referendum unaided or create a sufficiently large groundswell of enthusiasm among your faculty and administrators. The library of the future needs friends! Although you cannot possibly have something for everyone, you had best expand your definition of users to include these philistines at your gates.

The Monumental Majority

Somewhere along the way, you will discover that you must find a way for your proposed library to coexist peacefully with its alter ego, the symbolic library. We live in a world in which most respected institutions have been shown to have feet of clay. The presidency, the Congress, the medical establishment, and many other once-revered symbols of rectitude and respectability have fallen from their pedestals. For better or worse, the library has not succumbed to this fate.

Even though many people have not read a book in years, they revere the principles on which libraries are built—or at least the principles on which they think libraries are built. The library, they vaguely believe, is a noble institution glowing with the light of learning. The library represents lofty ideals for many, and such ideals should be enshrined in an equally noble edifice. City council members think that a stately library improves the tone of their municipality. Theirs is no hick town; it's a classy community because it boasts a snazzy monument to culture and learning. River City and Hemlock Falls can hold up their figurative heads proudly, and residents who've never seen the inside of the library can burst with civic self-importance when they view its exterior.

Naturally, architects can have a field day with such attitudes. Some may even compete to design the most pretentious, dysfunctional structures imaginable. University presidents are afflicted with a similar malady that I call the "hallowed halls of learning" syndrome. They lean toward oak-paneled conference rooms in which their portraits can most effectively be displayed. But enough already! Enough snobbish sarcasm! In their way, these too are library customers, and we must find a way to work with them. It is in our own interest to create an eye-catching library that says to the world: "Libraries are important, and they're not going away anytime soon." What we can't allow, however, is to sacrifice function for form or to fail those who need our services most.

PLANNING FOR HARD TIMES

Amid the hubbub of enthusiasm that accompanies the planning of a new library, it is hard to remember that libraries are experiencing difficult times. At this writing, the national economy is in especially bad shape. If you've been in the profession for any length of time, you can probably remember other grim periods when you held your breath through a series of staff cuts, when you endured a moratorium on book purchases, or when you were forced to cancel periodical subscriptions. Even though there are always financial constraints, a building project induces an artificial atmosphere of plenty. You find yourself dealing daily with staggering sums of money, hardware and furniture selections that cost the moon. Discussions with building professionals may lead you to look on these expenses almost as mere trifles.

Even library giants have inadequate budgets. A look back at the much-hyped San Francisco Public Library will serve as a reminder of what the real world holds for libraries. During the planning and construction phases, Director Ken Dowlin was the envy of librarians throughout the country. Corporate sponsors gave generously to the project, and the building that emerged was a design tour de force. Rich materials adorned every surface, and both library and architectural journals were enraptured by the opulence.

The problem was that the near-astronomical construction budget was not reflected in the library's operating budget. When the new library opened its doors, the public flocked to enjoy its many attractions, but there was no budget to support the many new or expanded services required. Staffing had been based on a projected 5,000 visitors daily, but the day after opening, the number jumped to 9,000. Long lines became common at the checkout desk, and for a while it took more than a month for books to be returned to the shelves.

Of course, initial activity eventually levels off, but the moral of the story is that you will never return to the kind of usage you are now experiencing in your older building.

When planning for hard times it is critical that you plan for efficient staffing. As mentioned earlier in the section on educating the architect, library staffs are small and getting smaller, while new electronic resources take an ever-larger bite out of the budget. It is important to design a library that can be staffed safely and efficiently by the smallest possible number of people. For example, arrange stacks and work areas so that staff can use their time more efficiently, and centralize light panels, security monitors, and other equipment so that the building can be opened, closed, and monitored by the fewest people. If times change and your budget zooms skyward, bask in your affluence and enjoy! However, it's still best to be prepared for more than one episode of belt-tightening.

Plan Now, Save Later

Wherever possible, spend money now to save money later. Planning to get the most for your money at this early stage will reap rewards down the line. For example:

choose workhorse equipment known for low maintenance

buy the best carpeting you can afford with the longest wear guarantee

choose energy-efficient systems that reduce the cost of heating, cooling, and lighting

Although it may sound contradictory, it's important to think big. Generous funding comes only to those who ask for it. Go ahead and design a library that will support exciting new programs and services. You might even plan for luxuries, but be sure you can do without them. Don't leave yourself out on a limb with higher public expectations than you can satisfy.

SELECTING A SITE

Before blueprints can be developed, the site must be selected for the proposed library. If you have the opportunity to participate in the selection of a site for the new library, you should feel blessed. Site selection is often a foregone conclusion determined by the availability of a lot that the county doesn't know what to do with or a piece of useless land a citizen or an alumnus has donated in exchange for a hefty tax deduction. If, however, you are consulted in the matter of site selection, here are some basic considerations:

- lot size
- real estate costs
- site quality and configuration
- security
- traffic flow (ingress and egress) and traffic controls
- visibility
- proximity to automobile pollution
- accessibility
- population demographics

- environmental consequences
- utilities
- zoning
- site conditions such as buried gas tanks or environmental hazards
- adjacent land and the possibility of future expansion

In addition, the site chosen has a lot to do with your ability to create an environmentally friendly, sustainable building. We'll talk more about that in the next chapter.

You might want to assign a point value to each site, depending on the criteria. If some criteria are more important than others, the points can be adjusted accordingly. For example, site size can be an important decision factor because larger sites allow more design flexibility, including a buffer around the perimeter of the building.

TIPS AND TALES

Going into the process, make sure you have established priorities that will guide the design and construction. Decide where you will put the emphasis if money runs short. In our case, the priorities I established were collections, staff safety and comfort, and education and event space, then everything else. As our funding has been cut a couple of times since we started, this prioritization has helped keep things on track and helped me make consistent decisions that allowed us to stay on time and within budget.

Build it and patrons will come! We have seen an incredible surge in circulation stats, reference stats, and new patron registrations. My staff feel overwhelmed right now.

Plan far ahead and begin building increased staff expenditures into your budget.

Security Issues

Depending on your library type and your neighborhood, security may or may not be the most important factor in selecting a site. If it does rank high in your priorities, it's helpful to break down the elements that contribute to a safe environment. Take a walk around the immediate neighborhoods of the sites under consideration. Consider topography, vegetation, adjacent land uses, sight lines, and potential areas for refuge or concealment. Give some consideration to the types and locations of utilities, including their vulnerability to tampering or sabotage. How much emphasis and therefore funding will need to be allocated for security at any given site? What areas will need special attention? What items of equipment and what personnel will be needed to protect vulnerable areas? After a site is selected, these observations should be integrated into the design of the building and building site as early as possible. Security planning is much more effective when it is an integral part of the planning exercise rather than tacked on at the end.

A good architect spends almost as much time thinking about what goes on outside the building as what happens inside. How will automobiles approach the site? How can library pedestrian and vehicle traffic be separated from off-site vehicle areas and pedestrian zones? How can planting beds, berms, fences, and walls best be used as barriers to control access? How can motor vehicle speeds be reduced around the perimeter of the site by the creative use of curves and turns, speed bumps, changes in pavement, narrowing of lanes, and medians?

As the number of criminal and occasionally life-threatening incidents taking place in libraries continues to mount, security becomes an ever more important issue. Keeping track of library visitors becomes essential. The architect must consider how patrons can be confined to designated areas through the installation of high curbs, median strips, planters, fencing, or walls. How can pedestrians, especially children, be kept out of the way of traffic? Crime has become so prevalent that it is not paranoid to consider drive-by attacks, which might necessitate obscuring sight lines from surrounding roadways.

Will the site include a parking lot? If the answer is yes, will the library be located in an area where parking is at a premium and your lot will attract people working in nearby offices and shops? Will there be a separate area reserved for staff parking? Creating and maintaining a parking facility may require the use of static barriers like bollards, planters, and walls as well as operable barriers like sliding gates, pop-up bollards, crash beams, booms, and even those nefarious tire shredders.

Will you require a safe, enclosed place to park bookmobiles and other library vehicles? Will you need a separate staff entrance? Is deterring vandalism an important consideration? If so, you may need a wall or fence that discourages climbing. Such a wall may require a special coating that facilitates the removal of paint and graffiti.

Will you need to screen an especially expensive computer lab or multimedia facility from view from the outside? A wall, fence, or plant screen may be needed. Other security barriers can include berms, plantings, ditches, bollards, or natural topographic separations.

Underground Sites

In an effort to find space for a new library or addition where none exists, architects occasionally go underground. For example, they may excavate half a dozen subterranean levels under an existing library. Another strategy is to dig into a hillside so that part of the library is aboveground and part surrounded by earth. Occasionally, an all-new library is built from scratch belowground. In general, underground buildings require the most sophisticated construction techniques and the most advanced materials. Few libraries can afford such expertise, and so in most cases, the idea should be strenuously opposed. Think about a roof that serves as a sidewalk with the constant scuffling and crunching of thousands of feet, the weight of service vehicles, and the freezing and thawing that occur with seasonal change. Because underground construction is usually approved when traditional buildings occupy the aboveground space, those buildings will inevitably be affected by the new construction. For example, blasting can endanger nearby foundations. Underground structures eventually leak, and drainage is a major problem. In fact, water damage poses the greatest danger to an underground building, and this can result in disaster in a library.

Differing Site Conditions

It is important that contracts with design professionals and contractors make it clear that they are responsible for performing pre-construction site investigations and for disclosing information about existing site conditions. The term *differing site conditions* covers occurrences or events that would not reasonably be anticipated by the parties involved in the construction process. These are often physical subsurface conditions, such as a rock ledge, unsuitable soil materials, or flowing water. Such unexpected conditions can considerably increase the labor and materials costs of construction without adding to the value of the project. A serious problem with the site could bring about major cost overruns and result in cuts in budgets for furniture, equipment, and other necessities.

If the worst happens, someone must be responsible for the added expense. Common law has tended to hold the contractor to his obligations when a job is more time-consuming or costly than had been anticipated—except in the case of differing site conditions. Such problems are more often the fault of the architect or engineer, but their contracts frequently protect them from liability. If you are using a design-build firm, the joint organization can be held responsible. Otherwise, be sure that design professionals are clearly held responsible in your contracts and that they are sufficiently financially stable to absorb these costs. Be certain that the language in your contracts makes it clear who is responsible in the event that any of the following errors or omissions occur:

  failure to undertake adequate pre-construction investigations or surveys of existing site conditions

  failure to describe existing site conditions accurately or completely in bid and contract documents negligence in the drafting of bid or contract documents with regard to the circumstances under which a contractor will be entitled to relief because of differing site conditions

failure to resolve contractor and design professionals' differing site conditions claims

If you have any particular reason to anticipate a problem, you might recommend that a geotechnical engineer be brought in for expert advice. In fact, negotiations should clarify the responsibility for furnishing any required geotechnical engineering or survey services. Prior to signing contracts, all of the building professionals should be encouraged to visit the site to become familiar with the site conditions.

SHARING A FACILITY

The idea of a building complex designed to meet a variety of community needs has become popular in many areas. Although academic libraries may be required to share their facilities with academic departments or classrooms, the demands on those areas are not markedly different from those on the library. For public libraries, the issue of shared facilities may be more complicated. For example, the West Des Moines Civic Campus was built after a flood left the city administration homeless. An older plan was resurrected that called for a joint civic campus that would include a police station, elementary and high schools, library, municipal pool, recreation fields, and city and school administration center.

Joint use of a facility may be made necessary because of a crisis like that in Des Moines or because of the need to achieve greater economy by combining two or more projects into one. A shared facility can make it possible for a library to fund a construction project when funding might otherwise be impossible to obtain. Although such marriages of convenience must be approached with care, they do not necessarily mean an adversarial relationship. When these partnerships work well, they allow you to combine forces and share the burden of maintaining a building. If the administrators of the other facility are team players, you will have the advantage of their experience and influence.

Marriage of Convenience

A congenial partnering of two or more complementary facilities can also allow for economies of scale not possible when building just a library or just a recreation center. Site costs as well as architect and contractor fees may be reduced. The Des Moines project gives residents a library they might otherwise have waited years for. In return, the library staffs an information desk that directs traffic to and from five city departments, collects city bills and payments, and provides training on the OPACs. The building has the advantage of close integration with other similar facilities. For example, fiber-optic cables connect the library with the community schools' learning resource center next door.

Cost savings is usually one of the major reasons why the multiuse model is so popular, but you may find that your funding agency expects far greater savings than can realistically be achieved. For example, a new library project may be tottering on the brink of approval when some community leader speaks up and says something like, "Why don't we spend a little more and build an athletic complex as well?" Your community leaders will soon discover that such a facility involves major capital expenditures. When the discovery is made that the shared facility will cost far more than anticipated, conflicts invariably arise.

Of course, some librarians have become adept at playing the same game. When that athletic complex is under consideration, librarians may be the ones who pop up with the suggestion that the funding agency spend a little more and include a new library or library addition. If you or your board chair is good at this sort of political strategizing, go for it, but don't delude yourself into believing that two facilities can really be built almost as cheaply as one.

Weigh the Pros and Cons

Joint facilities may pose unique problems. For example, the library and the swimming pool may be housed within the same complex and may have to share the same ventilation system. Noisy adolescents may have to walk through the library to reach the pool, or shared walls may force library patrons to endure sound from the pool. What can be even more devastating than the physical inconveniences that result from such strange bedfellows are their political ramifications. If you share a facility, you share planning and decision-making responsibility. Some librarians have found themselves pitted against assertive, politically astute athletic directors or recreation supervisors who virtually take control of the entire project. If this happens, the library may be deprived of funding for even basic needs while the competing activity wallows in luxury. This is, of course, an exaggeration, but it reflects the way battle-scarred librarians may feel after such a project.

Advance planning is a strategy for dealing with any number of difficulties, but it can be especially important with shared facilities. Such planning involves educating decision makers to library needs long before the bickering begins. When a facility is shared, the number of players multiplies, and so do the politics.

James Madison University, Harrisonburg, Virginia, East Campus Library, The Design Collective, designcollective.com. Photo: Michael Dersin Photography.

This makes it even more important to attract politically astute friends for the library. It also means reassessing your own political skills. Some librarians find that they are the ones best able to defend their projects from the onslaughts of rapacious fellow tenants. Others discover that it works best to stay somewhat in the background, providing ammunition while their politically experienced board chairperson engages in any necessary negotiations.

IDENTIFYING SPACE NEEDS

While different sites are still under consideration, you should also be considering the spaces that will make up the new library building. Although the architects have a much better idea of how large a structure can be built with available funds, the way the space will be used can affect site selection, and likewise, the site can affect the way space is organized. As you visit libraries, you'll quickly discover that some new buildings boasting a generous number of square feet of floor space seem cramped and crowded. Others that are actually smaller in their dimensions feel as if they have more available space.

The way the space is planned makes all the difference in the way your customers interact with the library building. Form should follow function, but you'll discover many architects for whom that phrase means little. For example, they may design the exterior of the building first and then chop up the interior space into oddly shaped areas. In many libraries you may find yourself wasting a lot of time and effort just trying to find your way around. Even though the signage system may be well designed, the space arrangement is counterintuitive. Therefore, it is important to identify space needs early in the planning process. The following sections focus on the space requirements of the overall building and on various internal spaces of the library.

Establishing Priorities

Since the publication of the first edition of this book, I've visited literally hundreds of libraries. No matter how old or new, I've often had the sense that something is not quite right. Although staff members complain that there isn't room to accommodate this or that customer need, I repeatedly discover an oversized book return room, a vast mechanical room, or a huge area intended to house the cataloging and processing staff of thirty years ago. The reason the library exists is to serve the needs of its customers. Therefore, most library space should be public space. All the other spaces are intended to provide support for that public space and the customers who occupy it.

Our customers, however, are not usually present when library space is allocated, and their interests are often overlooked. Each time an office is added or enlarged, the public area shrinks; when a storage area is added, the public area simultaneously contracts. We all want to work in spacious, functional surroundings, and so we tend to focus on our own space needs rather than those of our customers. Naturally, the custodian would like large janitorial closets located conveniently throughout the library, as well as a spacious, well-organized workshop. Facilities managers want plenty of space to store the lawn tractors and other equipment, with a well-equipped place where they can take them apart for maintenance. The library staff would like plenty of "backroom" space and a staff lounge that is larger and more convenient than the present one.

In addition, the professional team designing the library has its own priorities. I've visited a great many mechanical spaces in libraries and have decided that something is seriously amiss. Modern air-handling equipment is big, boxy, and takes up a lot of room. However, the amount of space allocated for this purpose varies to an astonishing extent in newer libraries. Why is it that one library manages to get along just fine with a mechanical room half the size of that found in another library of similar proportions? The answer frequently goes back to the mechanical engineers on the design teams. They know nothing of the needs of library customers.

Instead, they focus their energies on the spaces they understand, the ones that interest them. That frequently means designing ideal or near-perfect mechanical spaces. Because library directors usually know so little about the technical side of heating and cooling the library, they tend to accept the engineer's word and assume they have no options. In fact, they may not even notice the spaces devoted to building systems because those blueprint pages may not be presented to them for consideration. Yet a few miles away, a library of similar size may be enjoying an equally sophisticated HVAC system while having considerably more public space available for collection and services.

When Machines Are More Important Than People

The library director and the other staff members planning the library must view themselves as their customers' advocates. They have an obligation to represent them when important decisions are being made. If it came down to reducing the size of their beloved children's collection or sacrificing half a dozen public computers, you can be quite sure that customers would look carefully at the space being given up for other purposes. They would want you to find out precisely how large the mechanical room must be and what would happen if it shrunk by, let's say, 25 percent. Is there really any good reason for their sacrifice?

When I've asked such questions of mechanical engineers, I've frequently been told that the space is needed to accommodate future growth. Someday the library will be enlarged, and the mechanical room will be ready for the expansion. At the risk of taxing your patience, I have to repeat my mantra. Libraries are poor! It may be that building professionals are accustomed to dealing with more-affluent clients. Your capital budget is probably stretched to the max just meeting the library's current needs. None of the spaces you and the staff have pored over are intended to remain empty and unused until some future date. In fact, the budget can barely pay for the space you needed yesterday. The new library will attract new customers, and it won't be long before you are wondering how you can expand services and collections to meet their needs. Why should your HVAC system be accommodated in considerably greater luxury than your customers? Why should you be able to accommodate more mechanical equipment than your building requires?

As plans begin emerging, question every single space that isn't open to the public. What would happen if this room or that closet were a little smaller? What would happen if it disappeared entirely? By reducing the number of offices, might you actually increase the number of library staff members available to your customers? Of course, the custodians would like more space for their supplies, the facilities manager would like to spread out, and the library staff would like more space to hide their clutter. This is natural, and at least some of this space is badly needed. Past a certain point, however, the library's mission and goals are taking second place.

Optimal Floor Size

If you think about the last time you became lost and exhausted in a Walmart, you'll realize that there is a limit to how large a space a customer can comfortably traverse. In a Walmart or a large supermarket, however, you can push your cart through the store aisle by aisle. It is not possible to approach library resources in this efficient manner. If you were to follow most customers as they use the library, you would discover that they cover a considerable distance, trudging back and forth as they identify the materials they need. First they will probably stop at the OPAC, then zigzag among stacks and reading areas, and then maybe return to the OPAC. Later, they may seek out the computer area or the periodicals, with a detour to the reference desk or restroom. For many people, especially the elderly, this can be an exhausting experience. If they are also trying to find a copy machine while carrying a stack of books or lugging around a twenty-five-pound toddler, the experience is not one they will want to repeat.

Most public libraries should not exceed 50,000 square feet on one floor. Beyond this size, staff are unable to direct patrons to the resources they are seeking, signage is too distant to be useful, and both customers and staff exhaust their energy trotting from place to place. When more space is needed, multiple floors are one solution. Customers can move from floor to floor by elevator without becoming footsore. Many different levels, however, present security problems, since a floor to which no staff members are assigned is potentially dangerous. For a period of time, academic institutions were building "tower" libraries with ten or twenty stack levels ascending high above the campus. This layout can be extremely dangerous, isolating solitary patrons and staff members who cannot call out for help and must defend themselves unassisted from theft, assault, or unwanted personal advances.

So what is the answer to this catch-22? How do you design a large library that doesn't either endanger or exhaust your patrons? One way is to attempt to anticipate your users' needs and cluster functions that relate to one another. Another is to adopt the hub or spoke design of many airports with a service desk at the center of the hub. You might also design a series of small hubs, each with a service desk and each relating efficiently to other hubs. Your plan, however, should not be overly optimistic about the number of hubs you can effectively service.

Satisfying Proportions

As you may recall from your history classes, ancient Greek architecture was in part built around the axiom that the perfect proportion for a space is a ratio of 2 to 3 (known as the golden mean). With 2,000 years' experience under our belts, we recognize that the Greeks did indeed know what they were talking about. The most functional and aesthetically pleasing rooms are half again as long as they are wide. This formula usually meets the most sophisticated modern needs.

Although this may seem unnecessary to point out, a room should also have four walls and four right-angled corners with opposite walls parallel to one another. When you see the first floor plans for your new building, bear this truth in mind. If your architects have designed a round or curvy building, rooms will be fitted in at odd angles. Not only will room shapes not be governed by the golden mean, but they may not even have four walls. Instead, they may consist of odd angles and multiple small walls that jog out into the room, wasting huge amounts of space. Remember that triangles, trapezoids, pentagons, and hexagons do not work as efficient room shapes. Any circular room wastes nearly as much space as it provides, and fitting furniture, especially stacks, into it can be especially challenging.

The shapes and sizes of rooms are matters on which you and your architects must come to a satisfactory agreement. You can certainly be sensitive to their concerns about an ugly, "boxy" building. You share their desire to create a beautiful structure—but not at the cost of functionality. A few oddly shaped spaces needed to accommodate an impressive design feature are probably okay, but be sure bizarre geometry does not become a habit. Be certain your architects understand your views before they begin preliminary sketches. Then check each space on the plans to be sure it is rectangular, has roughly 2:3 proportions, and has no funny little extra walls. If you discover multiple problems, begin ringing alarm bells early enough so that a major redesign is still possible.

Service Desks

Early in the planning process, you'll want to decide how many service points you will need and where they will be located. Then consider each in turn. After you tentatively position a service desk, ask yourself if users will be able to see it from a distance or will it be obscured by stacks or structural elements? Is it located in a logical place near the resources and equipment that customers will be using? For example, the reference desk should naturally be near online reference sources and the print reference collection. However, it's also important that it should be reasonably near the circulation desk and the main exit. If you are planning to have a separate information desk, it should greet your customers as they walk in the front door so that they waste as little time finding their way around as possible. Consider traffic patterns and avoid service locations that are too far off the beaten track to serve their function effectively.

San Francisco Public Library, Noe Valley/Sally Brunn Branch, Carey & Co. Inc. Architecture, careyandco.com.
Photo: David Wakely.

Stack Areas

Even with the advent of electronic resources, storage for collections still occupies more space than any other function. It is therefore important to design a layout that will satisfy the requirements of both staff and library customers. Gone forever are the days of dark, ugly, closed stacks that used to be wedged into buildings two levels per floor, with most of their light dependent on slippery glass-block floors and accessible only by dangerous spiral stairways. Even though most of those horrors are gone forever, many newer library stack areas are almost as inconvenient. As you discuss stack areas with architects, consider the impact of shelving heights on visual control of public areas. Also consider the impact of tall stacks on lighting and remember how difficult it is to see the call numbers on the bottom shelf. Think about the kinds of users who will be seeking materials and the difficulty they may experience trying to reach books on the upper shelves.

Architects may assume that the stacks will neither shrink nor grow throughout the building's useful life. However, change is a constant in libraries, and some stack areas may eventually be transformed into computer and reading spaces. Although the proportion of your budget spent on print materials may be shrinking, a radical reduction in stack areas would be premature. You will be making some educated guesses about the future needs of the print and media collections, but allow for flexibility in case your crystal ball is faulty.

The Mystery of the Disappearing Bookshelves

While visiting newer libraries, however, I have discovered an unexpected problem. As libraries evolve into more attractive, people-friendly spaces, they tend to discard their full-height shelving (approximately 90 inches) and substitute mid-height units (often 42 or 66 inches). They also plan for wider aisles between stack ranges to comply with Americans with Disabilities Act (ADA) requirements. Even though architects may design new stack areas that are somewhat larger than the old ones, it sometimes happens that there isn't enough room to shelve even the existing collections, let alone accommodate future growth. No matter what the future holds, I know of no public librarians who are planning to open their new libraries with smaller book collections than their existing ones. Although the situation is a little different in academic libraries (where some collections really are shrinking), librarians are still expecting a substantial part of their usage to be generated by the book collection.

There is no substitute for precise measurements. Count every single shelf in every single stack range in your old library. Then have other staff members make the same count and be sure the numbers match. Your old 90-inch shelving sections usually have seven shelves to each section. Count the number of sections and multiply by seven. That is the number of shelves you'll need just to squeeze in your existing collection. However, optimal conditions mean shelves that are about

TALES

For archives, don't assume anyone knows how wide shelving should be. Draw up your own plan (no matter how crude), and think about where you plan to put things. Then actually give samples of boxes for those areas to the vendor, architect—whomever. They are always surprised at the variety of sizes and shapes.

I recently discovered that our rare book room will unfortunately be open stacks. (It was not my idea, but I knew I wouldn't win that battle.) It also won't have the added security of glass or a metal grating. Although I'll be the one to unlock the door and supervise visitors, they will still be able to take books off the shelf.

TIPS

Start estimating stack dimensions and aisle widths early in the project so you don't find yourself coming up short of space and having to make aisles narrower to accommodate the required number of stack units. Wider aisles are not only needed for ADA compliance, but they facilitate browsing and reshelving.

Remember how loud newer power-flush commercial toilets are, so locate them away from offices and reading areas. Even high-performance acoustical partitions won't entirely conceal the sound. On the other hand, locate restrooms close enough to high-traffic areas so that patrons don't wander around for fifteen minutes trying to find the women's room.

70 percent full, and yours are probably at capacity. That means you may need about 25 percent more space for your existing collection. Then consider that mid-height shelving may reduce the capacity of a section to three or four shelves, and ADA requirements will necessitate fewer sections in a given area. Once you have your numbers honed, you'll need to convince your architects and interior designers that stack spaces can't disappear as more interesting features are added.

Even though the architects are far more knowledgeable than you about technical requirements, be sure they understand that all stack areas or future stack areas must be able to handle a live floor load of at least 150 pounds per square foot. An earlier section described the Sleeping Beauty complex that seems to be rampant among architects. Five or ten years from now, you may find it necessary to install stacks in a space originally used for some other purpose. This means that most library areas must be able to accommodate the weight of fully loaded book stacks. Be sure that your architects do not create a library that is unable to respond to change. Consider, too, that compact shelving requires a floor with a live load of about 300 pounds per square foot.

Restroom Areas

After an architect has sketched out the larger spaces on the floor plan, a lot of small, oddly shaped spaces will remain. Some will be hidden behind other spaces and can be accessed only down long hallways. Others will take their shape from structural bracing or other functional necessities. Some of these spaces will inevitably become the library restrooms. In still another of your many gentle tussles with the architects, make it clear that restrooms must be easily accessible. A larger proportion of your patrons will be using the restrooms than any other resource or service in the library.

Location

Restrooms must be well marked and easy to find. For example, most people expect that if they see a men's room, there's probably a women's room nearby. When the two are on opposite sides of the building, you will inevitably have disgruntled customers. Libraries that decide to cut corners by locating men's rooms on even-numbered floors and women's rooms on the odd ones are even guiltier of wasting their users' time, sending them searching fruitlessly up and down aisles, investigating every possible nook and cranny.

Size

Be certain that restroom quantity and size are determined by probable use; this is almost always higher than anticipated. The availability of small, unused spaces should not determine the presence or absence of restrooms. Because everyone who comes into your library probably spends some time on the main floor, you will need to provide the largest number of stalls and sinks there. Since the second floor is next in terms of heavy use, it should be next in size and quantity of facilities, and so on as floors go higher. At least one men's and one women's room is needed even on the top floor. The principle of separate but equal does not extend to the planning of restrooms. Instead, anatomical needs should play some role in determining the number of stalls in each restroom, which means that women generally require more. Family restrooms are increasingly popular, and the notion that only women change diapers has been relegated to ancient history.

Convenience

Fortunately, design professionals are familiar with ADA guidelines for restrooms, but in making these accommodations, they may ignore the needs of the majority of users. For example, restrooms should be equipped with both wheelchair and walk-up-height mirrors or with extra-long mirrors that meet everyone's needs. (See p. 99 for additional discussion of ADA accommodations.)

Speaking of mirrors, be kind to your women patrons by providing good light and large mirrors. There is nothing immoral about using the restroom to comb one's hair or apply one's lipstick, but we sometimes treat such common creature concerns with contempt. Women do, indeed, spend more time than men in library restrooms, and so, rather than making snide comments, it is important to make these spaces as pleasant and inviting as possible.

Maintenance

Libraries are not noted for the quality of their custodial services. It is hard enough to obtain adequate funding to maintain a library, and it is only with great reluctance that we part with our precious pennies. Hence, custodial expenses are almost always kept to a minimum. At the same time, no one likes a dirty restroom. If you think back, you have formed some very negative impressions of stores, restaurants, and even libraries based entirely on an unpleasant visit to the restroom. Talk with your architect about building in easy-clean maintenance solutions. Floor tile, for example, should have a flat, nonslip surface with no troughs or valleys of light-colored grout. Otherwise, within a few short months, each tile will be framed in dirt that will eventually become petrified into antique dirt, remaining throughout the life of the building. Partitions should be easy to clean and resistant to graffiti. Bright colors work well because too-dark colors show cleaning smears and too-light ones become message boards.

Storage Spaces

On the one hand, no library ever has enough space for storage. On the other, it may be wasteful to dedicate large areas to this purpose, since storerooms do nothing but sit there crammed with things you're not using. You will fill every inch of space you devote to storage, and the more space you have, the more junk you will find to fill the vacuum. Do you remember the libraries of the past that had "dungeons" where mountains of uncataloged books gathered dust over the decades? Computers largely eliminated those huge cataloging backlogs, but now

TIP

Determine before the project even starts what will be stored in an archive area. This should not change and needs to be supported before even beginning.

we store antiquated or cannibalized computers in similar spaces. It's probably best to have a number of small storage spaces located throughout the building where you can store cleaning supplies, fluorescent tubes, paper and toner for printers, and replacement bulbs for microfilm readers near the areas where they will actually be needed.

Stairwells

How many times have you walked through an attractive library, entered the stairwell, and found yourself in the most appallingly ugly space imaginable? Although I think I understand why architects create some abominations, I've never quite solved the stairwell mystery. Just think about the stairwells in most modern buildings. Unpainted cinder block walls, cement floors, and gunboat-gray metal stairs are hardly designed to please the eye. I've been told several times that stairwells are the way they are because they must function as fire exits. If you're responsible for fire drills and building evacuation, you know that you're supposed to herd patrons out of open areas and into stairwells that are hermetically sealed with metal fire doors. Hence, the materials used in a stairwell must be fireproof.

Why, however, must being fire-retardant mean being ugly? Is gray paint somehow more resistant to fire than purple or blue or chartreuse? (Not that I'm advocating chartreuse stairwells, though it might be an improvement.) If you can paint the stairs, is there some reason why you can't paint the cinder block? Even interior decorators, doyens of aesthetic sensibility, seem to be blind to stairwells. Of course, only a limited selection of materials can be used, but then I'm not suggesting fabric wall coverings or broadloom carpeting.

Perhaps the problem arises because other buildings have stairs located out in the open, but that seems to be true only of older edifices with those grand, sweeping staircases. Do architects assume that everyone rides the elevator? Maybe library users are the world's only physically fit people who sometimes prefer to walk up a flight or two rather than wait for a slow elevator. Whatever the reason, your patrons will be using those ugly stairwells, and if you don't intervene now, they will take away with them a gunboat-gray impression of your library.

Even if you are blessed with a caring architect or are able to negotiate a reasonably attractive compromise, you cannot put the stairwell war behind you. Stairwells are a kind of "no-man's land." Custodians don't clean stairwells, painters don't paint stairwells, and remodelers don't appear to realize that stairwells exist. For example, each time the library is repainted, you're going to have to remind the painting contractor that the stairwells should be included and will require special equipment to reach some areas.

Display Space

If your library is like most others, your enthusiasm for exhibits and displays waxes and wanes with the seasons. Colorful displays attract public attention, increase circulation, and enlist your users in causes near and dear to libraries like

National Library Week or Banned Books Week. On the other hand, creating successful displays is a very time-consuming activity, and sometimes your staff simply cannot spare the time. All of this needs to be factored into your approach to display space in the new library. You will also want to consider the community's needs. For example, you may want to provide gallery space for local art groups.

Ideally, you will want display boards, cases, kiosks, and panels available when either your staff or your users feel inspired, but you don't want to live with that ugly, "undressed" look in between exhibits. Panels that can be folded up and stored in a closet between uses are ideal for displays (if you can store them close by). Covered bulletin boards (in other words, those that have some type of material covering the cork) are also good because when the boards are not in use, patrons needn't view the gouged-out holes left by ancient tacks and staples.

I personally have never been a big admirer of glass cases. They tend to be terribly expensive, gather dust, and block traffic. Nice exhibits are prone to theft, and ugly ones seem to stay forever. The glass can crack or shatter, so staff must spend precious time monitoring them to be sure patrons aren't piling on books or children aren't climbing on them. It always makes me nervous when Mr. Jones wants to exhibit his rare collection of Indonesian beetles. I know that we'll lose the key to the case, or Mr. Jones will be irate because we didn't treat his priceless collection with proper respect. Brightly lit display cases are a terrible environment in which to place valuable manuscripts or rare books, so glass cases don't satisfy any real needs of the library.

Artistic staff members, library pages, and student assistants can create remarkably professional displays with inexpensive ink-jet color printers, colored paper, and poster board. Copy centers can enlarge color and black-and-white photographs and mat them for surprisingly attractive and inexpensive displays. That way, you can feel more comfortable knowing that the library is not responsible for anyone's prized possessions. Original artwork should be displayed only in a well-supervised area, since prints and paintings are subject to theft and alterations by too-creative middle school students. In general, lean more toward graphic displays than real art or realia, so the library staff won't get trapped into discussions of what is art or what is appropriate for display. Your community may have other needs, however, so this may be an area in which you must remain flexible.

Staff Spaces

Now that you have the opportunity to design your "dream library," consider what it's been like working in your present building. I once worked in a beautiful library that had wall-to-wall carpeting everywhere except in staff areas. Cataloging, acquisitions, and processing staffs all worked on a cold, hard, cement floor. You've probably even known libraries where technical services are squeezed into a dark basement. Why should the people who spend the most time in the library enjoy the least comfort? In an environment in which quiet is almost a cliché, why must staff frequently be consigned to areas that are so noisy that it is impossible to concentrate?

TALES

In the old building, we could touch each other just by extending an arm. My acquisitions secretary's desk was only about three feet from mine. Papers were passed by just reaching across walkways. The new tech services room is more than sixty-six feet long and at least thirty feet wide. It is spacious and beautiful—all open landscape. Communication modes have changed. Now you have to walk a distance that is beyond normal hearing range. Written notes are used more. During the first few months, people noticed that they were simply worn out from a lot more walking.

Planning is absolutely essential. Invest in a solid planning effort before doing anything else. We used the first three months of our design process to study the way we work as it affects adjacencies and facilities layout. This has proven extremely valuable.

In addition, staff are sometimes the last to be considered when ergonomically designed furnishings are being purchased. Given the long hours they spend at their desks, staff can experience carpal tunnel syndrome as well as eyestrain resulting from poor lighting. Paying special attention to staff spaces will not only have a positive impact on morale, but will substantially increase productivity. Consideration given to acoustic issues, ergonomics, good lighting, and just plain comfort should be basic to the design of library staff areas.

How Much Staff Space?

How much staff space will you really need, and how should it be organized? Although the computerization of libraries is making existing formulas obsolete, some basic guidelines can help you make your decisions. The spaces in which the library staff will work should be large enough to allow each employee to do his or her job correctly and encourage logical and efficient organization. For example, staff members who must work together should have work spaces within reasonable proximity of one another. Space should be flexible enough to respond to changes in functions and to easily accommodate additional employees or evolving tasks

As a general rule, staff areas can be somewhat smaller than in the past. Computers have reduced both the number of staff members and the backlog of items awaiting processing. In fact, it's a good idea to consider whether some personnel can't move into public areas and do their work just as efficiently as when they were closeted in a staff-only work area. We simply don't maintain all those paper files anymore. Since computers can also facilitate communication, you may find it useful to blur that traditionally sharp line between public service and other library staff. However, any staff members you move to public areas will be asked questions. They can continue to spend most of their time on their regular duties, but they'll need some basic public service skills and a friendly attitude toward the library's customers.

By the way, while I was collecting accounts from librarians and support staff about their building projects, I came upon a potential problem. A few emphasized that they wanted their areas to be secluded, far away from the hubbub of public areas. I'm not sure there are many jobs in the modern library that lend themselves to seclusion. Most library staff members are more effective when they can wear a variety of hats and when they understand how their work affects the library's customers. It might work for someone who does nothing but routine tasks like processing materials, but those tend to be precisely the tasks we relegate to student workers and volunteers who need considerable supervision. Some tasks may require more concentration, a place to hide and avoid interruptions, but usually for brief periods of time. Although some staff members may prefer seclusion, one can't help but wonder whether they are really the right people to be working in the twenty-first-century library.

Fitting the Pieces Together

For more traditional staff spaces, you might think of them as a giant jigsaw puzzle. Explore the various ways in which the pieces might be fitted together and then choose the most functional arrangement. As you are already discovering, space, whether for public or staff use, is becoming more and more expensive, and using available space in the most efficient manner must be a high priority. It is sometimes possible to allocate fewer square feet per person while maintaining staff comfort and increasing productivity. To decide on the design that best uses available space, consider that staff need access to information, to one another, and to library customers.

Are there ways that the floor plan can save staff time? Here is an experiment you might like to try: at irregular intervals throughout the day, make the rounds of all areas where staff are working. Are they at their desks? Seated at work tables? Standing at counters? Meeting with one another? Pushing book trucks? Getting supplies? Be sure everyone knows you will be doing this so they won't feel spied upon. Then meet with staff to learn how they would describe their comings and goings. You'll probably find that by combining your observations and their perceptions you will arrive at a more complete picture of staff space needs.

Adaptability

None of us can be quite sure what the future will hold, and most of us are convinced we're in for a bumpy ride. This will mean that we must be able to adjust to change quickly. When new technologies replace older ones, we must be prepared to change as well. The future may require frequent physical relocation of personnel to meet changing library needs, and so we must be able to quickly reconfigure communications, computer services, and workstations.

Accommodating Individual Differences

Today's emphasis on team projects, team goals, and team meetings may be causing us to forget individual needs. We have moved so far in the direction of a teamwork-focused environment that the need for

TIPS

Involve staff in designing work spaces! The circulation area is beautiful in our new library, but function did not precede form. We are finding that the area is too small and does not have adequate shelving.

We involved staff heavily in the design stage. Dividing into teams of three or four, each team visited three libraries, took pictures, wrote notes about good or bad features, and put these into a report that was shared and discussed by all. We then wrote our building program to submit to our architect on the basis of that report. That was one very good thing we did. All bought into the final product.

individual concentration may be overlooked entirely. As you plan staff spaces, it is important to focus on maximizing individual performance by creating an environment in which each staff member can do his or her very best work. Individual staff members are very different in their ability or inability to screen out distractions.

Ask your library staff about their present work conditions. Find out what they like and dislike most about their environment. You'll get a good idea of how sensitive they are to environmental distractions including noise, temperature, and even odors. Don't criticize their responses. Although it's impossible to create a workplace that will please everyone, problems should be taken seriously or else productivity levels (and of course, personal satisfaction) will be affected. At some point, however, personal preferences may interfere with a staff member's ability to do the job that needs doing. For example, members of the circulation staff must be able to tolerate noise and confusion. Otherwise, they will keep retreating to work areas when they need to be available at the public desk. When staff members have duties that can be effectively performed in public areas, allowing them to sequester themselves may place an extra burden on everyone else.

The Great Office/Cubicle Debate

You needn't be a fan of the "Dilbert" comic strip to be aware of the trend away from private offices in many workplaces. Among the leaders of the movement toward systems furnishings and individual cubicles were the young, egalitarian computer companies that sought to escape the hierarchical status games played by hidebound businesses. They were interested in accomplishments, not in who got the corner office suite. Is such "office landscaping" appropriate for library operations? It offers many advantages but should be viewed with some restraint. On the positive side, systems furniture is usually very well designed, offering a generous work area in a small space. Everything the staff member needs is close at hand, and a quick swivel of one's chair brings the file cabinet or computer within easy reach. Office landscaping also tends to increase staff camaraderie and the sense of working together as a team.

On the negative side, privacy is almost nonexistent in cubicles. Everyone hears everything. Supervisors must seek out private spaces to discuss confidential matters or to evaluate subordinates, and such quests in search of privacy may be obvious to all.

If you choose to go with systems furniture for some or all staff members, it is possible to design a comfortable, productive environment, but success will require considerable forethought. For example, work areas in which a lot of people are housed in a small space are almost inevitably noisy. Since staff members vary in their ability to tolerate noise in their immediate surroundings, people with loud voices can sometimes drive their colleagues mad. Limiting the number of cubicles grouped together is one way to minimize noise problems. Make it clear to the architect or builder that the ceiling tiles, carpeting, light housings, furniture, and panel systems should be selected to absorb and mask sound. Be sure that all staff members can retreat to a quiet, unassigned space where they can hide for short periods to concentrate, to have a private conversation, or just to get away from it all. No staff member should be denied the right to a confidential telephone conversation with her physician or family member. These spaces, however, need not be assigned to any one person but can remain available for use by any staff member as the need arises.

Remember, too, that visual privacy is important, and the glass walls that may be ideal in public areas may not always be appropriate in staff spaces. Flexible spaces that can be opened up for use by a large group or partitioned for multiple smaller groups are a good idea. However, partitions tend to be expensive and difficult to move into place. Cheaper ones also tend to have poor sound absorption characteristics. Remember that group spaces may need phones, projectors, and screens as well as tackable or markable surfaces. Some informal spaces should be conducive to teamwork; these can be furnished with coffee tables and comfortable chairs.

Systems furniture can be easily moved and reconfigured over and over again. This is very convenient, but it does create problems for voice and data installation. Some systems units have what is called a "spine" that accommodates wiring, and some partitions have thicker walls with multiple channels for voice, data, and power. Such plug-and-play options provided with systems architecture allow for horizontal and vertical cabling. Wires may run through panels at the work surface level, as well as through horizontal, overhead raceways or raised floors.

If you choose systems furniture for some library areas, remember that it will affect the ways heat and air are distributed and the type of lighting that is needed. For example, systems furniture panels cast shadows and considerably increase the need for task lighting.

Locating Staff Spaces

In all too many libraries, administrative offices are located on separate floors or in distant wings, far from the madding crowd. This was never a very good idea, since the library director and department heads had little firsthand knowledge of what was going on in the library. With the staffing cuts of recent years, however, such ivory-tower aloofness has assumed more negative consequences. On the assumption that a great divide existed between public and backroom staff and never the twain would meet, older libraries also tended to isolate technical service areas in distant corners. In a modern library, all staff members, whether they be administrators or clerks, catalogers or reference librarians, bear a responsibility for a safe and efficient library operation.

Not only are the rigid lines between technical and public services disappearing, but library functions themselves are changing as well. Outsourcing of cataloging services is becoming increasingly common, while computer-related jobs are growing rapidly. As you design staff spaces, consider how backroom spaces can be changed to accommodate future staffing patterns. Load-bearing walls, for example, should not be used to separate staff and public spaces. Some libraries are also moving more tasks to the circulation area to make better use of available staff resources. This means that some creative planning will be needed to accommodate these additional people and work spaces.

Modern, less rigid divisions of labor may lend themselves to glassed-in offices surrounding public spaces. Staff members are visible and available to assist patrons, while at the same time they can carry on conversations without disturbing others or being overheard. However you choose to accommodate staff, you will need to think about supplies and reference sources that must be shared, book trucks that must be parked, and equipment used by more than one person. Planning for such interactions can best be done with the library staff, but this may not be the appropriate arena in which to decide who is entitled to a private office.

Loading Dock

While you're planning spaces designed primarily for staff use, you should probably have a talk with your architect about the loading dock. Although you certainly do need one, you will discover that they function quite differently in libraries than in other kinds of buildings. First, you don't use the area just inside the dock to store a large inventory of boxes that will be sent out to customers. In fact, not much leaves the building by the loading dock, and most incoming boxes go directly to the technical services area.

That means you need a loading dock that is convenient to technical services. Since boxes are very likely toted by pages, student assistants, and worn librarians with back problems, they should not have to traverse half the library. In fact, what is usually called the receiving room just inside the dock may actually become the technical services area. If that's the case, be sure that deliveries can be made without blasting staff with gusts of frigid air. Of course, you will indeed need storage space, but most of it should be located in convenient places throughout the library. Thus, a small loading dock/receiving area is probably just fine for your needs.

Lane Libraries, Hamilton, Ohio, Hamilton Lane Library, SHP Leading Design, shp.com. Photo: Nikki Shoemaker.

PLANNING A RENOVATION OR REMODELING PROJECT

New construction, whether an addition or a whole new library, gets more expensive every day. Take a good look at the cost of new construction in your area and the likelihood that the library can raise that much money. Maybe you've already sought approval from your county or university—only to be repeatedly turned down. Would a less expensive remodeling project meet most of your needs? Some projects might involve updating the look of the library. For example, you could replace outdated colors (say good-bye forever to harvest gold). You might purchase new furniture (although it's become astronomically expensive, and your old library furniture may be better made). You might add new millwork like accent panels, built-in cabinetry, and architectural moldings. Another change might involve replacing wallboard with glass to give a more open, airy feel and improve supervision. Getting new carpet can make a huge difference in the look and feel of a library. Likewise, lowering ceilings in old buildings will not only provide a more modern look, but acoustical panels will also reduce noise. Many of the green and energy-saving features described later in this book can be scaled down to a remodeling project and can reap big dividends in cost savings.

Without major construction, you will still have the same amount of space. However, you could reorganize library space to function more efficiently. A more efficient floor plan in public service areas could have a major impact on services at a relatively small cost. For example, you might remove non-load-bearing walls to open up cramped spaces, replace load-bearing walls with columns, or turn wasted space into conference, meeting, and study rooms. Some other remodeling improvements might be to

replace an inefficient heating, ventilating, and air-conditioning system

increase storage space with new storage closets

replace windows for improved energy effectiveness

upgrade electrical service to accommodate new computer equipment

replace outdated equipment like copy machines and computers

Do you think that these relatively inexpensive changes would meet most of your library's needs? Of course, an extensive remodeling project or renovation is never cheap, but depending on the specific changes you have in mind, it can probably be accomplished for approximately $20 to $30 per square foot. Considering the political climate in which your library functions, would it be significantly easier to obtain funding for a renovation or remodeling project than for an addition? In some other situations, you might as well go for a whole new building, since the effort involved in getting a big project funded is little different from that involved in a small one.

Reallocating Space

Unlike the librarian who has the luxury of planning a new library or addition, the remodeler's challenge is to find ways of making existing space serve present and future needs. Libraries seem to defy the laws of nature in that they appear to shrink a little with each passing year. After a few years of rapidly growing collections and the initiation of new services needed to keep up with modern library developments, you suddenly discover that your library building is full. Looking into the future, you realize that the library desperately needs more space to accommodate public computer areas, media collections, more extensive children's materials, and a host of new or expanded resources. Where are you going to put them all? If you are unable to build a new addition, how can renovating or remodeling give you the space you so desperately need?

Begin by considering how you can use your existing space more effectively. Reassess its arrangement and organization. How can you retrofit spaces to accommodate new requirements? Although it may not be possible to find new space in an old building, an increasing number of options such as high-density storage can accommodate growth. Smaller, more efficient offices and storage areas are another option, as are window wells that can turn dark basements into attractive public areas.

Take a cold, cruel look at the collections and services that are experiencing a decline in usage. For example, you may have an audiovisual department replete with filmstrips, eight-track tapes, and sixteen-millimeter films that is scheduled for extinction. It may be time to dispose of many older books since they are readily available elsewhere. Consider integrating traditional "behind the scenes" departments like acquisitions, cataloging, and technical services into a single department. As libraries replace printed periodical subscriptions with online full-text services, they may no longer need periodical-processing areas, and online check-in can be done at a public service desk. In fact, moving a variety of processing functions to public service desks can result in better use of available staff and improved public services. The vacated spaces can be remodeled into public areas like computer labs, classrooms, and meeting rooms.

The Unexpected Cost of Asbestos Removal

If your library decision makers have chosen remodeling or renovation over new construction because of cost savings, make sure these savings are not imaginary. A major renovation can actually cost more than a new building for a number of reasons, one of which is asbestos abatement and removal. Asbestos is a mineral substance that was used in building construction for many years. It was not until 1986 that the Environmental Protection Agency (EPA) banned the major uses of asbestos, so most library buildings probably contain at least some of this dangerous material. Exposure to asbestos dust and fibers causes lung disease as well as various cancers. If your library was built or remodeled between the 1940s and the early 1980s, it probably contains at least some tile work, asphalt, caulking compounds, roofing materials, or insulation containing asbestos. Older structures may also be at risk because asbestos-containing compounds were used for repairs.

Fledgling renovators almost invariably underestimate the cost of asbestos removal, and even experienced contractors sometimes appear to be blind to the potential investment involved. It is not unusual for a renovation contractor to keep finding more and more asbestos as the project continues. What you and your library decision makers really need is an accurate evaluation of the problem before a single worker arrives. You need the information at a point when it is still possible to call a halt to the project and reconsider a new addition or all-new construction. Most larger communities have specialized asbestos consultants who can make building inspections, monitor air quality, and provide complete laboratory analyses. If this service is not available in your community, building inspectors may be able to make a professional recommendation.

Buildings Not Designed as Libraries

Librarians experienced in renovation projects usually advise caution when city councils, school boards, or university administrators have a building on their hands that they don't quite know what to do with. Yes, it may be possible to transform such buildings into functional libraries, but these people probably have no idea of the amount of money and work involved. If this idea is being discussed among your bosses or board members, try to bring in an experienced library consultant as soon as possible. Don't allow the idea to build up steam (and enthusiastic support) before you react.

Few government buildings have much in common with the design of a library. For example, most buildings have a plethora of interior walls that make supervision almost impossible, thus requiring larger staffs and impeding traffic flow. Expensive demolition is needed or customers and staff must waste considerable time getting from place to place. Collections must be split in illogical chunks, and such buildings often have multiple entrances that defeat your best efforts to provide security.

Although I've seen very functional libraries that were once supermarkets, the kind of buildings usually available in academe or government simply don't lend themselves to our needs. Schools converted into libraries may have long corridors and cinder block walls that often must be tolerated because the cost of demolishing them is so great. How many library functions can you think of that can be entirely contained within a 400-square-foot area? Your library's collections should be organized with logical breaks, and merely accommodating natural growth in a well-designed library can pose a challenge. When spaces are created for a rigidly defined function, they tend to resist logical rearrangement. Compared with an office building, in which people in different departments tend to "stay put," library users seek out a variety of resources located throughout the building. Balconies and central atria can create ring-around-the-rosy traffic patterns, forcing everyone to walk in circles.

HISTORIC AND OTHER OLDER STRUCTURES

Most older buildings do not meet ADA standards. Those impressive exterior stairs, for example, were built long before anyone worried about barrier-free environments, and access ramps require major alterations to the facade. The handsome entrances of the past were flanked by heavy oak doors that are difficult for able-bodied football players to open, let alone people with disabilities. What does one do when confronted with a historical commission on the one hand and ADA guidelines on the other? The result may be a building that pleases no one.

Consider carefully whether it is really possible to transform a historic structure into a library. If you are renovating a historic structure, preservation considerations may get in the way of creating a functional library building. Architectural details and artistic appointments may be off-limits, and you may expect political

Highland Park (Tex.) Library,
Komatsu Architecture,
komatsu-inc.com.
Photo: Thomas McConnell.

battles if you are thinking of altering a local landmark. You may find that even though the building has long been ignored and allowed to fall into decay, it will have irate defenders coming out of the woodwork to protect their civic treasure. The architectural details that make an old building unique may be too expensive to refurbish but illegal to remove.

Evaluating Older Buildings

If plans call for renovating or adding on to an existing library, someone will have to decide whether the building has sufficient historical importance that its character should be preserved. This is yet another of those political land mines you must approach with caution. Since this is one of the critical points at which your job may actually be on the line, be sure your position has strong support. There should be clear agreement among the board members or key administrators representing your parent institution.

The library director tends to be the person who has day-to-day contact with the architect. Other participants may not be monitoring the project closely and so may be shocked and amazed when confronted by a delegation of preservationists. You will find that people who seem never to have known what street the library is on will rally to protect what they perceive as an endangered historic treasure. Deal with the issue before the first work crew arrives. Don't allow it to become a cause célèbre when it's too late to turn back.

Affection versus Practicality

Local residents are not the only ones who hate to lose their old buildings. Librarians love them too, and when it comes to updating our historic libraries, we have an especially difficult decision. Our buildings are like ancient great-aunts for whom we feel both affection and irritation. We love our old libraries, and we are daily frustrated by them. These once-glorious edifices are fraught with obstacles to modernization, from their ornate gabled roofs to their hand-stenciled stone walls and their elegant marble floors. In addition to all the rational, brick-and-mortar problems they present, we must deal with our own subjective feelings.

On the one hand, we tell our colleagues that we would happily volunteer for the demolition crew. We complain endlessly about the plumbing and the wiring, and we pine for central air. Librarians who have been forced to endure an old-fashioned, uncomfortable building usually choose function over form. They would like to see preservation enthusiasts devote their efforts to structures that don't require extensive data capacity, electric outlets at workstations, and walls catacombed with voice, data, and electrical equipment. Nevertheless, these annoying buildings are an integral part of our professional history, and a small internal voice urges us to save them if it's at all possible.

Added Cost

On what should such a decision be based? First and most important is the community of which the library is a part. It will usually cost far more money to both modernize and preserve an old library than to build a new one from scratch. Do your board members and administrators understand this? An institution like Harvard or an affluent community may derive great satisfaction from preserving its heritage while at the same time supporting the information needs of library patrons. When funds are less readily available, however, it is often necessary to choose between history and information access.

Some libraries have achieved successful compromises by building a high-tech, architecturally compatible addition and leaving the older structure much as it was. Even this is expensive, however, and the lounges, stack areas, and other lower-tech functions for which the older structure is used may require a substantial financial investment to meet building codes and ADA guidelines. The following are some other problems often encountered when remodeling or renovating older libraries:

Monumental stone buildings may crumble when walls are breached. Our ancestors often built walls of rubble-and-mortar mixtures and then faced them with thin slabs of expensive stone. Over the years, the mortar mix has turned to powder.

Imposing and elaborate circulation desks may take up far too much room, forcing staff to create makeshift work areas behind them.

Floors may be unable to bear the 150-pound-per-square-foot live loads that library book stacks require.

Areas originally intended for closed stacks are not wheelchair-accessible and may even be dangerous for able-bodied customers and staff.

Extensive telecommunications and electrical cabling may simply not be feasible (although wireless networking may eliminate at least some of the difficulty).

Libraries on the National Register of Historic Places

Although there are no firm rules about which buildings should be preserved, the decision may already be made for you if the library building is on the National Register of Historic Places. However, whole districts are included on this list, so there is still a lot of room for local decisions. A National Register listing does not mean that a building should be frozen in time or that each part of the building is equally significant. If it is decided that yours is a historic building that should be preserved, consider whether a new addition would damage or destroy the building's character. An addition to a historic structure should preserve significant materials and features. It should be architecturally compatible with the older section yet not pretend to be part of the original structure. In all probability, the building has been added to or altered many times over its history. It is really not necessary to preserve an alteration made in 1954. In other words, your project will require an architect skilled in preservation work to determine what should be preserved and what can safely be ignored.

The National Park Service provides guidelines for determining whether an addition meets the requirements of historic preservation. "A project involving a new addition to a historic building is considered acceptable within the framework of the National Park Service's standards if it preserves significant historic materials and features, preserves the historic character, and protects the historical significance by making a visual distinction between old and new."[4]

Although you will need an expert to tell you what architectural features of a historic building should be preserved, it is safe to say that exterior features are usually more important than interior ones. Features at the level of the main floor or "primary elevation" are more important than those at upper levels. In general, eighteenth- and nineteenth-century society placed more attractive and impressive design features where the passersby could see them and used poorer-quality materials higher up where they were less visible.

Preservation-worthy features might include windows, shutters, porticoes, entrances, roof shapes, cornices, or decorative moldings. Although the building site may determine location, when making an addition to a historic building, consider placing the addition where the loss of important historic features will be minimized. To achieve this, the addition will usually involve adding one or more floors or locating the new section to the rear of the present building. An addition to a historic building should also be fully compatible with the original building. Of course, the building is going to be larger after the addition is completed, but the proportions or relationship of the different areas to one another should be preserved.

The main goal of preservation is to protect the characteristics that were responsible for the building's being listed in the National Register of Historic Places. You and your community will have to decide whether it is possible to meet this goal while at the same time providing the kind of information access that will be needed by citizens of the twenty-first century. If the two goals are really incompatible, now is the time to come up with an alternate plan. Don't wait until the building's historic character has been lost or you discover that the building cannot possibly support the technical infrastructure required. If your grand old friend will not work as a library, all is not lost. It may still have a long and productive life as a community center, a historical museum, or in some other useful role.

ACCESS AND THE AMERICANS WITH DISABILITIES ACT

Whether planning a new building or renovating an older one, planning for the needs of people with disabilities must be considered at every stage of the building design process. Adding a few last-minute modifications to meet local codes is all too common, and despite the Americans with Disabilities Act and numerous volumes interpreting its provisions, library buildings often fail to serve users with special needs. The old saw about walking in someone else's shoes certainly applies. Again and again, architects and contractors fail to view the building through the eyes of someone with a disability who requires special accommodation.

The Spirit of the Law

The implementation of the Americans with Disabilities Act has been fraught with frustration for people whose quality of life depends on access to their workplace, school, library, and other buildings. The act, signed into legislation on July 26, 1990, prohibits discrimination on the basis of disability in employment, state and local government services, public transportation, public accommodations, commercial facilities, and telecommunications.

In an excellent article, H. Neil Kelley suggests that "the best approach to compliance with the ADA is the golden rule. Offer modifications and accommodations that will yield the access for others that you would like for yourself."[5] Try not to be overwhelmed with the difficulties. Remember that only 20 percent of people with disabilities need any special accommodation. Although some ADA requirements are costly and difficult to meet, the majority of accommodations are relatively inexpensive. You might even think of it as enlightened self-interest, since simple modifications can help keep you and your staff comfortable and productive for many years to come. Many people will experience a disabling condition at some time during their lives.

Understanding What's Required

Under Title II of the ADA, state and local government units, which include most libraries, must eliminate accessibility barriers that restrict their services by moving services and programs to accessible buildings or by making changes to existing buildings. Most of the few libraries not covered by Title II come under Title III guidelines, which require that owners of public accommodations make "readily achievable" changes that improve accessibility. These may include installing a ramp, creating accessible parking, or adding grab bars in restroom facilities.

The "Checklist for Buildings and Facilities," prepared by the Barriers Compliance Board, is one of the most comprehensive interpretations of the ADA, and it is well worth getting a copy of it. The checklist is intended as a supplement to the Barriers Compliance Board's Minimum Guidelines and Requirements for Accessible Design. It was created "to assist individuals and entities with rights or duties under Title II and Title III of the Americans with Disabilities Act (ADA) in applying the requirements of the Americans with Disabilities Act Accessibility Guidelines (ADAAG) to buildings and facilities subject to the law."[6] Not until you've read the checklist will you realize how many seemingly small details affect access. Although the use of this checklist is voluntary, you can bet that in any dispute its provisions will probably be upheld.

Structures Covered by the ADA

The ADA applies to all new construction. That is, it applies to any facility that was designed and constructed for first occupancy after January 26, 1993. According to the act, exceptions to its provisions are permitted only "where the alternative designs and technologies used will provide substantially equivalent or greater access to and usability of the facility."[7]

Remodeling projects or renovations, referred to as "alterations," should "be done in a manner so as to ensure that, to the maximum extent feasible, the altered portions of the facility comply" with the guidelines.[8] This means that most of the alterations of specific parts of a facility must be completed in compliance with the requirements for new construction, but full compliance is not required where technically infeasible. If yours is a qualified historic building, it

---

TIPS

ADA rules do apply, and don't forget it. This makes a huge difference in how wide your aisles are going to be and will affect the number of shelving units you can put in. A good vendor knows this and won't fudge but will make the most of the space you have. ADA also affects the width of your doors, hallways, and so on.

ADA works well for archives in this regard because the wider halls and doors work better for carts loaded with boxes and odd-sized items. You don't have to convince the architect that your carts are going to be heavy and need a wider turning point.

Follow the ADA codes religiously.

must comply with restrictions unless it is determined that compliance would threaten or destroy the historical significance of the building.

Although it is impossible to include all the issues raised by the checklist in this brief summary (and it often becomes extremely technical), it will be useful to just mention some of the most basic considerations. The following is a very small sampling of some of the points you should be aware of:

Pathways

Outside pathways should be level, or no steeper than 1:14 gradient.

Pathways should have a level rest area every 9 m (about 29½ feet) or less.

Pathways should have an unobstructed width of 1,000 mm (about 3¼ feet).

Entrances

Entrances should be sheltered from inclement weather.

Landings in front of entrance doors should have a clear circulation space of 1,550 mm (about 61 inches) in diameter.

Doors

Doors should be at least 760 mm (about 30 inches) wide, although 820 mm (about 32¼ inches) is preferred.

Doors and drawers should have "D" handles, not knobs.

Lever handles are preferred to doorknobs.

Floors and Corridors

Thresholds should not have steps.

Floors should be of slip-resistant vinyl sheeting, low-pile carpet, or unglazed tiles.

Corridors should have an unobstructed minimum width of 1,000 mm (about 39⅜ inches).

Corridors should have adequate lighting levels, at least 300 lux.

Restrooms

Accessible bathrooms should have side and rear grab rails fixed at a height of 800 mm to 810 mm (about 31½ inches).

The space beside accessible toilets should be at least 950 mm (slightly more than 37 inches).

TALE

We had bathrooms that were supposed to be built to ADA specs, and someone at the architect's office made a mistake, so they weren't to spec. These were the bathrooms for the meeting room. We had doors so heavy and hard to open that no one in a wheelchair could open them. They opened the wrong way, and the trustees were obstinate about changing or putting in a sliding door with an electric eye.

Access to Historic Buildings

In one sense, libraries bear a unique burden when it comes to complying with ADA guidelines. Our heritage is integrally tied to our nineteenth- and early twentieth-century Carnegie libraries that are nightmares of inaccessibility. The multistory structures seem to have steps everywhere, especially the steps averaging eight in number at front doors. On the other hand, many people would like to affirm the public library tradition by restoring their Carnegies to their former glory. Not only Carnegies but most libraries of the period, especially those with classical facades, suffer from major access problems. Older buildings may have no accessible route from parking lots, and if there are any entrance ramps, they are too steep. Elevators are also nonexistent or too small for most wheelchairs. Wheelchairs are also unable to move among the stacks in many historic buildings, and seating, water fountains, and restrooms are inaccessible.

If your board or administration is considering a renovation project, be sure it is aware of the difficulties involved in making an older structure ADA-compliant. For example, exterior stairs may leave no room for ramps, and elevators and automatic doors may be difficult if not impossible to install. Old-fashioned stack areas with their tortuous spiral stairs and narrow aisles usually must be completely removed. Still other features like steep terrain, monumental steps, narrow or heavy doors, decorative ornamental hardware, and narrow pathways and corridors make access difficult if not impossible. Older buildings also often have multiple levels, with a single step separating each stack area or reading room from the central area. Disabled users may be forced to travel long distances merely to reach a ramp that takes them up or down a step or two.

Critical Issues

Although the unique characteristics of your particular historic structure will determine the specific modifications that must be made, you would do well to use the following list of critical elements to do a personal assessment of your building. You need not even enter the building to get an idea of the scope of the difficulties that may lie ahead. If any of the following statements is not true of your site or structure, you can anticipate problems. This advance warning will allow you to be prepared and, hopefully, head off poorly informed enthusiasts.

The width, slope, cross-slope, and surface texture of walkways permit easy wheelchair access.

The distance between arrival and destination points is short.

Landscaping does not hinder wheelchair access.

Parking is provided conveniently close to the building (libraries serve many older patrons who may use canes or walkers).

Walkways are a minimum of 91 cm (3 feet) wide and preferably wider.

Pathways are appropriately graded and have a firm and slip-resistant surface.

Customers who use wheelchairs are able to come into the library through the main public entrance. (This may require changing elevation, steps, landings, doors, and/or thresholds.)

Space is available to position ramps at public entrances and at every location where one or more steps prevent access. The steepest allowable slope for a ramp is 1:12, or 8 percent, but gentler slopes are preferable. Such ramps should not significantly alter the historic character of the building.

It is true that wheelchair platforms and inclined stair lifts can be installed and used to overcome changes in elevation ranging from 0.9 m to 3 m (3 to 10 feet) in height, but local building codes may restrict their use. It may also be possible to create an entirely new entrance without significantly altering the look of the building. For example, you might make use of a not too prominently placed window opening. However, if such major changes are needed, it may be an indication that the structure is not really accessible enough to be used as a library.

Simple Modifications

On the other hand, there are many ways you can increase access while doing little damage to the original building. For example, creating designated parking spaces, installing ramps (where ample space exists), and making curb cuts are all reasonably straightforward. Inside the building, raised markings can be added to elevator control buttons, flashing alarm lights can be installed, accessible door hardware can be added, and offset hinges can be used to widen doorways.

Restrooms lend themselves to fairly easy alteration, and few zealots will argue that they should remain in their original antediluvian state. For example, grab bars and higher toilet seats can be added to stalls, partitions can be rearranged, and pipes under sinks can be insulated to prevent burns. Even repositioning the paper towel dispenser can make a big difference.

Getting Around

Most historic buildings are equipped with ancient elevators or, more probably, no elevators at all. Although it's certainly preferable to install a new elevator, control panels can be modified with a "wand" on a cord to make the control panel accessible. The timing device regulating the doors can also be adjusted.

Historic interior doors also pose serious access problems. On the one hand, historic buildings are often chock-full of fire hazards, so the local fire inspector may insist that interior doors be kept closed. On the other hand, antique door hardware, needed to preserve the look of the doors, severely limits accessibility. Power-assisted door openers can be installed, but they, too, alter the look of the door.

ADA Expertise

Evaluating the building and its potential ADA-compliance problems may require the assistance of an accessibility specialist who is trained to identify and assess barriers and who is an expert on local codes, state codes, and federal laws. Together, the accessibility expert and architect should develop a plan that provides the greatest amount of accessibility without threatening or destroying the features that make the library a historic building. This plan should be completed before any final decision is made to preserve the building as a library. The historic building under consideration must be able to support a sophisticated technical infrastructure, and it must be able to provide convenient access to all library patrons. If it cannot meet these two basic requirements, the project should be abandoned. It is far too costly, both in human and monetary terms, and it is doomed to failure.

The U.S. Park Service provides a list of priorities when making modifications to a historic structure. They are

1. Making the main or a prominent public entrance and primary public spaces accessible, including a path to the entrance
2. Providing access to goods, services, and programs
3. Providing accessible restroom facilities
4. Creating access to amenities and secondary spaces[9]

Making intelligent accommodations to meet the needs of your customers with disabilities is an excellent example of seeing the library through the eyes of our customers. As you continue the design process, remember that most of your customers will not have an opportunity to tell you about their needs or to veto decisions that make it more difficult or less enjoyable for them to use the new library. It's a good idea to carry around with you a mental picture of some of your customers—young women carrying a baby, adventurous preschoolers, elderly mystery readers. You've gotten to know them well over the years and you can do a pretty good job of walking in their shoes. As you look at those floor plans, imagine them in each area using each service. You'll be surprised how changing your point of view affects your design decisions.

NOTES

1. Will Manley, "The Manley Arts: Clean, Well-Lighted Stacks," *Booklist* 92 (October 1, 1995): 215.
2. Harold Hawkins, "The Uncertain Future of High School Library Design," *School Planning and Management* 36, no. 10 (1997): 7.
3. Anya Breitenbach, "Big Debut for Denver's Public Library," *Library Journal* 121 (January 1996): 20.
4. Kay D. Weeks and others, *The Secretary of the Interior's Standards for the Treatment of Historic Properties* (Washington, DC: Government Printing Office, 1995).
5. H. Neil Kelley, "ADA: Relax, Take a Deep Breath, and Do It Well," *Illinois Libraries* 74 (May 1992): 302–3.
6. U.S. Architectural and Transportation Barriers Compliance Board, Minimum Guidelines and Requirements for Accessible Design (Washington, DC: Barriers Compliance Board, 1993).

7. U.S. Architectural and Transportation Barriers Compliance Board, *Americans with Disabilities Act: Accessibility Guidelines, Checklist for Building and Facilities* (Washington, DC: Barriers Compliance Board, 1996), available at http://adata.org.

8. Americans with Disabilities Act, Public Law 336, 101st Cong. (July 26, 1990), available at www.usdoj.gov/crt/ada/pubs/ada.txt.

9. Weeks and others, *Secretary of the Interior's Standards*.

RESOURCES

School Library Design

Note: Since school library design differs in some ways from other types of libraries, school librarians will find the following resources helpful.

Baule, Steven. *Facilities Planning for School Library and Technology Centers.* Worthington, OH: Linworth Books, 2007.

Erikson, Rolf, and Carolyn Markuson. *Designing a School Library Media Center for the Future.* Chicago: American Library Association, 2007.

Ferro, Maximilian L., and Melissa L. Cook. *Electric Wiring and Lighting in Historic American Buildings.* New Bedford, MA: AFC/A Nortek, 1984.

Formanack, Gail. "Designing a Facility: Making It a Place Where Every Student Succeeds." Paper presented at the 12th National Conference of the American Association of School Librarians, Pittsburgh, PA, October 7, 2005. www.ala.org/ala/mgrps/divs/aasl/conferencesandevents/confarchive/pittsburgh/DesigningaFacility.pdf.

Hart, Thomas. *The School Library Media Facilities Planner.* New York: Neal-Schuman, 2006.

Renovation of Historic Buildings

Imagining the Future of the School Library. Minneapolis, MN: Designshare, 2006. www.designshare.com/index.php/articles/school-library-future.

Jennings, Jan, and Herbert Gottfried. *American Vernacular Interior Architecture 1870–1940.* New York: Van Nostrand Reinhold, 1988.

National Trust for Historic Preservation. *Old and New Architecture: Design Relationship.* Washington, DC: Preservation, 1980.

Turberg, Edward. *A History of American Building Technology.* Durham, NC: Durham Technical Institute, 1981.

Wisconsin Department of Public Instruction. *Design Considerations for School Library Media Centers.* http://dpi.state.wi.us/imt/desgnlmc.html.

Functional and Sustainable Buildings

When the first edition of this book was published in 2000, the move toward "green" buildings had begun in earnest. However, my interviews with librarians who had incorporated major environmentally friendly modifications in their new buildings were mixed. A number of them had been convinced by architects and enthusiastic environmentalists that some new innovation would both save the planet and save the library thousands of dollars. Many of those promises were never kept. It may have been a flaw in the engineer's calculations, or a product that wasn't really ready for market, or a company that went bankrupt soon after the library purchased its product or services. Simpler passive solutions like orienting the building to make the most effective use of sunlight did reap big benefits, but more elaborate technology often left disappointed customers in its wake.

WHOLE BUILDING DESIGN

In the past decade, the situation has changed markedly. Although libraries are occasionally making poor choices, many more options are now available to planners. Sustainable technologies have often been in use for several years, and many bad ideas have been discarded. This is not to say that you won't encounter a number of other bad ideas when you delve into the subject of sustainable buildings, but lots of good ideas have become cost-effective options. One of my favorite websites has become the U.S. Department of Energy's Building Technologies Program site.[1] You could profitably spend days at this site, but one section that is especially relevant to your planning concerns is the one entitled

Oldsmar (Fla.) Public Library, Harvard Jolly Architecture, harvardjolly.com. Photo: George Cott, Chroma Inc.

"Whole Building Design." The basic idea is that creating or renovating a high-performance, energy-efficient building requires a holistic approach to design. Traditionally, building planners consider each aspect or each system independently. By looking at the building as a whole and integrating all building components and systems into a single plan, it is possible to determine how they can work together to save energy and reduce environmental impact. The following is a very simplified outline of the recommended steps:

Begin with the design team. Choose architects and engineers who have extensive experience incorporating energy features into their buildings. Identify these members of the design team as early as possible. Don't choose professionals piecemeal. Include specialists in areas like indoor air quality, materials, and energy use.

Be sure professional team members are really committed to the goal of a sustainable, energy-efficient building. Then make sure they can communicate with one another. Once planning has begun, find ways to assure that they spend time together. When a decision is made that will affect the performance of another team member's design area, everyone must be involved. They will need to evaluate the consequences up front and make modifications as a team, not later on as individual participants.

Consider revising the standard contract used for your building project to include the project goals as well as consequences if the design team does not meet these goals. Verify that these goals have been met before providing payment for design team services.

Conduct a design charrette. It is common for professionals involved in a project to meet together early in the process in a peer review workshop or "design charrette." A charrette is an effective way of generating and discussing ideas and allows people to cut across disciplinary boundaries. Participants offer design ideas and solutions that are outside their areas of expertise, providing new ways of looking at issues. Participants can address organizational differences, reducing the natural competition and somewhat adversarial attitudes that can characterize relationships.

Be sure that participants in a charrette record the ideas expressed. Librarians should keep their own elaborate notes as well so that later they can revisit important ideas and make sure they are not forgotten. Make sure that building professionals are keeping their own records as well.

The building's location, orientation, and microclimate should be among the first topics to be discussed. Other important topics include the building envelope, interior spaces, fenestration, lighting, water, HVAC, exterior spaces, and monitoring equipment.

No matter what the topic, emphasis should be on energy use and sustainability. For example, the building should be oriented to maximize southern exposures and to respond to local climate conditions.

It is important that participants have solid data at their disposal, possibly including energy performance and lighting analyses. Data are also important if professionals are to make effective use of building-energy software tools. These ensure that mechanical, electrical, lighting, and other systems are sized to reduce energy demands.

Professionals should understand that throughout design and construction, green materials and energy-reduction choices should be part of all contracts.

Contractors should be selected for their expertise in low-energy design and construction. A contractor who considers these as "passing fancies" will not produce a successful building.

The HVAC and lighting systems must work hand in hand. Be sure that windows are sized and located to support the building's heating, cooling, and ventilation needs. Be sure the building envelope incorporates high-performance glazing and other energy-efficient materials.

COMMISSIONING, SUSTAINABILITY, AND WHOLE BUILDING DESIGN

The Building Technologies Program website strongly recommends the adoption of the commissioning process for as many building systems as possible. *Commissioning* is a term that's become widely used in the building trades to mean providing documented confirmation that building systems actually function according to criteria set forth in the project documents. The American Society of Heating, Refrigerating, and Air-Conditioning Engineers (ASHRAE) defines commissioning as "a quality-oriented process for achieving, verifying, and documenting that the performance of facilities, systems, and assemblies meets defined objectives and criteria." Commissioning uncovers deficiencies in design or installation and accomplishes higher energy efficiency, environmental health, and occupant safety and improves indoor air quality. It can be seen as a quality assurance–based process that produces preventive and predictive maintenance plans, operating manuals, and training procedures.

LEED

In the last decade, environmental enthusiasts have become more realistic in their expectations, experience has brought new insights, and technology has become more reliable. Nevertheless, during the first decade of the new century, environmental issues received little attention from state and federal agencies, and the building industry has had few incentives to become a more prudent guardian of the earth's resources. At last, however, the idea of the green building with less waste and more efficiency is coming out of the shadows and going mainstream. Goals have become more practical, and government agencies are gradually raising their standards. Because they must meet these new standards, architects and engineers have had to become more knowledgeable about the elements that contribute toward a building's sustainability.

The U.S. Green Building Council (USGBC) has developed a set of voluntary standards that define the goals of the green building industry. They have produced a variety of Leadership in Energy and Environmental Design (LEED) standards, and you will be especially interested in the Green Building Rating System for New Commercial and Major Renovation.[2] LEED provides a widely accepted set of expectations that clarify the goals of green construction and establish clear priorities. LEED makes it possible to certify that the design and construction phases of commercial, institutional, and high-rise residential buildings meet established standards.

LEED Certification

The LEED rating system is intended not only as a guide to creating high-performance buildings that cause less stress to the environment but also as a way to identify such buildings, recognize their designers, and allow them to serve as models. Buildings that receive high scores are healthier for the human beings who live and work in them and are ultimately more profitable than buildings that achieve low scores. Building projects earn points for satisfying specific criteria that address their impact on the environment. Design, construction, operation, and management of a building are all considered. The system is organized into six categories:

Sustainable Sites	Materials and Resources
Water Efficiency	Indoor Environmental Quality
Energy and Atmosphere	Innovation and Design

To become LEED-certified, a building project must score 26 to 32 points, 33 to 38 points to receive the Silver rating, 39 to 51 points to receive the Gold rating, and 52 to 69 points to receive the Platinum rating.

In developing the standards, the Green Building Council was concerned not only with the natural environment but with the commercial environment in which buildings must be profitable. LEED-certified projects cost less to operate and maintain, are energy- and water-efficient, facilitate more profitable leases, and contribute to the health and productivity of their occupants. Architects and contractors seek LEED certification because it serves as evidence of the quality of their work. Certification is a way of verifying that their buildings meet high national standards. The Green Building Council considers it a way of increasing owner confidence, and they compare certification to the nutrition label on packaged foods.

LEED for Libraries

"LEED for New Construction and Renovations" was initially intended for new office buildings, but its application has been expanded to many other building types. Institutional buildings like libraries, schools, and museums have embraced the standards because accountability is such an important aspect of government and nonprofit management. The standards were developed by USGBC committees composed of a diverse group of experts representing a cross-section of the building industry. You will probably want to learn more about LEED, and the USGBC website (www.usgbc.org) is an excellent place to start. A wide range of resources is available there, including training workshops.

Because LEED standards are becoming so widely accepted, library planners can feel confident that they are not making risky or idiosyncratic choices suggested by architects and engineers who may be out of the mainstream and acting entirely on their own personal values. Instead, they can have some assurance that their choices will have the support of the building industry. Perhaps the best way to understand how LEED standards can contribute to a more successful, more sustainable building is to take a look at two LEED-certified projects.

The Bronx Library Center

The Bronx Library Center is a branch of the New York Public Library System and the largest public library in the Bronx. Formerly called the Fordham Library Center, the original building opened to the public in 1923. The library was renovated and expanded again and again as use increased and collections grew. Finally, it became clear that a new building was essential to serve twenty-first-century needs, and planning began on a structure that would serve both the library needs of today's customers and sustainability goals. The new and very beautiful Bronx Library Center opened on January 17, 2006.

Rising five stories and occupying 178,000 square feet, the library is three times the size of the Fordham Library. It was immediately embraced by Bronx residents, lending three times as many items and issuing five times more library cards than in the old building. With 150 public-access computers and more than 200,000 items, it is a model of an effective public library. What makes it especially notable, however, is that the new building earned a LEED Silver rating, New York City's first municipal building to achieve this distinction.

Library planners wanted their customers to feel as if they were stepping into a modern chain bookstore. The teen center with speakers and flat-screen TVs, the auditorium, conference rooms, and classrooms all say, in effect, this is not your grandmother's library. The exterior glass window wall opens reading areas up to and makes the library part of the surrounding community. Called a curtain wall and made of high-performance glass and insulated frames, it allows daylight into much of the library. Light shelves and translucent shades provide better light control, while photo sensors and occupancy sensors assure that lights are turned off when rooms are unoccupied or lit adequately by daylight.

Window walls and computer-monitored electric lighting are not the only ways the building manages solar energy. In the densely populated Bronx, heat islands are a major problem, but the ENERGY STAR roofing reflects solar heat, considerably reducing internal cooling loads. A variety of carefully thought-out strategies like making efficient use of outside air for cooling reduce the library's energy costs by 20 percent.

Use of Materials

Recycling was, of course, an important part of the planning, and many materials were selected based on their environmental characteristics. Materials with high percentages of recycled content included the foundation, structural steel, carpeting, and terrazzo and linoleum flooring. Eighty percent of the wood used in construction was certified to Forest Stewardship Council standards. Paints, adhesives, and sealants were chosen, in part, for their low chemical emissions, and composite wood products had no added urea-formaldehyde. The project's central location made it possible to purchase many materials that were manufactured within 500 miles of the site. In fact, more than half of the building materials were produced in the region. The project included demolishing the older library, and 90 percent of all construction and demolition waste was recycled.

The Hillsdale Library

On a smaller scale, the Hillsdale Library in Multnomah County, Oregon, was awarded the LEED Gold certification. The choices made by library planners, architects, and the contractors make it clear that libraries of all shapes and sizes can be both user-friendly and friendly to the environment. Hillsdale's design reduces air and water pollution, as well as solid waste creation. It minimizes depletion of natural resources while at the same time improving indoor air quality, reducing operating costs, and optimizing performance over the life of the building.

Planners began with the building site, choosing a site served by multiple bus lines. They provided ample parking for bicycles, as well as parking space and a charging system for electrical cars. They also developed an erosion control plan and restored more than 50 percent of the site's open space as habitat areas with native or adaptive vegetation. To manage storm water, they built large planters at the front of the building and a "bioswale" (a low-gradient channel filled with plants) at the back. These plantings hold and filter rainwater runoff from the roof, and elsewhere on the site, the use of permeable materials such as pavers and planting soil further reduces runoff. To reduce the need for large, paved surfaces exposed to sunlight, underground parking is provided to library customers. The ENERGY STAR roof is also treated to reflect sunlight, thus reducing heat islands.

Water conservation is one of the most important issues addressed by LEED standards, and the Hillsdale Library has done an excellent job of choosing the plants and trees surrounding the library. They were selected, in part, because they require little water and need little in the way of pest control or maintenance. Native, drought-resistant plants make an irrigation system unnecessary. Further savings in water consumption are achieved with "low-flow" restroom faucets and toilets.

The Hillsdale Library was designed to be 21 percent more energy-efficient than conventional buildings intended merely to meet local energy codes. This goal is achieved through the use of a daylighting system that lessens the need for artificial light; energy-efficient, high-performance windows with "low-E" glass; and insulated, translucent skylights. It is not enough to achieve theoretical energy savings, however. A plan was developed to measure and verify that the anticipated lower levels of energy use were actually achieved.

Environmentally Friendly Materials

Like the Bronx Library Center, recycling was an important consideration both during construction, when 75 percent of construction waste was salvaged or recycled, and after opening, when areas throughout the building were designated for the separation, collection, and storage of recycling materials. In addition, more than 50 percent of the building materials used in construction contain significant recycled content. This includes carpet, wood flooring, restroom tile, acoustical ceiling and wall panels, drywall, concrete, and the structural steel. Approximately 20 percent of the building materials were manufactured locally, and 50 percent of the wood used in the ceiling and walls is from sustainable forests. Wall paint, steel structure, and all adhesives and sealants are low VOC (volatile organic compounds) and contain few of the other chemicals that can endanger both the environment and human health.

Air quality was an important consideration for Hillsdale Library planners, so fresh air was mixed into the mechanical ventilating system for health, safety, and comfort. Filters were used during construction to prevent contamination of the water and mechanical systems by construction debris. The mechanical system ran for two weeks after construction was complete and before the building opened, bringing 100 percent fresh air into the building. Filters were then replaced to eliminate the possibility of contamination.

The Cost of Sustainable Buildings

When the first edition of this book was published, eco-friendly modifications invariably added to building costs. More than one librarian I queried pointed to some purchase or building modification that was simply taking up space and serving as a reminder of money wasted. One example I recall was a thermal mass that was intended to store heat during the day and release it at night. It functioned more or less as intended, but the electric fan required to distribute the heat cost so much to operate that the project reaped no monetary or environmental rewards.

As librarians look at twenty-first-century innovations, they can't help but wonder how much they will cost and what the payback will be. It turns out, however, that the cost of building green structures is just about the same as standard construction. A study published in July 2007 by the cost-management consulting firm Davis Langdon found that sustainable buildings were not usually more expensive than nonsustainable buildings. Although construction costs had risen 20–30 percent since 2004, most of the LEED-based projects achieved their goals within budget. A total of 221 building projects were analyzed; 83 incorporated LEED goals and 138 did not. Of these projects, 57 were libraries.[3]

LEED and Sustainable Sites

Although many site considerations were discussed in chapter 3, you will also want to consider some of the environmental and energy-related decisions that impact LEED certification. As you evaluate different sites, give some thought to the following questions:

Is it possible to locate the library in an area of existing development rather than on land that has never been developed for human use?

Is it possible to minimize the use of open space by selecting disturbed land?

Is erosion likely to be a problem at the site? Has thought been given to controlling erosion through environmentally sensitive landscaping practices? Has consideration been given to preventing erosion and stabilizing hillsides by using vegetation and grading? These modifications can be expensive and will need to be included in cost projections.

Is storm water runoff likely to be a problem? Will it be possible to capture and retain runoff with features like permeable pavements or vegetated swales and depressions?

Has some thought been given to installing retention ponds and berms to control erosion and manage storm water? (These can also serve as physical barriers to control access to a building.)

Although it's preferable to locate the library on a site that has been used before, heavily populated areas produce heat islands. Are your building professionals concerned about this problem? Are they committed to reducing heat islands by using a variety of methods, including landscaping, building orientation, and design?

Will construction affect the habitat of any threatened or endangered species?

Can your project be designed to restore the health of a degraded site and improve the habitat for indigenous species (for example, with native plants and closed-loop water systems)?

Will it be convenient for local residents to use public transportation when they visit the library? Can children and adults safely ride bicycles to the library? Will the library offer a safe and convenient place to store bicycles?

Have your architects considered the amount of sunlight the site will receive and how it can be used most effectively? Are they planning to integrate both passive and active solar strategies?

Will the library adjoin or be in close proximity to other buildings? Have designers considered how this will impact natural ventilation? How will they make certain that natural ventilation will be sufficient?

How will future development adjacent to the site affect green library planning, like solar applications and daylighting?

Will it be possible to design a building whose "footprint" keeps land disturbance to a minimum and retains as much existing landscaping or vegetation features as possible?

Has thought been given to maximizing the use of existing trees and other vegetation to shade walkways, parking lots, and other open areas?

Is consideration being given to water conservation through xeriscaping with native plants? (Xeriscaping is a landscaping method that uses drought-tolerant, low-water-demand plants, mulching, and other strategies to reduce water use.)

Will it be possible to locate parking and pedestrian areas for maximum sun exposure?

Houston Public Library, Central Library, Prozign Architects, prozign.com. Photo: Prozign Architects.

Has some thought been given to how the library might enrich the community in which it is located? Examples include controlling sprawl, reusing existing infrastructure, helping to create a walkable neighborhood, and locating the library where people live and work (using existing roads and utilities is preferable to building new ones).

Has some thought been given to the nighttime environment? Will it be possible to protect dark skies through high-quality and thoughtfully planned outdoor lighting?

SUNLIGHT AND HEAT GAIN

Designing a sustainable building requires a lot of attention to managing sunlight. Using sunlight effectively means reducing both the cost of heating in winter and cooling in summer. In commercial buildings, 33 percent of the cooling load is the result of solar heat gain through the windows. To reduce the heat load, consider the sun as it arcs high in the summer sky. Much of the sun's heat is concentrated on the roof and on the west facade of the building. By designing a structure with smaller east and west dimensions, it is possible to considerably reduce this summer heat load. If the west side of the building is well insulated and opaque in surface treatment, heat gain is minimal. Since west-facing windows raise the building's temperature to an alarming extent, they should be small in size, providing only enough light to meet daylighting goals. Because of the sun's lower arc in winter, windows on the south side of the building should be larger, allowing more of the sun's heat to enter the building during that season. If some kind of overhang shades the windows in summer when the sun is higher in the sky, the larger windows are even more beneficial. No overhang is needed on the north side, and the low winter sun makes such an overhang ineffective on the east and west sides.

Passive Solar Design

Using the sun's energy without the use of mechanical collectors, commonly referred to as passive solar design, can reduce operating costs significantly and help save the environment at the same time. Sunlight can

- allow artificial lights to be dimmed or turned off
- reduce summer cooling caused by heat from artificial lights
- reduce winter fuel consumption through passive solar heating

However, passive solar design requires knowledgeable building professionals to integrate heating, cooling, and lighting in such a way as to maximize the efficiencies and cost savings. The pieces must interrelate with one another, so architects, engineers, and contractors must all be involved. Encourage your building professionals to consider incorporating passive solar design into your building plans. Not only is it more environmentally friendly, but it can reduce heating-cooling bills by 20 to 70 percent. Building components such as windows and masonry can be used to collect, store, balance, and distribute heat and light. For example, if much of your light is natural, you will not require as much air-conditioning to counteract the excess heat given off by artificial lights.

Passive Solar Uses

Approaches to passive solar heating can be divided into three basic categories: direct gain, indirect gain, and isolated gain. With direct gain, solar radiation enters a space directly through large areas of glass. When it's sunny, heat is stored in floors and walls and released when it gets cold. Direct gain is most effective when glass and heat-storage capacity are correctly balanced. Indirect gain means that solar radiation is collected and stored in a thermal wall separating south-facing windows from the rest of the library. The heat is distributed through the building over a period of several hours. With isolated gain, solar radiation is captured by a separate space, like an atrium, and distributed by natural airflow or by other methods.

Careful attention to site conditions and the orientation of the building is essential. For example, shading is an important component of passive solar planning. Overhangs or natural landscaping can prevent harsh sunlight from entering a facility in the summer and can direct winter sunlight into the building. This is possible because of the angle of the sun's rays in different seasons. The building should be oriented in such a way that overhangs can shade high summer sun while allowing low winter sun to enter the building.

Windows, Lighting, and Passive Solar Design

Windows should be considered when incorporating passive solar design elements. Low-E coatings can increase a window's thermal performance. Some coatings block solar gain or allow solar energy to pass into a building, depending on the climate and the orientation of the building. Selecting appropriate windows can be a complicated matter, since east and west windows typically require different glass than south windows if they are to contribute effectively to the overall energy management of the building.

More light does not necessarily mean higher energy consumption. First, your project team will need to determine the proper illumination levels for each space. For example, a lighting power density of about one watt per square foot is adequate for a typical building; however, more light may be needed in some areas to ensure adequate reading levels, especially in the stacks. Explore the possibilities of task/ambient lighting systems. (Task lights are used to provide higher illumination levels at the work surfaces.)

One commonsense lighting-efficiency strategy is to install motion-sensor controls where the lights are likely to be left on in unoccupied spaces. (As mentioned earlier, controls should be incorporated into the lighting design from the beginning.) Another is to use light-colored surfaces on modular furniture, wall coverings, and ceilings in order to minimize the need for artificial lighting.

Yet another energy-efficient measure is to install LED exit signs. (They use just a few watts and last for twenty-five years or more.) Of course, you will also want to use natural daylight to supplement artificial lighting.

Artificial Lighting

Fluorescent lamps are approximately five times more efficient than incandescent lamps and three times more efficient than halogen (tungsten-halogen) lamps; therefore, use fluorescent fixtures where appropriate. Use compact fluorescent lamps instead of incandescents for recessed cans, wall sconces, table lamps, pendants, and other wall and ceiling fixtures. Use four-foot, single-tube fluorescent fixtures where applicable. Specify electronic, high-power-factor ballasts in all compact fluorescent fixtures. The following are some additional aesthetic and energy-saving suggestions:

> Use lamps with a Color Rendering Index (CRI) of 84 or more. (Color rendering is the effect of an illuminant on the color appearance of objects. A Color Rendering Index is a quantitative measure of the ability of a light source to reproduce the colors of various objects faithfully.)
>
> Use tungsten-halogen flood lamps instead of incandescent floods.
>
> Use high-pressure sodium or metal halide lamps instead of mercury vapor ones. (Metal halide fixtures can be used indoors in high-ceiling areas and outdoors where color rendering is important.)
>
> Use high-pressure sodium fixtures in parking lots and on the exterior of buildings for security lighting.

MINIMIZING MUNICIPAL WATER USE

Large public buildings like libraries both use and waste an extraordinary amount of water. Early in the planning process, talk with your architects about the impact of groundwater on library planning. Rainwater is usually considered a waste product and is channeled off the property by a drainage system, deposited in sewers, and dumped into creeks and rivers. This rapid runoff is responsible for many environmental nightmares since it becomes contaminated by weed killers and fertilizers and negatively affects wildlife and recreation. Municipal drinking water is then used to irrigate the plantings and lawns that surround the building, wasting a valuable resource.

It is not difficult to slow and harvest groundwater by providing vegetated swales and filter strips. Rainwater collection tanks ranging in size from 50 to 30,000 gallons are another option. The resulting water can be used instead of municipal drinking water in irrigation systems, fountains, and custodial applications. The library wins with considerably reduced water bills, and the whole community enjoys the benefits of reduced flooding, water contamination, and soil erosion. The use of scarce municipal water can be further reduced in the following ways:

Install water-free urinals, low-flow faucets, and lower-volume toilets.

Install toilets that use reclaimed groundwater and cooling towers that are upgraded to use water more efficiently.

Reduce water pressure to lessen the likelihood of leaks. Pressure-reducing valves can be installed.

Plumb the building for gray water separation. Gray water includes most wastewater, excluding toilets. If you are not ready to actually separate and use gray water, installing the needed plumbing separation now will make it easier later.

Consider providing dual plumbing so that recovered water can be used for toilet flushing.

Minimize lawn area, since lawns require large quantities of water (as well as fertilizers and pesticides).

Plant grass varieties that are more appropriate to your climate, like buffalo grass in the arid Southwest.

Use xeriscaping.

Design sprinkler systems to put water only where it is needed.

Install efficient watering systems like micro-irrigation, drip-irrigation, and soaker hoses.

THE BUILDING SHELL

Once your site is chosen and consideration has been given not only to green grass but to an integrated "green" environment, it's time to think about the building itself. In fact, you're nearly ready to clothe your thus far imaginary building in brick and mortar, or possibly a more sustainable alternative. At any rate, there are a great many decisions that must be made about the exterior, including the roofing system and the design of the building exterior.

Everyone enjoys being in an attractive library, but don't allow yourself (and your board or committee) to be consumed by an "edifice" complex. As you know from your own domestic experience, there's a huge difference in cost between good-quality "off-the-shelf" fittings and their custom-made "designer" counterparts. Sure, you'll want to go for a little drama here and there, but don't sacrifice precious library space for a few showy touches. When it comes to priorities, practical matters like electrical capacity and HVAC systems must be placed far above a marble entryway.

Building Materials

If you are building an addition to an existing library, you will have less flexibility than if you are building a new library, especially with regard to materials for the exterior of the building. Although it is not necessary to precisely match the existing structure, you will want to choose materials that have a similar look and roughly the same degree of formality. Some postmodern architectural styles provide an excellent transition from old to new. Unless you must match an existing structure, relatively inexpensive, functional materials like brick, block, and drywall will serve you far better than trendy substitutes costing several times as much.

Some librarians report that the selection of the basic materials is the area where they most often come to blows with their architects. Make your priorities clear from the very beginning. Inquire about the materials that will be used and ask to be consulted about expensive extras that might drive up the cost of the project. When you're assured that a premium material is just a little more expensive, be sure to ask how much more expensive it is. Make a list of what you consider absolute necessities and only then a wish list for luxuries. Share the lists with everyone involved in building decisions, explain the logic behind your choices, and try to get them to buy in to your vision before egos and architects take their toll.

THE ECO-FRIENDLY ROOF

At one time or another, it seems that every library building in which I have worked has had a leaky roof. In some buildings, the leaks persist year after year with no permanent solution to the problem. Paneling has warped, carpeting has been badly stained, and saddest of all, valuable collections and important reference sources have been damaged. In addition, sensitive electronic equipment can be jeopardized, data lost, systems furniture damaged, and other building contents destroyed. The mold and bacteria resulting from moisture inside a building can also produce sickness and disease.

Why is a roof leak allowed to continue? Although there are probably as many reasons as there are libraries, perhaps the most common one is poverty. The government unit or academic institution of which the library is a part is simply unwilling to allocate the funds needed to install a new roof. Instead, each emergency is treated in isolation. The roof is patched, the mess is cleaned up, and the problem is forgotten until it recurs the next year or the next. The moral: do it right the first time. While you're involved in the building process, you have a rare opportunity to insist on the best roof you can afford. Be sure that your new roof is designed to last at least twenty years or longer if possible.

What Makes a Good Roof?

Proper installation is just as important as the right materials. If the best available roof is installed incorrectly, it will not work right and will soon fail. For example, supports and penetrations for mechanical equipment must be built into the system, so the finished roof does not have to be punctured. It is also essential to have an owner's representative, such as a roofing consultant, on the job site during construction. This can help ensure quality and eliminate the need for cutting out part of the roof for tests at completion.

To begin with, a good roof requires a slope that effectively removes water, a structurally sound deck, and good attachments. The roofing system should use lightweight and versatile materials. High-quality, easily installed materials offer a broad range of design choices, such as roof color, surface treatment, and edge material. The roof should have a long life cycle and be able to resist rot, fire, solar ultraviolet radiation, and climatic extremes. In addition, it should be easy to maintain and repair.

Flexible Membrane Systems

Most of the better roofing choices fit into a category called flexible membrane roofing systems. These are factory-fabricated "sheets" of roofing. The following are the basic types:

Thermosets membrane is a vulcanized, cured material. Thermosets are seamed using adhesive or butyl tape.

Chlorosulfonated polyethylene, or "Hypalon," is a synthetic rubber material that self-cures when exposed to ultraviolet radiation after installation. Hypalon is usually seamed by welding.

Thermoplastics (including polyvinyl chloride [PVC], the various blends of PVC, and thermopolyolefins) are almost always reinforced with polyester and are welded using hot air or solvents.

Modified bitumens and styrene butadiene, often referred to as "mod bit" in professional parlance, uses hot or cold asphalt adhesives or a torch to melt asphalt in the seam area.

"Single-ply" products are manufactured and installed as a single layer. However, in reality some of the "single-ply" membranes consist of multiple layers (plies) that have been put together during the manufacturing process.

Catwalks

While your building is still in the planning stage, think about all the workers who will be walking around on your roof. Roofing systems were never really intended to have people walking on them or dragging heavy equipment across them. Think of the satellite dish, antenna, air-conditioning condenser, and other equipment that will require installation and repair. Inevitably, this kind of usage compromises the integrity of the system. Workers will also be walking across one part of the roof to repair another section. You should suggest that extensive catwalks be installed to prevent damage. Remember, the catwalks are a lot cheaper than a new roof.

Be sure that you or the contractor posts a sign by the access to the roof providing the following information:

◆ roof type
◆ name, address, and phone number of the installer

- warranty information
- a warning not to damage the roof

Keep a complete set of technical information in the library file and copy it for workers when the roof is repaired. Such information is vitally important because repairs can create new problems unless workers know what they are dealing with. For example, some types of roofs should not be repaired using bituminous materials, and rubber roofs require special adhesives and special techniques for repair. The same thing is true of plastic roofs.

Metal Roofs

In recent years, metal roofs have become very popular. They have a number of advantages, but there are some disadvantages as well. On the positive side, metal roofs are

flexible	energy-efficient
durable	lightweight
almost maintenance-free	recyclable
fire-retardant	

In addition, they can be made to resemble other roofing materials and can be installed over existing roofs. However, they do have downsides that should be considered before selecting one. They are

complex and need to be installed by experts

costly to install

more expensive than other roofing materials

inappropriate for buildings near seawater; salty air
    can drastically shorten the roof's life span

noisy when it rains or hails

easily damaged by hail and flying debris

A Truly Green Roof

The Ballard Library in Seattle, Washington, is an environmentally sensitive project that shows how much can be done on a small scale. Like other green libraries, it is an inviting, eco-friendly building that focuses on customer comfort. However, its roof design really sets it apart. In fact, the library's roof is literally as well as figuratively green. It occupies approximately 20,500 square feet and cost approximately twenty dollars per square foot. At its base is a waterproofing membrane, insulation, and drainage/moisture retention elements that are all part of American Hydrotech's "Garden Roof." The roof was planted with a mix of drought-tolerant, indigenous grasses and sedums. It is truly like having a garden on the roof.

A seamless waterproofing membrane composed of a hot fluid–applied, rubberized asphalt forms a long-lasting bond to the substrate. The water retention/drainage/aeration element is made of lightweight panels of recycled polyethylene molded into retention cups and drainage channels. Water can drain freely from the roof, achieving flow rates significantly higher than conventional drainage methods while providing water through capillary action and evaporation to the rooftop vegetation and ground-level greenery surrounding the library. Storm runoff is filtered through the vegetation-planted roof or absorbed by the site landscape. Both roof and building water are conserved through a computer-controlled irrigation system, low-flow fixtures, sensor and timed faucets, and waterless urinals.

The green roof is part of an integrated strategy to conserve energy. Solar (photovoltaic) panels are installed on the northern edge of the roof and monitor the amount of electricity captured and collected. Energy generated from these panels is fed back into the city's power grid, thereby reducing the library's energy bills.

EVERYONE LOVES AN ATRIUM (EXCEPT A LIBRARIAN)

Throughout the Tips and Tales sections, you'll notice librarians criticizing the popularity of the atrium. Even Elizabeth McCracken, in her book *The Giant's House*, advises librarians to never trust an architect because "he will always try to talk you into an atrium."[4] I strongly doubt that architects have any special atrium fixation. They've probably found that they get pats on the back and design awards when they include them, and so they assume that everyone likes them as much as they do.

Librarians, on the other hand, have a tendency to talk about the "A" word because atria do, indeed, present many practical problems. They tend to leak, they interfere with climate control, and they go hand in hand with balconies and open, echoing spaces that amplify noise. Nevertheless, architects are probably right that people are drawn to an atrium. Mortals that we are, we love a sunny, spacious environment. On a cold winter day we want to bask in the sun, and nothing cheers us up more than these bright, plant-filled spaces.

In my own library, we have two large atria. Fortunately, the building was actually designed more than a decade before it opened its doors, so no one on the present staff need accept responsibility for the "A" places. The library is also wildly popular with the university community, having exceeded attendance projections by an extraordinary number of visitors in its first year of operation. Library colleagues were generally right in anticipating the problems that we encountered with the atria, although recent technology and a commercial "plantscaping" service have reduced these concerns to more manageable proportions. However, every day a student comments on how light and bright and inviting the library is.

Designing a Functional Atrium

If those around you are clamoring for an atrium, you may decide it's best to graciously concede defeat. If you can convince your building professionals to give some thought to the matter, there are a number of ways to reduce problems and make an atrium more energy-efficient. Here are just a few.

Orient the atrium in an east-west direction. That way you can maximize exposure to light, minimize skylight size, and reduce excessive heat gain.

Install photocells to turn off atrium light fixtures when the light level reaches a certain brightness.

If you use clerestory windows on the sides of the atrium, you can have a smaller skylight with comparable light and fewer leaks, less breakage, and less direct sunlight.

Use slightly tinted glass if glare is a problem.

Consider your location and the average amount of sunlight your area usually enjoys. Once you are above a certain light threshold, additional sunlight merely means additional cooling loads.

Take into consideration the natural air convections in an atrium (cooler air collects at lower levels and hot air rises) when designing cooling systems. This means that in summer, hot air should be mechanically vented or naturally exhausted from the roof. Locate return air ducts near the bottom of the atrium to supply cool air during summer, reducing energy consumption. In winter, recirculate rising hot air. Maintain air circulation to keep cool or warm air in the desired areas.

TALES

We now have a three-story atrium that serves as a combination echo chamber/den of spiders (cool webs, which can be seen from the first floor).

Where the first and second floors of this library "meet," there is an atrium. It is aesthetically pleasing, but in the summer it heats up and funnels extremely hot air into the second floor of the library. And in this atrium we have a red-brick cube that obstructs our vision through the stacks.

WINDOWS AND NATURAL LIGHTING

In a nutshell, here is the truth, the whole truth, and nothing but the truth about natural light:

- ◆ sunlight is bad for books
- ◆ sunlight is bad for viewing computer monitors
- ◆ sunlight is bad for viewing television screens and projected images

- ◆ sunlight is bad for carpets
- ◆ sunlight is bad for upholstery
- ◆ users love sunlight
- ◆ users win

After grim years in the 1960s and 1970s when libraries, classroom buildings, and corporate headquarters were built without windows, architects finally realized that windows are essential to our human sense of well-being. Look around the library reading room. Tables and study carrels by windows are occupied first. The attraction is not simply a matter of light and ventilation; these can be dealt with artificially. Rather, there is something about sunlight that we crave, and we will put up with all sorts of inconveniences to get it.

One might say that librarians have a love-hate relationship with windows. Yet the windows you select for your building will determine to a large extent how both the library staff and the library's users respond to the new library. Depending on your part of the country, large windows on all sides of the building are probably not advisable. There can actually be such a thing as too many windows. The orientation of a window really matters, and northern lighting is usually best for reading and general lighting, although windows on any side of the building, if they are well designed, may meet your needs.

To Open or Not to Open

Windows that do not open provide greater climate control than the type that can be opened and closed by staff or users. However, it is not uncommon for air-conditioning systems to fail, forcing occupants to swelter. Modern buildings are very nearly airtight, and inadequate ventilation is all too common. Sick building syndrome results when air is merely recycled and pollutants emitted by construction materials are not carried away from the building. Under these circumstances, there are few luxuries that surpass that of being able to open a window and breathe cool, fresh air. Unfortunately, books do not thrive in fresh air. They respond adversely to dust, mold spores, and pests that commonly enter through open windows. Your library will, therefore, depend for most of its climate control on a high-quality HVAC system. However, e-books are rapidly replacing older printed books, so this is becoming a less important consideration than in the past.

Daylighting or Daylight Harvesting

Although it sounds a little simplistic, daylighting, a buzzword among sustainable building enthusiasts, is the practice of using natural light to illuminate the interiors of buildings. The use of artificial lighting can be cut drastically during the day when sunlight is harnessed and managed effectively. Daylighting

TIP

Make sure that the architect has planned for the cleaning of skylights and clerestory windows, both inside and outside. For example, the addition of a rail at the sill of the clerestory windows can make cleaning easier and reduce cost. Too often, relatively new buildings have dirty windows. The regular window cleaners have concluded that the windows are too difficult or dangerous to reach and have abandoned them to the elements.

TIPS

Don't let design engineers talk you out of installing operable windows! If your windows don't open, and your air-conditioning goes out, you close your library (unless it is small enough to be ventilated by opening doors). It doesn't have to be very warm outside to become unbearably hot inside without air-conditioning.

We had huge, beautiful windows with low-E glass (holds heat in), but no safety bars outside. The decision makers insisted on windows that opened, so that on nice days we could have fresh air. (Yankee frugality, but no thought of little kids falling out of the windows.)

involves bringing indirect natural light into a building, thereby providing pleasing and often glare-free light. Though it sounds elementary, daylighting is a complex field of study involving precise calculations of lighting power density, illuminance levels, contrast ratios, and window-to-wall ratios. Technology comes into play with a variety of devices, including sensors that turn off electric lights when they are not needed. Climate and geographical region, building type, and building orientation are all factors that must be taken into consideration when designing a successful day-lit building.

Light Shelves

On many newer buildings, we see solid structures attached to windows a little like awnings, or perhaps more like bookshelves, floating between the top and bottom of the window. Light shelves are an extremely effective way to use the light coming in from windows. They consist of white or reflective metal shelves that protect the interior of the building from direct summer sun. Blocking glare yet allowing light to enter the building, the shelves are angled in such a way as to create shade in the interior window area. Simultaneously, the shelves or eaves reflect sunlight upward to illuminate the ceiling. Reflected light contains less heat, and this ceiling illumination is a more pleasant, more desirable kind of light, reducing shadows and creating a bright, attractive ambience. Although building occupants would otherwise draw the blinds and turn on the lights, light shelves allow them to experience considerably more comfort and reduce energy use at the same time. In winter, a natural light shelf is created when the ground is covered with snow. The snow reflects light through windows, illuminating the ceiling and increasing solar gain.

Room Darkening

Many rooms in the library like auditoriums, classrooms, and meeting rooms need to be darkened occasionally, especially for projecting media. Blinds are a good choice for most areas because they provide the most flexibility and can be adjusted for different times of day and varying light conditions. However, they may not darken a room sufficiently for film, video, or computer projection. Specially fitted shades are made just for this purpose. Be careful that you do not go to the effort and expense of installing light-blocking shades only to realize later that you forgot about the glass doors or clerestories through which light pours in.

It will be necessary to turn off the lights in any room in which media is projected, so be sure your building professionals are given a list of all rooms that require separate lighting controls. Since people may be taking notes when programs are being shown, you will also want to be able to darken a room without plunging it into total darkness. Ask that emergency lights be located away from projection screens or the resulting glare will reduce visibility.

TIP

Don't install mini-blinds on metal (exterior) doors. We had problems with them and eventually removed them. They swing, get in the way, get bent, make noise, and so on.

THE ENTRANCE

The library's front entrance must serve multiple functions in addition to providing a doorway into the library. It should accommodate such security activities as observation, detection, and inspection. It is the point at which customers make the transition from cold, rain, snow, or excessive heat into a climate-controlled space. It is the spot where they watch for their rides, wait until the rain lessens, shake their water-drenched umbrellas, and track in mud on boots and shoes. Where should the main entrance be located? How should it be designed?

Location

If you have a choice, it's probably better to locate an entrance on a side street rather than on a main thoroughfare. Side street access reduces the volume and speed of the traffic approaching the site, thus adding a measure of safety for pedestrians. Although most librarians are accustomed to a single entrance for patrons, architects are not. Make it clear that additional entrances are needed only in the loading dock area and as emergency exits. Insist on a single public entrance. Since many people, especially administrators and board members, can't understand why this is such a "big deal," it may be helpful to read the following tales of librarians who must live with the problem on a daily basis.

TIPS AND TALES

Provide a safe, dry place for daily newspaper delivery. Libraries get lots of newspapers, and it's no fun to have them disappear or become wet, sodden masses.

Locate outside book drops where the staff can easily get to them. Remember that staff will be wheeling loaded book trucks and can negotiate uneven sidewalks and steps or curbs only with difficulty.

Make sure that the staff entrance is well lit and protected from the elements. Imagine staff members fumbling for keys in the dark or struggling to swipe access cards through a reader while being pelted by rain.

We have two entrances and the second one, although it is very popular, is a constant problem. We have a circulation desk and security gates there, but making sure we have student staff is not always possible. The tendency, when a student is absent from his or her shift, is to leave the door unstaffed. This is not a good idea because if the alarm goes off, no one can reach the entrance in time. Using permanent staff to sit at this desk is also much too costly.

When our older building was restored last year, there was some pressure to open yet a third entrance. I convinced the administration that purchasing a security gate and hiring a student assistant for ninety-plus hours a week was not worth the "convenience" of giving patrons a third entrance. I have had only one complaint about this, and once the patron knew the money situation, she agreed with our decision.

TALES

We are in a four-story building that serves dual purposes. The library occupies floors two through four, with the entrance on the third floor. The first floor is offices and classrooms. The library was not designed with such use in mind. We convinced the administration to install a security code system on the elevator that allows only authorized individuals to get to the first floor from the library.

Our library is located in a large building of offices and classrooms. Prior to getting a security system in the early 1980s, we had two entrances/exits, and the library was like another corridor for people to pass through. We experienced losses of 3 to 4 percent of our book collection annually. When we got a security system, the back entrance was made into an emergency exit with an alarm, and we have kept it that way ever since.

My library has one entrance but takes up four floors of a six-story multipurpose building. The problems you should watch out for are the stairs and the elevator. The stairways have doors with alarms, but that doesn't stop the walkers. The elevators go to two lower floors, and too many people (staff and students) have keys. They simply bypass the library floor, leave via the lower floors, and go directly to another building entrance. There is no way we can afford to staff or provide an extra security gate. Students go to the lower floors and leave without checking materials out.

Our main concern has always been about how users exit the building. The fact that one can take the elevator into the library from the first floor but not vice versa has been a livable, if not an ideal, situation. One thing to keep in mind when configuring traffic flow is the fire code. You need to be aware that certain entrances/exits, even interior ones, may not be locked under your local fire code.

Entries for Multiuse Facilities

It is not unusual for the library to be housed in a building that serves other functions. Public libraries are often part of civic center complexes, and academic libraries may be housed in a larger classroom building. These multiple access points create special security problems that can be extremely difficult to address. Not only do you have to worry about a number of outside entrances, but you must also consider internal access through elevators and stairways that connect the library and nonlibrary areas. Once again, the experiences of other librarians will alert you to potential problems.

As you can readily see from this chapter, planning a new library or addition involves a clear understanding of library goals, technology, and environmental issues. Without considering all aspects of the project in a holistic way, it is easy for both your planning group and your building professionals to be led astray. It is important that you take some time to reflect, looking back on your experiences with libraries and with your library customers. You will discover a precious reservoir of insight that, when paired with a better understanding of building design and construction issues, will result in a successful twenty-first-century library.

NOTES

1. U.S. Department of Energy, Energy Efficiency and Renewable Energy, www1.eere .energy.gov/buildings/commercial/whole_building_design.html.
2. U.S. Green Building Council, "LEED for New Construction and Renovations" (2005), www.usgbc.org/ShowFile.aspx?DocumentID=1095.
3. Lisa Fay Matthiessen and Peter Morris, "The Cost of Green Revisited: Reexamining the Feasibility and Cost Impact of Sustainable Design in the Light of Increased Market Adoption," Davis Langdon, July 2007, www.davislangdon.com/upload/ images/publications/USA/The%20Cost%20of%20Green%20Revisited.pdf.
4. Elizabeth McCracken, *The Giant's House: A Romance* (New York: Avon, 1997).

GREEN BUILDING DESIGN RESOURCES

American Solar Energy Society (ASES)—www.ases.org

Architects Designers Planners for Social Responsibility (ADPSR)—www.adpsr.org

Association for Environment Conscious Building—www.aecb.net

Center for Livable Communities—www.lgc.org/center/

Ecological Design Institute—www.ecodesign.org/edi/

Energy Efficiency and Renewable Energy (EREN)—www.eere.energy.gov

Environmental Building News and GreenSpec Product directory—www.buildinggreen .com/index.cfm

Global Green USA—www.globalgreen.org

GreenerBuildings—www.greenerbuildings.com

Green Resource Center—www.greenresourcecenter.org

iGreenBuild.com—www.igreenbuild.com

The Long Now Foundation—www.longnow.org

REDI Guide, Resources for Environmental Design—www.oikos.com

Resource Renewal Institute—www.rri.org

Rocky Mountain Institute—www.rmi.org

Smart Communities Network, Green Building—www.smartcommunities.ncat.org

Solar Living Center, The Solar Living Institute—www.solarliving.org/overview.cfm

Sustainable Buildings Industry Council—www.sbicouncil.org

Sustainable Sources—http://directory.greenbuilder.com/search.gbpro

Urban Ecology—www.urbanecology.org

U.S. Green Building Council—www.usgbc.org

Human Needs and Energy-Efficient Buildings

If your present library building dates back to the period from about 1960 to the mid-1980s, you may be living with a structure that makes little accommodation for human beings. Although some beautiful buildings emerged from this period, many others were based on design trends that emphasized modernism, sleek lines, and an overconfidence in the technology of the time. For example, we went through a period when windows were often eliminated from public buildings. Of course, it made for sleeker lines and fewer complications. Designers imagined that the climate control systems of the time were so sophisticated that they could precisely regulate the interior environment, and windows just interfered with these perfect systems.

DESIGN FOR HUMAN BEINGS

Whatever else we've learned during the intervening years, we've rediscovered the truth that human beings must feel comfortable in a space or they will avoid it. Rooms without windows make us feel claustrophobic and airless, even when HVAC systems are functioning correctly. Another painful discovery is that every mechanical system will break down, and it will do so again and again. When style, aesthetic considerations, efficiency, or technology become the designers' focus instead of the people who will be using the building, the resulting structure will be a failure. Although it may win design awards, its occupants will do little but complain until it is ultimately torn down. As your project team becomes increasingly enmeshed in technical details, it is possible to lose sight of the users who will be spending many hours in the new building. If the library program is to be successful, users' needs, whether for comfortable chairs, sunlight, or disability accommodations, must be given serious consideration.

Human Needs and Energy Conservation

During those years when designers were planning those sleek slabs of concrete, they were also increasing energy consumption to an alarming extent. At last we are realizing that we cannot continue to consume the quantities of coal, natural gas, and petroleum products that we currently use. Supplies of fossil fuels are diminishing, the planet is suffering, and we grow ever more dependent on oil-producing nations that may not share our values. Therefore, this chapter will give some thought to how our library buildings can provide comfort and efficiency while at the same time reducing their consumption of scarce energy resources.

FUNCTIONAL, ENERGY-EFFICIENT LIGHTING

When you investigate the subject of lighting, you may find it a little overwhelming. Whether considering natural light entering through windows and skylights or artificial lighting, lighting tends to be the focus of much of our discontent. Can you think of a single library where overhead lights are positioned in such a way that they illuminate every stack range? If by some remote chance you happen to know of such a library, are lights changed routinely as soon as they burn out? You've probably criticized the lighting of every library you've ever visited, and that's only to be expected.

Although your architect will hammer out the details, you should be prepared with very clear, specific lighting recommendations. How can you hope to emerge from the project with a functional lighting plan when so many before you have failed? First, get the architects on your side. If at all possible, take them on a field trip, not only through your present library but to other local libraries as well. (You might go on a reconnaissance mission ahead of time to scout out the darkest areas.) Point out the inaccessible lightbulbs that never get changed because the custodians simply can't get to them. Pause below the buzzing, nonstandard fluorescent tubes that are always on back order or only available through a supplier in Montana who went out of business three years ago.

Ask tour participants to find a call number that's impossible to read because the book is on the bottom shelf of a remote stack range. Let them watch a video or read a computer screen that has been washed out by glaring afternoon sunlight. Then be prepared to discuss these experiences. You might also want to visit several newer libraries in your region to examine the lighting fixtures used and the kind of light they provide. In fact, you might also want to see these libraries' electric bills, because the differences among them might amaze both you and your architects. Ask some library users how they feel about the lighting. Is the light from windows too bright or glaring? Does the area appear gloomy?

Library Lighting Problems

Although lighting decisions for libraries are not so very different from those for other large buildings, there are some ways in which the library is unique. Architects sometimes forget that library users are usually reading. In fact, architects may tuck lighting fixtures into places just because they are out of the way of other design features. This may mean recessing them in the ceiling, thus directing the light straight down rather than diffusing it. It might be a nice, attractive idea in other environments, but such installations simply don't work in libraries. Factors such as building orientation, blinds, and furniture arrangement as well as the type and number of lighting fixtures all affect the lighting of an area.

As you're talking with your architects, suggest that they avoid decorative lighting fixtures that don't really provide much light. The bulbs they require are often expensive special orders, and your custodial staff will waste a great deal of time changing them. Be sure that any light fixture you have in the library really illuminates the space it was designed for. Help your architects understand the importance of keeping the number of different types of fixtures as small as possible so you're not always running out of one type of lamp or another.

A Brief Primer on Lighting Theory and Terms

Like other aspects of library design, lighting has language and some basic concepts that you will need to master to discuss the subject with your architects. The following sections provide a very brief tutorial.

Direct Lighting

Light that is directed downward into an area is direct lighting. In general, it is an efficient way to deliver light to work surfaces. It can, however, create problems. For example, bright lamps or luminaires against a dark ceiling can cause reflective glare on computer monitors, glossy magazines, and photographs and can result in a "cavelike" atmosphere. Harsh shadows are another unpleasant effect of direct lighting. Although we usually choose direct lighting for reading, it tends to illuminate unevenly, and scalloped patterns can occur on books and walls.

Narrowly focused lights may highlight an architectural detail dramatically, but they cause irritating shadows outside the small pool of light and make reading extremely difficult anywhere in the library and impossible in the stacks. Also remember that you will eventually tear down and rearrange book stacks as your collection grows and your priorities change. Will you have a crisis if the lights no longer line up properly? Patches of light and dark are the last thing you need in a library.

Indirect Lighting

When a space is indirectly lit, light is "bounced" off the ceiling and dispersed throughout the space. For obvious reasons, this type of light is also called "uplighting." Both our users and our staffs find this kind of soft, uniform lighting environment very pleasant. Uplighting is frequently a better choice for areas of a library in which people are reading both print and computer text. In general, direct lighting systems provide higher illumination levels, and indirect systems supply a higher quality of light at lower light levels. Libraries really need a combination of direct and indirect lighting. Indirect fixtures create uniform illumination throughout the space, while direct lamps improve efficiency and light work spaces. Many newer fixtures can provide both. They can be adjusted so that more light is directed up toward the ceiling or more shines down on users. The combination results in a more attractive, inviting environment in which objects have shape without harsh shadows.

Color Perception

The ability to distinguish and interpret different wavelengths of light is called color perception. Color is not really a property of an object, but the way that different wavelengths of light make the object appear. A light source sends out many different wavelengths, and objects absorb some of them. They reflect the rest of the light, and it is this reflection that makes an object appear to be red or green or blue. Color perception affects not only the colors users see but their sense of comfort, pleasure, or even anxiety. Light determines color, and color affects your users' experience of the library. Color perception is the reason why librarians often complain that the colors they selected from swatches, carpet samples, and paint chips look completely different as walls, carpets, and upholstery in the new library. Even though the samples match one another perfectly when first viewed in an office or in the interior decorator's studio, they may look totally different in the new environment.

LIGHTING SOURCES

Although lighting fixtures come in every imaginable size and shape, the light they emit allows them to be divided into two major classifications: incandescent lamps and gaseous discharge lamps. (The term *lamp* is being used here to mean a light source.) Gaseous discharge lamps can also be divided into two subcategories: low-pressure and high-pressure or high-intensity discharge (HID) lamps.

Incandescent Lamps

Incandescent lamps were invented by Thomas Edison. These lamps have not changed a great deal through the years. One recent development, however, is the tungsten-halogen regenerative cycle lamp. These lamps are more efficient than traditional incandescent lamps and can produce more light because the bulb is made out of quartz glass, which permits a higher temperature inside the lamp. You will hear them called quartz lamps, tungsten-halogen lamps, quartz-halogen lamps, or just halogen lamps. The bulbs are quite a bit smaller than the common lightbulb. The most popular, the MR-16 lamp, is only about 2 inches in diameter. Halogen lamps produce a whiter light; standard incandescent lamps shed a yellowish glow.

Gaseous Discharge Lamps

When we think of gaseous discharge lamps, fluorescent tubes come immediately to mind. These are actually part of the group called low-pressure discharge lamps. Another lamp that falls into this same category is the low-pressure sodium lamp, although it is usually not used indoors since it produces a yellow light that turns everything yellow and brown. In all probability, your library depends almost entirely on fluorescent lamps, as do most stores and offices. The most common fluorescent lamp is usually 4 feet long and 1½ inches in diameter (although a 1-inch-diameter version is becoming more common). They are extremely cost-effective, since they are several times more efficient than incandescent lamps. It is not as easy to direct them to specific locations, but new compact fluorescent lamps can be inserted into almost any socket designed to hold incandescent lightbulbs. In the past, the stark white tubes often seemed harsh because their color-rendering properties were poor. However, newer fluorescents can actually simulate a variety of lighting conditions and even imitate the yellow glow of incandescent lamps.

The bluish-greenish street lamps popular a few years ago were mercury vapor lamps, the first high-intensity discharge lamps to be developed. They're no longer used because metal halide lamps provide better color rendering, and high-pressure sodium lamps have also been greeted with enthusiasm. HID lamps are extremely energy-efficient. Their small size (measured in inches, not feet) allows for good control of light. Although they were once used almost entirely for streets and other outside lighting, they are gradually becoming available in small wattages for indoor use.

Incandescent versus Gaseous Discharge Lamps

As you make your lighting decisions, consider every use of incandescent lighting carefully. Until recently, your choice was between an attractive environment lit by incandescents and a stark, glaring, supermarket-like space lit by the epitome of gaseous discharge lamps, the fluorescent tube. This is no longer true, but most of us haven't yet realized how much the world of lighting has changed. In general, fluorescents use 75 percent less energy than incandescents. They also last about ten times longer. However, fluorescent lamps require a ballast to regulate current and provide a high start-up voltage. In the past these noisy, temperamental mechanisms drove library staff and customers to distraction, but electronic ballasts have solved most problems. They outperform standard ballasts by operating at a high frequency that eliminates flicker and noise.

Librarians have long accepted the four-foot-long tubes that marched across their ceilings, but they have continued to use incandescents wherever they felt that comfort really mattered. Lounge areas, staff spaces, and task-lit workstations often fell into this category. Compact fluorescent lamps (CFLs) can now create cozy environments almost as well as incandescents, but extensive planning is required. The reason we dislike typical supermarket lighting is that the cheap lamps score poorly on the Color Rendering Index. Color rendering is the way lighting engineers describe the way a light source makes the color of an object appear to human eyes and how well subtle variations in color are revealed. The CRI is a scale that goes from 0 to 100 percent, and incandescents usually have a CRI that's close to 100. They may also shed a warm, golden glow. To achieve a similarly attractive environment with fluorescent lamps, you will need to compare different products carefully. The extra work will pay off, however, in greatly reduced costs and greater comfort for your customers.

Lighting Terms

The following are commonly used technical terms for lighting. They are based on either English or metric measurements. Although you probably don't need to understand each term, you will hear them used often.

Candela (cd). Unit of measurement of luminous intensity; the candela has replaced the standard candle.

Foot-candle. Unit of illumination on a surface that is everywhere one foot from a uniform point source of light, the brightness of one candle.

Illuminance. Amount of light that strikes a surface.

Lambert. Unit of brightness or luminance; equal to the brightness of a perfectly diffusing surface that reflects one lumen per square centimeter.

Lumen. Used in calculating artificial light; amount of light from a uniform point source having an intensity of one candela.

Luminance. Brightness or intensity of light on a surface.

Lighting Requirements

When we consider what good lighting means in the library, it is almost inevitable that we think of the way available light illuminates a book. Books and periodicals continue to be an important part of a library and so we must never forget the user, standing with open book in hand in a shadowy stack area. That same user, however, will probably be spending some time at a computer workstation before she leaves, and so we must expand our picture.

Using the library for reading and study has traditionally meant working with black characters printed on white paper on a horizontal surface. Since printed matter is read by reflected light, it has been assumed that the brighter the illumination provided, the higher the contrast between characters and background. Now that many workstations are equipped with desktop computers, users are looking not at a flat sheet of paper but at a vertical screen that emits, not reflects, light. This means that the lighting requirements for computer use and paper-focused activities are very different.

Lighting for Computers

At desk level, 100 foot-candles of light has been accepted as a normal office standard. Although architects may plan for this level in a library, the result is almost always uneven, with some areas too light and others too dark. Today's computer monitors can be read in almost total darkness. The ambient light in most library and office areas may be so bright that it causes glare or washes out computer screens. In fact, there is evidence that given a choice, employees who spend their entire workday at a computer will switch off the lights completely. Obviously, this is not desirable in a library, but it points up the enormous difference between reading a book and reading from a light-emitting screen.

Any decisions you make about lighting computer areas should take into consideration the following visual tasks that your staff or users will be performing:

- reading text displayed on the screen
- recognizing keyboard letters, symbols, and function keys
- reading written or typed text in a book or on a sheet of paper placed nearby
- copying notes into a computer

Users should be able to perform these tasks with ease and in comfort. Good readability for paper text requires a higher light level than for computers, but that same light actually reduces the readability of the text displayed on the video screen. When the text on the computer screen is light-colored on a dark background, the problem is exacerbated. The ambient light actually veils the image on the screen. Since it is impossible to fully satisfy the lighting needs of both computer users and those reading printed text in the same areas, you will inevitably find yourself making compromises. Just be careful that some flexibility is possible. Since you can expect rapid change in the next few years, try to create environments where a variety of activities can be carried on in proximity to each other and in reasonable comfort. Just consider, for example, the recent appearance of e-readers like Amazon's Kindle in libraries. They provide electronic text that is not backlit like computer monitors, and some models require bright light for adequate contrast.

One solution to the problem of lighting for print, e-text, and computer work is having a light installed in each study carrel or workstation that can be turned on or off by the user to suit the particular task. In general, the more control the users have over their environment, the happier they are. Another solution is to select monitors that have improved the contrast of their screens through dark-surround phosphors; antireflective coatings; and optically coupled, built-in, antiglare filters. Installing shades on windows and controlling the placement of light sources are still other options.

Light Switch Panels

Imagine the small group of staff members who must close the library in the evening. When I was in that situation many years ago, I remember that I had to walk through each and every area of the library turning out lights as I went. Each time I turned off a light, I had to feel my way in darkness until I reached the next brightly lit area, bruising my shins in the process. If at all possible, you will want to be able to control the lights in your building from one central location while retaining the freedom to turn individual banks of lights on and off as needed. Switches controlling individual spaces (such as storerooms and media rooms) are a necessity, but you don't want staff members walking into walls while feeling for switches in a dark building. Not only does a central light panel save staff time and reduce the need for first aid, but it is important for security as well. Even more important, your library needs a bank of real, honest-to-goodness light switches (or their high-tech equivalent), not just circuit breakers. When one circuit breaker looks exactly like another, all sorts of equipment can be shut off accidentally.

Despite your efforts, it often happens that your library ends up with light switches that cannot be centrally controlled. This situation is difficult enough to live with, but it becomes a great deal worse when switches get put in electrical and mechanical closets. Such things sometimes happen because the electrical contractor is in a hurry to finish the job and looks for shortcuts, paying little attention to the chaos that will inevitably follow. It may also be the architect's error or yet another misguided cost-cutting measure.

Electrical and mechanical areas are dangerous. Huge quantities of electrical current are pouring into your building, and you certainly don't want staff or student pages mistakenly pulling the wrong breaker. These are the very same areas that often bear signs reading "Danger! Keep Out" for good reason. If the light switch panels are in such "off-limits" areas, you may even find yourself in the position of being denied keys to turn on your own lights.

TALES

We have a sophisticated lighting system that we don't use. All we really wanted was an on-off switch.

We still have no idea what some of the wall switches do.

Our restroom lights were tied into a switch that controlled a bank of lights in a distant area. This was a problem at closing because we turned the lights out on people who were still using the restrooms.

Exterior Lighting

Exterior lighting has become a somewhat controversial subject. In many communities, residents are battling to protect the night sky. Light pollution has become so ubiquitous in many places that it is no longer possible to see the stars or sit in one's own backyard enjoying the beauty and grandeur of the night. As discussed in the last chapter, exterior lighting can disrupt ecosystems, make it difficult to sleep, and otherwise cause adverse health effects. In addition, exterior lighting wastes a huge amount of energy. Fixtures have improved considerably in recent years, but much of the light is still wasted, illuminating clouds rather than the activity that surrounds the library at night. Often bright lights remain on all night, annoying neighbors and wasting precious energy resources when lower light levels can provide adequate security. Some type of exterior lighting, however, is an absolute necessity if the library is to remain open after dark.

Security Lighting

To a considerable extent, the nature of the site determines the kind of exterior lighting needed. Security lighting is needed for observation, inspection, deterrence, and safety. The choice of lighting fixtures and their locations depend on

TIPS

I think the most important thing you can do is have your maintenance staff in on the planning, especially if they have experience in reading electrical plans. They will also see that your light fixtures and ceiling tiles are standard.

Take precautions against children turning task lights on and off.

See that switches are sufficiently tough to accommodate heavy usage.

Outdoor lights should be low enough to change bulbs easily, but not be in or near the ground. We have had a lot of trouble with in-the-ground fixtures, from vandalism (smashing lens covers) to water leakage when seals were not tight enough. One fixture a couple of feet above the ground has been hidden by shrubbery (our fault), and another was broken by a patron who tripped and fell into it.

Flagpole lighting should be mounted on the building, not in the ground.

site size, vegetation, topography, and building location. The aim should be to provide a uniform level of lighting with overlapping cones of light and with a minimum of shadow areas. If you plan to use closed-circuit television cameras, the lighting system should provide the correct level of intensity for the cameras. Exterior lighting fixtures should be resistant to vandalism and sabotage. Wiring should be concealed, and access to equipment should be via locked cabinets or receptacles. Before deciding on the type and the extent of external lighting, be sure that you and your architects have considered the following questions:

What is the present level of light in the area and on neighboring buildings? Is the library in a populated area where existing lighting will help illuminate the building?

How big a factor is security in your decision?

How safe is the neighborhood? Has crime or vandalism been a problem in your present library?

Where will the fixtures be placed? The placement of fixtures plays a major role in determining the mood and effect created by illumination of a building exterior. Lighting fixtures should be located as unobtrusively as possible. Because they are very bright and can get quite hot, they must be placed where people are unlikely to touch them.

How will your lighting plan address the concerns of local residents?

ENERGY EFFICIENCY AND NEW BUILDINGS

Whether your hypothetical crystal ball predicts hard times or times of plenty, energy conservation should be part of your building's future. Not only do reduced energy costs mean more money for library resources, but our environment profits as well. Unfortunately, the librarian is often not consulted about energy matters in the design of the building shell, HVAC, lighting, and other energy-consuming systems. Ideally, your building's various systems should interact with one another in a synergistic manner. This may require more cooperation among building professionals than normally occurs. If, however, you make your concerns about energy efficiency clear from the start, you are more likely to emerge from the experience with an environmentally responsible building.

Life-Cycle Costing

As mentioned earlier, construction funds are often more generous than ongoing operating budgets. It makes good sense to pay a little more for systems and equipment that lower your energy costs later. In other words, it is not really cost-effective to make decisions on the basis of the initial price tag. Long-term or life-cycle costing takes into account the initial cost as well as the costs associated with operating and maintaining the building during its useful life. In the case of lighting, for example, the cost of the fixtures and lamps really accounts for only about 10 percent of the real cost. The rest is the cost of electricity and the ongoing labor costs involved in changing lamps and repairing fixtures.

Convincing your building team to invest in energy efficiency is not always a battle you can expect to win, since most people involved in the project do not envision themselves being around to reap the savings created by energy conservation. However, the more dramatically you can present the long-term savings, the greater your chance of success. During the construction phase, the cost of making the building more energy-efficient is really not as high as commonly believed. Because new lighting, heating, and cooling equipment is being purchased anyway, there is no need for expensive retrofitting.

New buildings are inevitably more energy-efficient than those built in the past. Code requirements and new materials ensure better insulation, more efficient water use, and so on. However, new buildings also use far more energy than in the past due to the increased amount of power- and water-guzzling equipment required to meet contemporary expectations.

Insulation

Perhaps the best way to make your building more sustainable is to cut down on energy use, and there is probably no better way to do so than installing high-performance insulation. In fact, a recent construction industry report named insulation as the single most cost-effective way to improve energy efficiency. Fortunately, it is relatively easy to compare insulation values because of the standardized insulation rating system, which grades products based on their insulating efficiency. The R-value measures resistance to the flow of heat; the higher the R-value, the more resistant the material is to heat. U-values are the opposite; they represent the amount of heat that escapes through a material. Obviously, you will be looking for material with a low U-value since the slower the rate of heat flow, the better the insulating material. Since air has excellent insulation properties, R-value is proportional to the insulation's thickness or density. The more air pockets the product possesses, the higher the R-value. The following guidelines will contribute substantially to an energy-efficient building:

> The amount of insulation needed for one-story buildings where the interior is mainly influenced by the flow of heat through the building envelope is greater than for multistory buildings.

> Drop ceilings should not be treated as part of a building's thermal envelope, so insulation should not be placed on top of a drop, grid-type ceiling.

> Fiberglass batts should not be placed between roof rafters with a drop ceiling below. Use blown insulation instead of fiberglass batts where possible.

HEATING, VENTILATION, AND COOLING

Most of us rarely consider that climate control—a term that encompasses temperature, humidity, and air circulation—can have an enormous positive or negative impact on the library's ability to serve the needs of its users. Yet it may not be an important consideration among library planners. In one library, both architects and contractors were smitten with a very high-tech HVAC system but failed to carefully consider how it would function in the library's real-world situation. Soon after the building opened, the library director discovered that the state-of-the-art air conditioner, which could easily have chilled a small city, inflated the electric bill to such an extent that it had to be shut down. Because the windows were not designed to open, the sun's rays, shining through vast expanses of glass, heated the building to egg-frying temperatures. The state-of-the-art heating module might have worked as predicted if cost overruns had not resulted in a decision to reduce the number of temperature zones. The same quantity of heated air spewed forth in the already toasty window area as in the basement.

This meant that both the library and maintenance staffs spent their time designing clumsy work-arounds, wedging exterior doors open, disconnecting gizmos, and tinkering with other gadgetry. They managed to achieve a reasonable semblance of comfort until a few years later, when an electrical consultant arrived. Computerization, he promised, would save the day. All the dampers and vents and valves would open and shut, and all the fans and motors would spring magically to life at the touch of a key. After weeks of workers strewing lengths of wire and electrical conduit across the carpet and the constant ringing sound of metal striking metal, the project was complete. The entire HVAC system would be controlled from a console located in the physical plant office. (Naturally, the consultant reasoned, librarians didn't understand the technology, so it could not be located in the library.) Never again would staff need to adjust a thermostat, so the thermostats were removed. In their place appeared electronic sensors labeled with zone identification numbers. Yes, unfortunately, they were the same old zones. Once again, funds had been exhausted before new zones could be added.

Soon winter descended upon the library, and the temperature in the cataloging room fell to 50 degrees. Librarians in woolen gloves edited MARC records at frosty computers. Since all thermostats had been removed, staff learned the actual temperature only after a trip to the nearest hardware store to purchase thermometers. They carried them from room to room, exclaiming in amazement at the rapidly descending mercury.

When the library director phoned the maintenance supervisor, the latter eyed the building plan on his computer screen and announced confidently that the temperature in the cataloging room was 75 degrees. Eventually some adjustments were made, and life went on. A year passed and then another. However, the temperate nirvana that had been prophesied remained just beyond reach. Why were conditions no better than in the past? Why, in fact, were they actually somewhat worse?

At last the maintenance supervisor (not the one mentioned above, but his successor or possibly his successor's successor—turnover was a serious problem) made an astounding admission. No one on the present maintenance staff understood how the computer software program worked. Actually, since the computer that monitored the equipment had ceased to function a while back, this didn't matter a great deal. The system was on "autopilot." Like Hal in the film *2001: A Space Odyssey,* a runaway computer was calling the shots.

Couldn't the software be loaded onto another computer? Possibly, except that the disks had been packed in a box that had somehow disappeared in an office remodeling project. Then couldn't the computer program be manually overridden? This elicited the blankest of stares. How? No one on the present mechanical staff possessed any experience with the system, but a custodian remembered the heaps of scrap metal when the manual controls were torn out. Couldn't they get in touch with the engineering firm that installed the system? Yes, of course, that is, if anyone could remember who installed it. Those records too had been lost in the remodeling project.

Was this crisis inevitable? The director did an excellent job fulfilling what he considered to be his planning responsibilities. In other words, he correctly estimated the amount of space needed for the library's collections. He identified convenient locations for offices, computers, lounges, and photocopiers. However, he quite reasonably saw the technical requirements—what you might call the building's innards—as someone else's responsibility. In conferences with the architect, library board, and others, it was impressed upon him that he need not concern himself with these matters. They should be left to the professionals.

The Basics of Climate Control

The term *HVAC* encompasses all heating, cooling, and ventilating equipment in a building. The purpose of an HVAC system is to control temperature and humidity at levels that human beings find comfortable, distribute outdoor air to meet the ventilation needs of library staff and users, and isolate and remove odors and pollutants. HVAC systems vary from very simple to ultrasophisticated. In some areas it is possible to rely only on natural ventilation; there may be no need for mechanical cooling equipment, and humidity control may not be part of the system. The following are some basic classifications of HVAC systems. Each type has endless variations, but almost all systems fit into one category or another.

Water or Hydronic Systems

You probably have plenty of experience with water or hydronic systems that are characterized by fan coils or radiant pipes. These systems use a network of pipes to deliver water to hot water radiators, radiant pipes set in floors, or fan coil cabinets. Boilers produce hot water or steam; chillers produce chilled water. Thermostats are usually used to control the temperature by zone. Piped systems are easy to install because the pipes are smaller than ductwork. However, they are subject to hidden leaks and to burst pipes in winter.

Newer piped systems often called geothermal heat pumps may route a liquid through the ground, heating or cooling it before it is piped through the building. Until recently heat pumps could only make use of the heat in outside air, but newer geothermal heat pumps use the ground instead. They provide heating, air-conditioning, and, in most cases, hot water by collecting the heat that is stored in shallow ground (the upper ten feet). This top layer of earth is heated by the sun and maintains a very stable temperature year-round. Much like a cave, the shallow ground is warmer than the air above during winter and cooler than air in summer. A geothermal heat pump is therefore able to heat in winter and cool in summer by putting the heat back into the ground. Because they have few moving parts and use the earth's natural heat, these pumps are extremely efficient and cost-effective. The system's costs are returned in energy savings in about five to ten years.

Central Air Systems

Most central air systems distribute air rather than water and are designed for low-, medium-, or high-pressure distribution. Compressor drives, chillers, condensers, and furnaces are usually components of the system, depending on whether the air is heated or chilled or both. Ducts are usually made of sheet metal or flexible plastic and can be insulated. Registers can be installed in ceilings, floors, and walls, and thermostats control the temperature in each zone. Central air systems control interior temperature, humidity, and filtration. Heat pump systems extract latent heat from the outside air or from the earth itself and use it to evaporate refrigerant vapor under pressure. When heat is needed, the condenser and evaporator trade functions.

Solar applications are rapidly reducing the cost and improving the effectiveness of newer forced-air HVAC systems in a variety of ways. For example, solar ventilation air preheating is a recent innovation made possible by a sophisticated transpired solar collector. It is inexpensive and extremely effective. Preheating the air with solar energy before it is drawn into the ventilation system greatly reduces the energy costs associated with running the HVAC system. Solar ventilation air preheating is really a surprisingly simple, low-cost, and reliable addition to almost any climate control system. Since it has no moving parts except the fan, it is very low in maintenance and very high in efficiency (up to 80 percent). Unlike other HVAC system components, there are no breakdowns caused by freezing or fluid leaks. Unfortunately, there is also no practical way to store the heated air for nighttime use, but even if confined to daytime use, solar preheating is well worth the investment.

It is the innovative transpired solar collector, a painted metal plate perforated with tiny holes, that makes the system work. Although it may require a physics lesson to understand why these small holes allow the sun's heat to be absorbed more efficiently, there is no question that they work. In a moderate climate, the preheated air may be all that's needed to maintain a comfortable temperature. On cold winter days, additional heating by gas or electricity will be needed. Mounted to the south wall of a building, the transpired collector allows heated air to be delivered to an air handler destined for the heater or directly into the ventilation system.

Combined Air and Hot Water Systems

These systems combine the ease of installation of piped systems with the control of ducted systems. Air-handling units may be located throughout a building and are served by a central boiler and chiller. Water is sometimes delivered from a central plant that takes care of a complex of buildings.

Innovative HVAC Technology

A number of recent developments are coming together to gradually change the way HVAC systems are designed and move the industry in the direction of more energy-efficient systems. New technical innovations have made it possible to raise standards, and higher standards have in turn encouraged the development of new technologies. Changes to ASHRAE standards, the federal Energy Policy Act, and changes in equipment and controls are achieving energy-conservation goals with very modest modifications of existing systems.

For example, ASHRAE 90.1 mandated more stringent energy-efficiency requirements for controls and equipment, as well as building construction and operation. Similarly, ASHRAE 62.1, the standard for ventilation, has also been updated. These changes are spurring the development of performance evaluation methods for facilities that encourage resource conservation, indoor environmental quality, and comfort. ASHRAE is also developing tools to look at new and existing facilities to see if they are performing as intended. Outside the United States, the International Energy Conservation Code is similarly going through updates designed to reduce energy use.

The growing interest in commissioning systems is sending large numbers of technicians back to school to be certified through the North American Technician Excellence Inc. (NATE) program. NATE offers installation and/or service certification in five specialty areas: air-conditioning, air distribution, heat pumps, gas heating, and oil heating. Make it a point to find out about the certifications of the technicians who will be installing your system. The expertise behind NATE certification can have a huge impact on your building's energy use.

An increasingly important industry goal is to design "net zero energy use facilities," in which as much energy is produced as consumed. The day has not arrived when this is actually possible, but considerable progress has already been made. The use of energy-recovery ventilators is one example. They make it possible to recover some of the cooling energy as cooler air is exhausted and warmer air is brought into the building. Variable speed drives can be included with new equipment or retrofitted to existing equipment, saving up to 40 percent in energy costs. Variable air volume systems make it possible to damper off spaces that are not occupied or are infrequently used. Frictionless chillers that operate with oil-free magnetic bearing technology also reduce energy use. Since they don't require oil to run, they don't need an oil cooler, oil pump, or oil heater.

Natural Cooling

Natural ventilation or convection can also make a big difference in the long-term costs of energy consumption. For example, holes in the bottom of a facility can allow cool outside air into the building. As the air warms, it rises to the top of the space and exits through holes near the roof. Living in the Southwest, I became accustomed to the humble "swamp cooler," a simple evaporative cooling apparatus composed of a fan blowing air through what looked like a wet doormat. In a more sophisticated design, the water is sprayed in a downdraft cooling tower on the library's roof. The air filters through the tower and into the building. In dry climates, evaporative coolers can sometimes replace air conditioners entirely. Any of these cooling methods is well worth investigating.

HVAC Terminology

Like so many of the specialized trades involved in constructing a new building, climate control professionals have a language of their own. To talk intelligently with your building team, you will need to be familiar with at least some of the most frequently used terms.

ACCA (Air-Conditioning Contractors of America). National trade association in the field of heating, ventilation, and air-conditioning.

AFUE (annual fuel utilization efficiency). Measure of furnace heating efficiency.

Air handler. That part of a central air-conditioning or heat pump system that moves air through ductwork.

ARI (Air-Conditioning and Refrigeration Institute). Nonprofit, voluntary organization of heating, air-conditioning, and refrigeration manufacturers that publishes standards for testing and rating HVAC equipment.

BTU (British thermal unit). Amount of heat required to raise the temperature of one pound of water by one degree Fahrenheit.

COP (coefficient of performance). Ratio calculated by using the total heating capacity and the total electrical input in watts.

DOE (Department of Energy). Federal agency charged with setting industry efficiency standards.

EER (energy-efficiency ratio). Ratio calculated by dividing the cooling capacity by the power input efficiency method of rating HVAC equipment; the higher the rating number, the more efficient the system and the lower your fuel consumption.

Heat source. Solid, liquid, or gas from which heat is collected.

HSPF (heating seasonal performance factor). Measure of heat pump efficiency; the higher the HSPF rating, the more efficient the heat pump.

Kilowatt. 1,000 watts.

Sound ratings. Higher sound levels mean more noise when the HVAC system runs; measured in decibels (To get an idea of what a rating means, think of the human voice as about 7 decibels and an electric blender at 8 or 9 decibels.)

Ton. Each ton equals 12,000 BTUs; unit of size for heat pumps and air conditioners.

Watt. Unit of electric power used to rate electrical appliances and equipment.

Zone. Area that one thermostat controls.

TIP

Building interiors get hot and humid for reasons other than weather, such as proximity to the mechanical plant and use of equipment in a confined space. It may be desirable to locate storerooms near the building's mechanical plant.

Energy Savings and HVAC Design

The cost of operating an HVAC system accounts for the largest part of the library's energy costs. Therefore, success in designing an energy-smart building depends in large part on putting time, effort, and expertise into the design of your system. With careful forethought, it is possible to reduce both the library's operating budget and its negative impact on the environment. At the same time, your staff and customers can reap the benefits of a healthier, more comfortable environment. It is actually possible to lower energy costs by 50 percent while reducing maintenance costs. Such energy savings do not, however, come without a clear focus, a lot of work, and expert knowledge. More specifically, they require a thorough knowledge of best-practice guidelines, based on Department of Energy research.

Commissioning the HVAC System

As discussed in the last chapter, "commissioning" is a concept that's sweeping the building trades, and it offers a way to set goals for the performance of building systems and make certain they are met. HVAC is perhaps the system most often selected for commissioning. ASHRAE publishes guidelines for commissioning HVAC systems that can be accessed through its website.[1] Your building professionals should know exactly what they want from the HVAC system. If they follow the ASHRAE guidelines, this means that they will need to abide by the following procedure:

They should meet with your library planning group to clarify your requirements as well as the library's planned activities and equipment.

They will need to verify the fire and life-safety code requirements for the number of building occupants, and the ventilation requirements for the occupants and their equipment.

They should consider how the HVAC system can be designed with sufficient capacity to provide outside air for library staff and customers and for the anticipated heat-producing equipment.

Professionals involved in the project should review the documents to confirm that the system is properly designed for its intended uses.

Your project team has the option of including other systems like lighting and security in the commissioning process. That means you may also want to prepare design documentation and design criteria for these other systems.

Working with Your Building Professionals

Since this book can provide only an overview of the commissioning process, bring up the subject with your design team shortly after its members are selected. Ask how they understand the concept of commissioning and how they might implement it on the library project. If it is decided to adopt commissioning, be sure that the process is addressed in contract documents and construction meetings. The architect should be asked to describe the commissioning process at any pre-bid or pre-construction conferences. The next step is to designate a commissioning authority. This is the qualified person, company, or agency that will plan and carry out the overall commissioning process. This might be a design professional, the contractor, the building owner, or a commissioning consultant or agent. The role of commissioning authority might even be divided among two or more people. You might also wish to consider hiring an independent commissioning agent to make sure that commissioning is performed properly.

You might next ask how the commissioning authority will set about determining which system design to choose and, later, whether the chosen system is performing properly. There are actually several widely accepted ways of doing this, one of which is the "cost analysis method." This method considers how the added cost of building a high-performance system compares to the cost of fuel saved each year. How long will it take for specific improvements to pay for themselves? How does modifying one building system help to reduce energy costs in another? However, other criteria should be considered besides cost and payback when choosing a system. The commissioning authority must also consider reliability, safety, conformance with building codes, occupant comfort, noise levels, refueling issues, and space limitations.

Life-Cycle Costing

Life-cycle costing is another important tool available to the commissioning authority. It involves an analysis of the total cost of a system, device, building, or other capital equipment or facility over its anticipated useful life. Of course, determining how much a system will cost over its entire lifetime is a complex process and involves factors like initial capital cost, operating costs, maintenance costs, financing costs, the expected useful life of equipment, and future equipment salvage values. Energy-efficiency measures that have a short payback period (one to two years) are, of course, the most attractive and should usually be considered first for implementation. If capital outlay funds are short, energy efficiency measures that have payback periods from three to five years may be possible candidates for third-party financing through energy-service companies or equipment-leasing arrangements.

The Library's Conflicting Needs and Requirements

As you investigate various types of climate control, you will soon discover that some of your priorities are actually in conflict with one another. For example, computer equipment generates an extraordinary amount of heat, and it is especially important to continuously cool the rooms containing file servers. However, in too many library buildings the servers, modems, routers, and other networking equipment are housed in small closets, often with no thought given to cooling and ventilation. If electronic equipment is to be housed in a small, confined area, install fans to blow the warm air out of the closet into the ceiling plenum. In addition, you will need a chilled water source for year-round, twenty-four-hour cooling.

Maintaining the optimal environment for your equipment can mean increased energy consumption. The equipment itself consumes considerable energy, and additional energy is used to cool it down. The federal government now requires that energy consumption data be available for most appliances and machinery. Ask to see the literature for any piece of energy-consuming equipment under consideration. One must ask, however, why it is necessary to store heat-generating equipment in a small space anyway. Why not explore ways that expensive equipment can remain secure, for example, behind a metal grille, and yet remain in an open space where heat can be readily diffused?

The use of climate control systems has implications for many environmental and quality-of-life issues beyond simple energy conservation. As you consider the advantages and disadvantages of various systems, the EPA recommends that you consider a wide spectrum of related issues. These might include

ozone depletion

exposure to toxic emissions

global warming and other ecological effects

energy efficiency

flammability

MANAGING HUMIDITY

If there is any one problem that afflicts most libraries, it is excessive moisture. In the course of my own career, moisture in one guise or another has seriously imperiled or even destroyed important collections in my library. For example, one time the reference collection sprouted a summer coat of mold that quickly proceeded to infest nearly every volume. It proved to be impossible to make the physical plant director understand that this was an emergency situation. He was accustomed to removing mold from restroom walls, and throughout the course of a long and bitter battle, he never really understood that hundreds of thousands of dollars' worth of materials, some irreplaceable, were in jeopardy. In another library, seepage coming through the walls of the vault destroyed other valuable materials.

There is no real agreement on what constitutes an ideal environment for printed materials and computers, but you might think in terms of a humidity level in the winter of around 40 percent (plus or minus 5 percent) and about 50 to 55 percent (plus or minus 5 percent) in the summer. Humidity, however, must be correlated with temperature. To preserve materials and provide an environment in which computers can function effectively, the temperature should not rise above 72–73 degrees Fahrenheit.

I hesitate to throw these numbers around because of the enormous amount of research that has been done on the subject, some of it conflicting. Since the floods that devastated the art treasures of Florence, preservation studies have become one of the most active and exciting specializations in our profession. Take the time to peruse some of the literature. It is truly massive, and you will only be able to read a small sample. Nevertheless, excellent information is available both in print and on the Internet. Your only difficulty will be in convincing your building professionals of its importance.

Too little humidity should also be avoided. Modern library buildings frequently have computerized building systems that calculate the moisture content of the air and the dew point and adjust the humidity accordingly. Another recent innovation, the water-atomization system, uses compressed air and water, mixing and spraying it out through a nozzle to raise humidity to recommended levels.

Archival Collections and Humidity

Rare books, manuscripts, art, and historic artifacts require special climate controls and low-light conditions. At the same time, library users want comfort and sufficient light for reading. Separate archival facilities usually place the needs of the materials first and have considerably more options for protecting materials. A special collection housed within a larger, multipurpose facility has considerably less control over its environment. Even our own staffs will complain that we are trying to give them pneumonia when we turn down the heat, so compromises must be made.

According to the Smithsonian Institution's Conservation Analytical Laboratory Research Group, humidity in archival institutions doesn't need to be controlled as tightly as we've been taught.[2] Given that even the most sophisticated climate control systems with every conceivable bell and whistle often don't work, this is very comforting. It is going to take every ounce of determination you have to achieve even relatively minimal climate control for your archival collections. Even under the best of conditions, we know that all we can hope for is a compromise between protecting and preserving fragile collections and serving the public.

Climate control in special collections may require humidification to maintain a constant moisture level. Therefore, you will need to be aware that adding humidity to a building can also cause problems. The most frequently encountered difficulty is that condensation occurs when humidified air comes into contact with a surface that is below the dew point temperature. Many drier areas in the United States are in the West, where high-altitude temperatures may plunge at night. The need for a continuous insulation and vapor barrier system is especially important when humidification is a function of the HVAC system. Be sure that the mechanical engineer who is designing the HVAC humidity control is in close communication with the architect designing the vapor barrier system. Cold conditions will slow down the inevitable degradation to a snail's pace. Dry conditions will prevent mold, mildew, and chemical breakdown.

MOLD AND MILDEW

Whether it affects the interior or the exterior of your new building, mildew can cause serious problems. Although especially troublesome in damp, humid areas, mildew can become a problem under a wide range of conditions. Not only can it scar the building's facade, but the enzyme produced by mildew can cause

TIPS AND TALES

While it is true that the northern British Isles do not often have prolonged periods of heat by American standards, they can have prolonged periods of elevated humidity. The difference is that the greatest humidity is in the winter, not the summer. So although air-conditioning may not be needed so much as in most of the United States to control heat, it is certainly needed to control humidity. And anyone who thinks you need temperatures above 70 degrees for active mold growth has never encountered British mildew!

You must make it very clear when working with architects and engineers that there will or will not be people working in the archives. Otherwise, they will base their temperature estimates and levels on the fact that people will be working in the area on a consistent basis. We couldn't get it through the engineer's head that the media was the determining factor for appropriate temperature levels.

Because of excessive moisture, most of our rare books won't be shelved in the rare book room, as planned! They'll have to move to the archives, which means there will be less room for growth than I thought! I'll also have to spend more time supervising visitors.

We should have gotten the specs on ultraviolet light emissions from windows and lights and on the separate controls for the HVAC system for archives.

structural damage to some materials, including wooden and painted surfaces. In addition, mildew can affect indoor air quality by producing an unpleasant odor and triggering allergic responses from susceptible individuals. Mildew is a mold, the spores of which are present almost everywhere. It grows and spreads rapidly when

- organic materials such as soil, grease, or food are present
- the temperature ranges from 77 to 86 degrees Fahrenheit
- the relative humidity ranges from 70 to 93 percent

If mildew is a problem in your area, be sure that mildew prevention is considered in both the site plan and the landscape design. Avoid planting trees and shrubs too close to the library building, since plants can block air circulation and sunlight, preventing the exterior from drying out after a rainfall. In recent years, high-tech finishes have been developed that have built-in mildew resistance. For example, the exterior insulation and finish system results in a finish that inhibits the growth of mildew itself and that repels airborne dirt and pollutants, cutting off the mildew's food supply. For controlling interior mildew in a wet climate, your building engineer may need to use air conditioners, dehumidifiers, and exhaust fans during much of the year to keep temperature and humidity out of the optimal ranges for mildew growth.

Source of Moisture

It is often extremely difficult to tell where moisture is coming from. For example, what is assumed to be a leaking roof may actually be condensation coming from any one of a variety of sources. Whatever its source, excess moisture can not only cause collection damage but also result in rot, corrosion, peeling paint, water stains, and eventually building structural failure.

As was mentioned previously, some geographical areas are more prone to mildew than others. If you live in an area where the humidity remains high for long periods of time, ask your contractor what precautions are being taken to keep the building dry. Rain leaks are frequently the culprits, especially with hilltop and waterfront sites where driving wind makes every instance of caulking and flashing failure a potential time bomb. Remember that caulk has a limited life expectancy, and your physical plant personnel or a private contractor must inspect it regularly. HVAC systems include louvers and exterior exhaust grilles that require caulk around each exterior mechanical penetration. Flashing is also essential around HVAC penetrations. It is not uncommon for a contractor to take shortcuts, leaving these openings unprotected.

Failure to properly install moisture barriers or house wrap is another source of moisture and can cause extensive rotting within a year or two of a building's construction. These wraps, composed of such materials as spun bonded plastic fiber sheets, provide good rain protection and act as an infiltration barrier. In addition, roof overhangs may not provide sufficient protection from rain leaks. Sloped roofs must have substantial overhangs or walls may become sponges, sopping up rainwater.

Doors and windows are yet another source of unwanted moisture due to poor design and inappropriate specifications. Windows are made to differing code standards for wind/rain velocities, and your architects should require tests to determine which standards are appropriate for your specific site. Your building may be more vulnerable to rain and wind damage than those at a site a block away.

Ice Dams

Although high humidity may be a problem in warm southern states, ice dams caused by water runoff unable to get past ice-clogged gutters are responsible for many leaks in northern climates. Sometimes HVAC equipment installed in attic spaces generates so much heat due to uninsulated flues, ventilation exhaust ducts, and poorly sealed duct joints that the temperature of the attic area rises to room temperature or higher, melting snow on the roof and creating ice dams. Such simple solutions as attic fans for better ventilation are usually inadequate. It may be necessary to remove all the shingles, tape the roof sheathing joints airtight with a rubberized asphalt tape, and insulate the entire roof with 1½- to 2½-inch-thick isocyanurate foil-faced insulation board. This is certainly not a project you want to undertake a year or two after the building is completed.

Groundwater and Condensation

Groundwater that leaks into basements or crawl spaces is another source of excessive moisture. Where groundwater is a problem, it may be necessary to hire a geotechnical engineer to prepare a report on the soil and water table around the building site.

Occasionally, a crawl space is left unprotected by a concrete slab to cover the earth below. This is a near-catastrophic error that can create endless problems. Dirt floors in crawl spaces, except in very dry climates, are almost always a culprit when water damage occurs. In addition to making sure there is a concrete slab, one very effective precaution against moisture is the installation of a cross-laminated, high-performance polyethylene film under the concrete. When installed at the appropriate point in construction, it is extremely inexpensive and almost guarantees a dry slab. Concrete block foundations are usually more prone to leakage than poured foundations because of problems at joints and cracks. Underground waterproofing systems such as rubberized asphalt sheets and bentonite clay panels can help prevent these problems.

Condensation is most commonly found in modern buildings. In older structures, the use of minimal insulation and the average building's tendencies to leak large quantities of air meant that moisture was not easily trapped in inaccessible places. Good, thick insulation is essential for an energy-efficient building, yet air flows easily through insulation, bringing with it unwanted moisture. A vapor barrier must serve as an air barrier as well. The best kind of wall insulation system is probably a combination of foam insulation, glass fiber, and a good, sealed vapor barrier.

Poorly Installed Insulation Systems

It is not uncommon for contractors and architects to forget that insulation systems must be continuous. In other words, any place there are openings or holes, there will be air leaks. The insulation system includes not only the insulation itself but also the vapor barrier, adhesives, tapes, and fastening clips that hold everything in place. The system is continuous only if the wall vapor barrier is sealed to the floor and to the roof or ceiling vapor barrier. Special precautions must be taken any place that the system is penetrated by structural elements. All electrical, plumbing, and HVAC elements—even sprinkler protrusions—must be sealed and impermeable to air and vapor. Folds and staples in the vapor barrier also destroy the seal. Furthermore, unless the vapor barrier joints are sealed with a suitable adhesive, the barrier is all but useless.

Chilled water running through pipes throughout the building is still another cause of condensation. Piping requires properly installed foam-insulation systems with vapor barrier protection, or you will find yourself coping with ceiling drips and stains from the pipes above the ceiling.

Incompatible Neighbors

If your public library is being planned as part of a community complex and will share a wall, roof, or ventilation system with a swimming pool, the best advice is probably to campaign against such incompatible bedfellows. If, however, funding depends on togetherness, bear in mind some of the potential problems. In winter, for example, the facility will be bringing in outdoor air, which can create a cloud inside the building. Using air-to-air heat exchangers can improve humidity control as well as energy conservation. Dehumidifying heat pumps can provide year-round humidity control, allowing waste heat to be reused to heat pool water.

If your environment requires special humidifiers to maintain a constant moisture level, you may discover that you have still other problems to worry about. Condensation occurs when humidified air comes into contact with a surface whose temperature is below the dew point temperature. Again, the only way to prevent serious consequences is to ensure an absolutely continuous insulation/vapor barrier system. If a mechanical engineer is designing your HVAC humidity controls, do your best to see that adequate communication takes place with the architect who is designing the insulation/vapor barrier system.

As a rank amateur, you are certainly not going to presume to tell your architects how to moisture-proof the building. However, it is not out of place to have a chat about the terrible damage that moisture causes in libraries. It is also acceptable to suggest that extra precautions need to be taken and to nod wisely when the architects enumerate their brilliant and innovative solutions. The point of the discussion is simply to raise the issue to the level of a high priority.

A QUIET ENVIRONMENT

As HVAC and other building services equipment become ever more powerful, they also become louder. Some buildings even use diesel-powered generators to provide standby power backup for building services. Such generators can create noise in the 100-decibel range and cause excessive vibration and noise in adjacent spaces. Solutions to such acoustical problems are few, so look carefully at the location of your mechanical room and other spaces where service equipment will be running.

Designed-In Noise

The current practice to include atria and other spaces that are open from ground floor to roof in new library designs means that on each floor, stack and reading areas are separated only by balconies from the open space, thus allowing noise to be heard throughout the building. We librarians are extremely sensitive about the "shush" stereotype and may feel guilty enforcing quiet zones. However, we are finding that our users are not so reticent. "For heaven's sake, this is a library!" they complain. This has been quite a surprise for modern, liberated librarians who thought their "quiet" signs should go the way of the dinosaur and the dodo bird. You will be amazed at how traditional some of your younger users are in this regard, and you should include several quiet areas in your plans. Bear in mind that a quiet area means full-height walls, sound-baffling carpet, and the absence of loud mechanical noises.

Since the advent of systems furniture, the wall barriers that we traditionally relied on to decrease noise are no longer adequate. Modern management and learning theory encourage people to work together in groups. Therefore, increased sound absorption is needed at the ceiling. "Quiet zones" or separate rooms to provide quiet and privacy are another option. As you're investigating different manufacturers of systems furniture, be sure to check the barrier rating, or the amount of sound that can penetrate through the panel.

Rather than permanent walls, you may want to consider mountable partitions that are roughly equivalent acoustically to drywall. Nevertheless, these may not be appropriate for quiet areas, since sound can penetrate at the joints between panel and panel, between panel and ceiling, or between panel and wall. To keep out noise, consider having some spaces built with multiple layers of construction and insulation materials that include several insulating "sandwiches" of drywall, lumber, and fiberglass.

ENERGY EFFICIENCY AND OLDER BUILDINGS

You may be amazed to discover that the buildings with the poorest energy efficiency are actually those built between 1940 and 1975.[3] Surprisingly, really old buildings actually use less energy for heating and cooling than buildings of this "in-between" period. Therefore, buildings built before 1940 or after 1975 may require fewer weatherization improvements. Historic buildings were built at a time when craftsmanship was important, as was the desire to achieve maximum physical comfort by making the most efficient and effective use of natural heating, lighting, and ventilation. If you are confronted with the task of modernizing a historic building and have been agonizing over wiring and plumbing dilemmas, take comfort in the fact that there are some bright spots on your horizon.

Among the most obvious (and often ignored) energy savers are windows that open and close, providing natural ventilation and light. Your building may also include interior light/ventilation courts, rooftop ventilators, clerestories, or skylights bringing in fresh air and light and ensuring that energy-consuming mechanical devices are used only to supplement natural energy sources.

Historic buildings were constructed long before climate control became a buzzword. However, before making sweeping changes and installing massive HVAC equipment, consider that such structures may be naturally energy-efficient. Even though the windows in historic buildings usually have poor thermal properties, their number and size are limited, and the ratio of glass to wall is often less than 20 percent. In other words, the windows are just what is needed to provide adequate light and ventilation. Another energy-friendly characteristic of older buildings is their use of exterior shutters or exterior awnings to effectively control the amount of light and air entering the building.

In the South, exterior balconies, porches, wide roof overhangs, awnings, and mature shade trees are often part of the design of historic buildings. Their exterior walls are light-colored to reflect sunlight away from the building. In the North, heavy masonry walls, fewer windows, and the use of dark paint colors had the opposite effect. In recent years, engineers have come to realize that masonry walls can considerably improve thermal performance, and walls of large mass and weight possess high thermal inertia, known as the "M factor." Inertia can alter the thermal resistance or "R factor" of the wall, increasing the time it takes to absorb heat at its outside surface and transfer it to the interior. This is why many older buildings without air-conditioning feel cool when you enter them on a hot summer's day. It takes most of the day for the heat to penetrate the building, and by then it is evening, so the heat has plenty of time to dissipate during the night.

Simple Changes

Begin making your historic building more energy-efficient by initiating passive measures to permit existing systems to function as efficiently as possible. You may find that you need to make fewer major alterations than you thought necessary. For this purpose, however, you will need an architect who has a real appreciation for older buildings and not one who wants to rip everything out and start over. Preservation retrofitting is another course of action, which involves taking appropriate weatherization measures to improve thermal performance.

Preservation Retrofitting

Retrofitting older buildings must be done with care and sensitivity so that it does not jeopardize the historic character of the library. In general, limit your efforts to those that achieve the most energy savings at a reasonable cost, while at the same time altering the character of the building as little as possible. This is why these activities are usually referred to as "preservation retrofitting." Your architects should take special precautions that retrofitting measures do not contribute to the building's deterioration by trapping moisture. Depending on their location, old buildings usually contain large quantities of moisture in their interiors. In winter, moisture can condense on cold surfaces such as windows; it may also condense as it passes through walls and roof, creating potential problems. A common solution for making modern buildings more energy-efficient is to incorporate vapor barriers into interior and exterior walls. In older buildings, such thoughtless, ill-considered solutions can spell disaster.

Incompatible Materials

Another problem that frequently occurs in the course of retrofitting an older building is introducing materials that are chemically or physically incompatible with existing materials. For example, some cellulose insulating materials that use ammonium or aluminum sulfate as a fire retardant can react with moisture, forming sulfuric acid. This is an extremely powerful acid that can damage lumber and wiring as well as building stones, brick, and wood. One particularly distressing horror story concerns a building insulated with cellulose that collapsed when sulfuric acid weakened the metal framework.

Your architects or engineers should check to determine how your building was constructed, and what kind of insulation, if any, was used. They can determine what sort of retrofitting has been done in the past and whether it is the source of any problems.

Before your architects begin planning extensive new systems, be sure they have given full consideration to the smaller changes that can be remarkably effective in increasing the energy efficiency of historic buildings. The following are some basic concerns that can be addressed by preservation retrofitting. Not all of them may be appropriate for your building, but you may wish to use it as a checklist when you're talking with your architect.

storm windows and doors	replacement windows
attic insulation	duct and pipe insulation
vestibules with tightly fitting doors	wall insulation
	awnings and shading devices
basement and crawl space insulation	waterproof coatings for masonry

In addition, controlling air that infiltrates the building through loose windows, doors, and cracks in the outside shell of the building can be a very effective energy-saving measure. Consider weather stripping doors and windows as well as caulking open cracks and joints to reduce this infiltration. You don't, however, want to completely seal and prevent moisture migration in the building. Air infiltration is essential to prevent condensation problems. In addition, don't use too-colorful caulking and weather stripping materials that alter the look of the building. In general, air infiltration might be a good place to begin a retrofitting plan, since it is low in cost, requires little skill, and results in substantial benefits.

If it is necessary to replace existing HVAC equipment, ask your contractor to install any new equipment and ductwork in such a way that it can be easily removed and will not cause irreversible damage when it is installed, updated, or removed later. Weigh the merits of invisibility, which involves hiding piping and ductwork within wall and floor systems, against the damage that such installations may cause. Remember that the technologies involved in retrofitting and weatherization are quite recent. Little research has been done on the impact of new materials on old buildings, so caution should be a byword.

NOTES

1. American Society of Heating, Refrigerating, and Air-Conditioning Engineers, "ASHRAE Commissioning Guideline Helps Achieve Sustainable Design," www.ashrae.org/pressroom/detail/13522.
2. Michael Kernan, "Around the Mall and Beyond: Work of the Conservation Analytical Laboratory Research Group of the Smithsonian Institution," *Smithsonian Magazine,* March 1996, available at www.smithsonianmag.si.edu/smithsonian/issues96/mar96/around_mar96.html.
3. Baird M. Smith, "Preservation Briefs 3: Conserving Energy in Historic Buildings," http://ewingrestoration.com/Briefs/brief03.htm.

RESOURCE ORGANIZATIONS

American Council for an Energy-Efficient Economy
2140 Shattuck Ave., Ste. 202
Berkeley, CA 94704
(202) 429-0063

American National Standards Institute
430 Broadway
New York, NY 10018
(212) 642-4900
www.ansi.org

American Society for Testing and Materials
1916 Race St.
Philadelphia, PA 19103
(215) 299-5400
www.ia-usa.org/k0043.htm

Building Industry Consulting Services International
10500 University Center Dr., Ste. 100
Tampa, FL 33612-6415
(813) 979-1991
www.bicsi.org

Electronic Industry Association
2001 Pennsylvania Ave. NW
Washington, DC 20006
(202) 457-4900

E Source, Inc.
50 Walnut St.
Boulder, CO 80302-5140
www.esource.com

Federal Communications Commission
455 Twelfth St. SW
Washington, DC 20554
(202) 418-0190
E-mail: ccinfo@fcc.gov

Institute of Electrical and Electronic Engineers, Inc.
Operations Center
445 Hoes La.
Piscataway, NJ 08854-4141
(732) 981-0060
www.ieee.org

National Electrical Manufacturers Association
2101 L St.
Washington, DC 20037
(202) 457-8400
www.nema.org

National Fenestration Rating Council
1300 Spring St., Ste. 120
Silver Spring, MD 20910
(301) 589-6372

U.S. Architectural and Transportation Barriers Compliance Board
1331 F St. NW, #1000
Washington, DC 20004

Technology in Twenty-First-Century Buildings

If an early twentieth-century builder could be transported to the twenty-first century for a tour of a modern building, he (definitely "he" during that period) would be astonished at the changes that have taken place over the last 100 years. However, to the casual visitor, the majority of these changes are invisible. Modern technology has transformed practically every building system, and library buildings have been affected by technology even more than most structures. If you were to choose the most difficult part of planning your twenty-first-century library, it would probably be that of correctly forecasting technology needs.

The mention of the word *technology* probably brings to mind the vast expanses of computers found in many libraries. However, if you look a little closer, you'll discover that the entire library is run by computers, and these aren't necessarily the ones on staff and user desks. Computer chips can be found in the library's climate control, lighting, security, and other mechanical and electrical systems. At the time the first edition of this book was written, librarians had been coping with earlier generations of these computerized systems for some time, and many of the tips and tales I received were extremely critical.

The trouble was that the people who installed the high-tech building systems didn't really understand them. The absence of standardization and the likelihood that a new system would become obsolete within two or three years wreaked havoc on the library environment. Fortunately, we have come a long way, and high-tech equipment is far more stable than it once was. Nevertheless, technology has added a new level of complexity and sophistication to the job of selecting, installing, and adjusting new building systems, and local technicians and building professionals may lack the expertise to do the job correctly.

As you have gone about your work, you have been aided by a wealth of books and articles on library planning. You have been able to examine other libraries, picking and choosing the features you want to incorporate into your new library. Most important, you have been able to take advantage of a network of librarians who have already gone through the process and are usually delighted to share their experiences. No matter how helpful all these resources may be, no manual and no experienced individual can tell you exactly what technical requirements should be incorporated into a twenty-first-century library. By the time you read this book, some state-of-the-art solutions suggested here will undoubtedly be obsolete. All that library literature can do is point out general considerations. The rest is up to you.

INTELLIGENT BUILDINGS

Although there is really no standard definition of the term *intelligent building*, it is not difficult to describe one. In an intelligent building, for example, it is possible to integrate different electrical and mechanical building systems in such a way that they can be controlled centrally using a computer interface (web browser) and a shared computer network. It also becomes possible to communicate with these building systems, and they in turn can exchange information with one another. Intelligent management of building systems can maximize performance and increase the efficiency of lighting, HVAC, safety, power management, and security systems. Intelligent building technology can add long-term, sustainable value, decrease cost, increase the comfort of occupants, make systems equipment last longer, and reduce negative environmental impact. They can also cause you and your fellow building occupants a lot of grief if innovations are not approached with care.

Although some of these technological innovations are well tested and in widespread use, others are clearly bleeding edge and probably not appropriate for library buildings. Each group of library planners will have to decide how far they are prepared to go, considering the budget, library location, availability of high-tech expertise within their area, and the sophistication of the custodial staff. Naturally, the expertise of the building professionals involved in the project must be considered, and even the extent of local government involvement. Because intelligent buildings merge building design and management, designers must take into consideration the library's past experience dealing with maintenance issues and funding crises. The last thing any library wants is a meltdown that involves not one building system but all of them.

Most intelligent buildings have a shared cabling infrastructure that connects systems to a central controller, although wireless connectivity is increasingly common. Initially, the use of wireless to communicate with building systems was considered less reliable than cabling because it was more susceptible to interference. New mesh networking technology has to a large extent solved the problem. Mesh networks can automatically form their weblike structure, creating multiple redundant communication paths. Messages can be rerouted to avoid interference. By eliminating the need for wiring, installation becomes faster and cheaper.

Centralized Control

In a traditionally designed building, the HVAC system is controlled manually or from a computer console, while the lighting is handled separately with different controls. Even if the lighting is computerized, the computer program functions as if it were completely unaware of the existence of the HVAC or security system. Each has its own controls and probably a different method of cabling.

To create an intelligent building, almost everything—in other words, most electrical and mechanical building systems—becomes part of a common network infrastructure. Once systems are integrated onto one network that uses routers and switches, communications are converted to Internet Protocol by the centralized control system. You might call this a universal language that allows machines to talk to human beings and to one another. After translation, data such as sensor readings are delivered to the network and become accessible in a secure web browser.

Utah Valley University Library, Orem, Alspector Architecture, alspectorarchitecture.com. Photo: Paul Warchol.

To control all building systems from one user interface is no longer revolutionary, and operating your building via the Internet no longer requires a huge budget. Control of the system does not evaporate when new equipment is installed or staff members retire. Building systems can be monitored on the Internet twenty-four hours a day, seven days a week. They may be monitored from the library or from the facilities supervisor's home or even cell phone.

There are still many proprietary systems on the market, however, and it is important to specify that equipment purchased for your library be open protocol or open standards-based. Interoperability between building systems is essential, or it will be necessary to go through the manufacturer's service staff or a unique software gateway every time modifications are made to the system. Open standards also free the library to choose less expensive vendors and contractors, taking full advantage of competitive bidding. A common protocol allows contractors to work closely with one another and make more effective use of their time and expertise.

Advantages of Intelligent Buildings

Intelligent buildings have many advantages over traditionally designed ones. The following are some of the benefits that can be reaped.

Operating costs are lower because intelligent buildings are energy-efficient buildings. Since it is easy to monitor all building systems and fine-tune settings, operating costs are significantly lower. Systems can track energy use precisely, revealing where and when energy is being consumed.

The needs of building occupants can be addressed almost instantly. Conditions in different parts of the building can be monitored and controlled, making it possible for staff and customers to experience a comfortable climate and optimal lighting conditions anywhere at any time.

Computerized work orders can be easily integrated into the system so that problems can be solved and no time is wasted on paperwork.

Custodial staff needn't spend their time on many routine tasks like taking pressure readings or adjusting valves by hand. Adjustments are made from any computer with a few simple keystrokes.

Intelligent buildings are safer and more secure. In the event of a fire, alarms sound and other building systems begin to react: exhaust dampers open, the intercom system issues instructions to occupants, the access-control system unlocks doors for evacuation, and cameras provide emergency responders with a view of the fire.

In seismically active areas, an earthquake sensor or a signal from the national geological service can be connected with building systems. In the event of an earthquake, the building can automatically shut off gas lines, shut down computers, and notify occupants of the earthquake.

As mentioned above, careful measurement and monitoring of energy use made possible by intelligent building technology makes it feasible to reduce energy consumption. One example is daylight harvesting, which can coordinate a number of building systems to make the most efficient use of sunlight for heat and light. Consider carefully whether the building professionals on your team are up to the challenge of creating an intelligent building. They will need to work closely together, sharing responsibility for the design of electrical, mechanical, and structural systems. Architects must work with engineers, and it's best to involve contractors in planning from the start. When members of the team do not even know one another, when they work in isolation without consideration for the needs and opinions of the others, you have a recipe for failure.

PROMISING TECHNOLOGIES

Alternative technologies have come a long way since the first edition of this book. Unfortunately, they have not progressed as rapidly as many people hoped, but nevertheless, library planners can now explore a variety of tested technologies that both reduce dependence on fossil fuels and reduce operating expenses. Let's begin with the most popular one.

Solar Technologies

We've all become accustomed to seeing solar panels on rooftops, one example of an alternative technology. The field of photovoltaics has progressed from being a space-age novelty (for example, providing power to satellites) to being a cost-effective choice to help power public and commercial buildings. It's been incorporated into building codes and certifications; performance ratings are now available, making it possible to select systems with a degree of confidence that was never before possible. Photovoltaics is the field that deals with the conversion of sunlight into electricity through the use of solar cells. Photovoltaic production (solar cells and photovoltaic arrays) has been doubling every two years, making it one of the world's fastest-growing energy technologies.

Solar Cells

Perhaps the biggest difference between the solar technology of ten years ago and today's is the development of thin-film solar cells. Those heavy silicon panels we have become accustomed to seeing were expensive to produce, difficult to install, and often required roof modifications. The new thin-film cells are cheaper and much more flexible. Ultrathin sheets of flexible plastic are coated with a series of chemicals including indium, gallium, and diselenide that allow the film to turn sunlight into electricity. The term *thin* refers to these superthin layers of photoactive chemicals. Most of the barriers to producing thin film in large quantities with few defects have been overcome, and at this writing, the use of the technology is expanding at a rate of 45 percent a year. Producers of the older crystalline-silicon panels sell modules at a cost of approximately $3 to $4 a watt; newer thin film sells for approximately $2.40 a watt, and the price is steadily going down. In fact, in 2008 a company announced that it would begin selling thin-film panels at $1 a watt.

Flexibility and Adaptability

It has become possible to integrate the thin films with the roofing system, making them almost invisible; they may even look like skylights. Thin-film photovoltaics can be adhered to the flat part of raised-seam metal roofs without changing the roof profile. Although thin-film products are about half as efficient as larger silicon-crystal arrays, the cost per watt is about the same. It is in the area of thin-film development that the building industry believes there is the greatest potential for growth. Although film is more efficient when facing due south, newer products allow more freedom in placing them. Little efficiency is lost when either type of solar system is rotated toward the east or west. In addition, solar companies have become more experienced at working with builders and consumers. For example, some companies provide web-based monitoring of photovoltaic electric output, notifying consumers if problems arise. This means that solar systems can be integrated with other "intelligent" systems to produce greater energy efficiency.

Practical Considerations

At long last, government at all levels is supporting solar development. Utility companies may also provide incentive payments for solar system types and will often buy back photovoltaic electricity not consumed on-site. The use of solar power to heat water has been perhaps the most popular choice and has proven stable and reliable. This is a good first step, an opportunity for libraries to get their feet wet. However, it's important to talk with your building professionals about other solar applications and the possibility of controlling them centrally. The experience of many building owners indicates that although photovoltaic technology is initially more costly, it quickly pays for itself and ultimately saves many thousands of dollars over the life of the building.

Ground Source Heat Pumps

Ground source heat pump (GSHP) systems exchange heat from an underground source in either a heating or a cooling system. GSHP is one of the most efficient heating and cooling systems available today, with heating efficiencies 50–70 percent higher than other heating systems and cooling efficiencies 20–40 percent higher than air conditioners. It can be designed as a combination heating/cooling and hot water heating system.

Also called geo-exchange or earth-coupled, ground source heat pumps make use of the earth's ability to store heat in the ground or water. The term *geo-exchange* identifies them as ground source as opposed to air source heat pumps. GSHPs most often draw energy from shallow ground. Despite the commonly used name *geothermal*, the energy originates from the sun, not from the center of the earth. What you might call real geothermal energy is available only in places where volcanic activity comes close to the earth's surface. What makes GSHP technology work is the stability of underground temperatures. The shallow ground, in other words, the upper ten feet of the earth's surface, has a very stable temperature throughout the year: between 50 and 61 degrees Fahrenheit, depending on the location's annual climate. The shallow ground temperature is warmer than the air during the winter and cooler than the air in the summer. A geothermal heat pump uses that heat in the winter. In the summer, air temperature is warmer than the ground, so pipes carry the heat from the building back into the cooler ground, thereby cooling the building.

A Practical Alternative

The cost of most ground source systems is returned in energy savings in 5–10 years, although there are reports of systems recouping their cost in just three years. System life is estimated at 25 years for the inside components (depending on the specific equipment chosen) and 50 or more years for the ground loop. The GSHP contains fewer mechanical components and is very quiet, providing a pleasant environment. There are no noisy fan units to disturb library users. The buried pipe, or ground loop, is the most recent technical advance in heat pump technology. New heat pump designs and improved buried pipe materials have made GSHP systems the most efficient heating and cooling systems currently available.

There are two main types of GSHP systems: closed-loop systems and open systems. Variations in closed-loop systems are based on the configuration of the pipe, the type of antifreeze solution (if used), and how much heating or cooling is required. These systems rely on the contained circulation of fluids through an underground loop of pipes. The loop acts as a subsurface heat exchanger, which transports the heat to or from the ground. The loop of pipe is installed either vertically or horizontally. Traditional loop systems contain an antifreeze solution. Open systems vary according to the use and disposal of groundwater. They typically depend on the circulation of groundwater from a supply well to a discharge area. The source for heat, in other words, the groundwater, is moved from the ground to the heat pump in the building; then the water is disposed of by surface or subsurface methods.

Evaporative Cooling

Few cooling methods are as old as evaporative coolers. For example, in the desert Southwest, people have long used small swamp coolers that are both effective and inexpensive. Such direct cooling systems are typically roof-mounted and provide cooling as hot, dry outside air is blown through an evaporative medium that is kept moist. A modified spray-irrigation system can be used on the roof of a large building to drop daytime roof-surface temperatures from roughly 135–160 degrees to 85–90 degrees, reducing interior temperatures considerably.

Radiant Cooling

Night-sky radiant cooling is a recent and very innovative use of evaporative cooling. In climates with large temperature swings between day and night and generally clear nights, water can be sprayed onto a low-slope roof surface at night. The water is cooled through a combination of evaporation and radiation. Typically the water cools to 5–10 degrees below the night air temperature. The cooled water drains to a tank in the basement or circulates through tubing embedded in a concrete floor slab. In the daytime, water circulates from the tank.

Absorption Cooling

Although absorption cooling has been around since the nineteenth century, it is taking on new importance with our current struggle to lower energy use. Large, high-efficiency, double-effect absorption chillers using water as the refrigerant have been much more popular in Japan than in the United States, but the situation is changing rapidly. Absorption cooling is most frequently used to air-condition large commercial buildings.

You might call an absorption cooler a refrigerator that uses a heat source to drive the cooling system, or an air conditioner driven by natural gas, propane, solar-heated water, or geothermal-heated water. An absorption cooler changes the refrigerant gas back into a liquid using a method that needs only heat and has no moving parts. Because absorption coolers can also make use of renewable energy like solar, they are especially attractive.

In all large absorption systems, cooling is distributed by chilled water. The actual refrigerant is water at very low pressure. An absorber, usually the salt lithium bromide, is used to move water vapor through the system. Absorption chillers can be teamed with electric chillers in "hybrid" central plants to provide cooling at the lowest energy costs. In that case, the absorption chillers are used during the summer to avoid high electric demand charges, and the electric chillers are used during the winter when they are more economical. Because absorption chillers can use waste heat, they can provide free cooling in certain situations.

Desiccant Dehumidification

Desiccant is a term for materials that attract and hold moisture. Desiccant air-conditioning systems dry air before allowing it to enter an air-conditioned space. Large amounts of fresh air are required in healthy buildings, so removing moisture has become increasingly important in many areas. Desiccant dehumidification systems are popular because of their ability to remove moisture from outdoor ventilation air while allowing conventional air-conditioning systems to simply control temperature. Desiccant dehumidification offers solutions for many current economic, environmental, and regulatory issues. For example, indoor air quality is improved through higher ventilation rates. Since dehumidification can sometimes use even more energy than actual cooling, these systems can have the potential to considerably reduce energy costs.

Desiccant dehumidification systems have the ability to recover energy from conditioned air that is normally exhausted from buildings. Greater comfort is achieved with dehumidified air, and desiccant systems may make it possible to take advantage of preferential gas cooling rates from utility companies. The systems offer the potential for significant energy savings (0.1 to 0.4 quads nationwide) and inhibit microbiological growth, mildew, and rot damage to building materials.

Painting Yourself into a Corner

Unless yours is an unusually affluent library, a certain number of the items on your wish list will not be funded. Some items may be funded, but delays and other mishaps may mean that you'll be without them for a year or more. Still other items, especially sophisticated, high-tech systems, will malfunction or will not work as anticipated. When some crucial library service or building function depends on one of these "no-shows," you may be in big trouble. Elsewhere in this book, we have discussed the need for windows that can be opened when the air-conditioning goes on the fritz and the thermostats that were removed because a computer program would take their place. However, there are a number of other ordinary, everyday, low-tech devices that some architects imagine have been made obsolete by technology. Don't believe it! For example, you certainly do need those old-fashioned outdoor water spigots. When that supersophisticated irrigation system somehow fails to put in an appearance, all that expensive new landscaping will crumble into dust if you can't get water to it.

TECHNOLOGY FOR CUSTOMERS AND STAFF

Superficially, most library buildings look somewhat alike. Most have lots of computers and lots of telephones. Television monitors are sometimes visible, as are fax machines, printers, and scanners. All this really tells you nothing. Two installations that look similar to the outsider can be worlds apart when it comes to functionality. However, if you were to identify and interview the technicians who take care of a building's electronic innards, a great many issues would come to light.

It would be well worth your effort to get to know some systems administrators in your area. The information you amass will provide an overview of typical library technology. Of course, technology is changing rapidly, but taking a clear, detailed snapshot of the present state of library technology can be extremely helpful. The following description might be applicable to a recently built library.

- Computers are located throughout the building, not just in the workrooms and OPAC corrals. They are linked with one another through a local area network (LAN or WLAN).

- Wireless or Wi-Fi technology has largely replaced the old cabled network infrastructure within the building. The network broadcasts radio waves that can be picked up by Wi-Fi receivers attached to computers throughout the building.

- Stations (components including computers and printers that can connect to the wireless network) are equipped with wireless network cards.

- Access points (normally routers) serve as base stations for the wireless network. They transmit and receive radio frequencies for wireless-enabled devices.

The wireless network is protected by the WPA (Wi-Fi Protected Access) or WPA2 wireless security specification rather than the older WEP security. Firewalls or separate virtual private networks isolate public computers from other network functions.

An Internet service provider has been selected to provide Internet access. The connection may be digital, cable, or wireless (broadband). The library's own network distributes it to all library computers.

Technology does not exist in a vacuum. In a modern, well-designed library, every element works in unison with every other element. Because technology is changing so rapidly and needs vary across libraries, it is not possible to dictate what should be included in a specific library. Instead, the best way to approach the subject is probably to analyze individual libraries and the configurations they chose. Some aspects of their plans might be applicable to your new library. Other solutions address the specific needs of the local environment.

Planning for a High-Tech Future

Although it may not be possible to anticipate tomorrow's technology, there are some steps you can take now to ensure that your library will be able to accommodate the needs of tomorrow's library users. For example, you should allow more space for ventilated server maintenance areas than you will need immediately. If there is any prediction you can make with certainty, it is that computers and other media will increase rapidly and will have ever-greater power requirements.

Bear in mind that with technology changing so rapidly, it is probable that there will be a long line of technicians reconfiguring your system, upgrading the electrical service, and otherwise accommodating new technical developments. It is, therefore, important to avoid designing a building in which technicians will have to drill holes in walls or knock down walls to get to the building's "innards." Although it is inevitable that technology will change rapidly, the pathways and spaces allocated to the technological infrastructure will remain for the life of the building and should be designed to support many generations of technological change. Above all, you don't want your building to be obsolete the day you open. Retrofitting is an extremely expensive procedure and one you certainly want to postpone as long as possible.

Wireless Networking

Wireless networks are gradually replacing wired LANs in most library environments. They eliminate the necessity to wire around obstacles and can save a considerable amount in cabling costs. Such networks use electromagnetic airwaves instead of hard-wired connectivity. Wireless and wired equipment can coexist in most situations, and wireless components can take the place of any segment of a network. Purchasing wireless equipment can be somewhat confusing, and there are a lot of issues to consider.

Signal Strength

First of all, you'll want to know more about your building's walls. Wireless signals are usually capable of passing through walls and other obstacles relatively easily. However, some walls are thicker and more solid than others, so they may block some of your wireless signals. Only interior walls need concern you. In fact, you'd prefer that people outside the library not have access to your network. Of course, you may have a patio area where customers bring their laptops to work and enjoy the pleasures of Mother Nature.

If your library has more than one floor, you will need to consider floor construction. Drywall, plywood, other kinds of wood including doors, and glass do not pose any difficulty, but brick, plaster, cement, metal, stone, and double-glazed glass may present a challenge. It really depends on how porous the building material is. If your walls are composed of these materials, your connection may have a shorter range or a slower speed. If this is the case, you will need to purchase equipment that will overcome these structural barriers.

Another potential problem can be interference with the wireless network's frequency range. Interference can slow down a network or even keep your connection from working at all. A common source of wireless network interference is wireless telephones. The most common wireless network frequency, 2.4 Ghz, is also a popular wireless phone frequency, although you can find phones that operate on other frequencies. It is a good idea to work with a professional to identify the problems you are likely to encounter and the equipment you will need. This person may already be available to you as a member of your design team, or you may need to look elsewhere. If you will be installing a very large network, it will be worthwhile to bring in a consultant for the purpose. Consider the distances you need to cover and whether you have to go through stone or brick walls.

Practical Issues

Next you will need to decide how much you can spend. The more problems you identify, in other words, problems that will interfere with connectivity, the more difficult and inevitably the more expensive your network will be. Early in the planning process, begin reading expert reviews and discuss your readings with your consultant, electrical engineer, or other professional. One of the reasons why many consultants recommend Windows-based PCs is that it will be easier to implement your wireless network. Since Apple has a much smaller market share, vendors of software, firmware, and hardware tend to focus on Windows compatibility. However, if other factors lead you toward Mac, you will still be able to find quality hardware and software that meet your needs.

Network Configurations

Most wireless systems begin with a central "access point" transceiver (a term that combines the concept of a transmitter and a receiver), which communicates with both the network and with each workstation client. The transceiver is very much like a hub of an Ethernet network and communicates with a wireless adaptor or plug-in card in each network computer. Each adaptor comes equipped with an integrated antenna, and software converts data into radio signals and back to data again.

Protocols developed for the purpose minimize interference among transmissions and ensure reliable communications. Although wireless systems are somewhat slower than wired systems, the difference is not great; in most situations users are unaware of the difference. The distances over which the radio waves can travel vary with the particular situation, and as we mentioned, walls, metal, and even people can get in the way. A typical range for a WLAN is 500 feet in a normal library environment or 1,000 feet in open space. One access point usually provides approximately 50,000 to 250,000 square feet of coverage, depending on the library's design.

Some people occasionally ask whether it's safe to have all those microwaves passing back and forth. In actuality, the power output of wireless LANs is quite low and is typically only a fraction of that of a cellular phone. Since radio waves fade over distance, users experience very little exposure to radio frequency energy, and the energy emitted is called nonionizing, meaning that it does not damage cells if it is absorbed by the human body.

Public Computers

Whatever the specific components of your technology plan, the Internet should be a primary focus. In the last few years we have witnessed one resource after another becoming available on the Internet. OPACs are Internet-accessible, allowing users to dial in from home. Indexes and full-text journals are also available, as are cataloging and acquisitions utilities. These developments simplify your planning in some respects, but they also make greater technical demands on a library. The description of a modern library provided in the previous section is only the beginning. Libraries have unique requirements when it comes to meeting the information needs of their users. Here, for example, is a description of a sophisticated library emphasizing its broad access to information resources on the Internet:

> Technology is designed to support and facilitate both casual information seeking and the research process.
>
> Desks and carrels are equipped with desktop computers or with power outlets to accommodate laptop computers.
>
> All library-owned and personal laptop computers can connect to the Internet from any area in the library.
>
> The network offers a variety of information resources, including local and regional materials, productivity software, graphics, and statistical software packages.
>
> Scanners, fax machines, laser printers, and other hardware serve the needs of library users and staff.
>
> From a single library-designed web browser menu, users can connect to a wealth of networked utilities.

Wireless technology facilitates the digital transmission of data, graphics, audio, and video resources, and the library provides whatever peripheral equipment (like headphones or graphic tablets) is needed to make effective use of this digital delivery system.

In academic libraries, the library is an extension of the campus information network and ably supports electronic scholarship. Information technology is a natural, fully integrated part of the public library environment.

In public libraries, the library is an extension of local government and other community services, offering residents the opportunity to be fully informed of local resources.

Comfortable furniture encourages users to spend extended periods of time studying, researching, and writing.

Carpeting incorporates antistatic properties that safeguard computers, and it also creates an aesthetically pleasing environment.

Sophisticated daylighting technology permits exterior vistas and natural daylight without interfering with the visibility of projected images or posing a hazard to paper resources.

HVAC systems offer zone control, providing comfort for human users and adequate cooling for heat-generating computer servers.

Noise is controlled with an appropriate level of comfort-inducing "white noise" to facilitate viewing, reading, and study.

Spacious instruction rooms are equipped with up-to-date equipment to teach groups how to use online resources safely and effectively.

Collaborative or teaching spaces are wired to accommodate multiple workstations with access to the library network. High-quality, easy-to-operate projection equipment is mounted to the ceiling with controls adjacent to the team leader's workstation.

Contracts with database suppliers permit enough simultaneous connections to accommodate large numbers of users.

One or more firewalls separate public and library functions; protect against viruses; and routinely monitor, adjust, and redirect system traffic.

Hardware or software solutions prevent changes from being made to computer settings, or they return computers to their original condition at the end of each user's session.

The Learning or Information Commons

Most modern academic libraries have created technology spaces that offer especially sophisticated, high-end electronic resources and equipment. Usually called learning or information commons, they allow users, often working collaboratively, to produce sophisticated media programs, participate in videoconferences, use top-of-the-line modeling software, and otherwise take advantage of technological innovations usually found only within corporate communities.

Many public libraries have created similar spaces, although they go by a variety of names.

The information commons is an excellent place to make available high-end software that might be too costly for purchase by academic departments. However, libraries are nearly all underfunded and cannot afford bleeding-edge technology. No matter how attractive a new technology might be, we must let the for-profit world with its deep pockets take most of the risk. In visiting different information commons, I found elaborate installations with equipment that was once state of the art. Whatever the reason for its purchase, the workstations were rarely used.

When designing the information commons, it is essential to consult with faculty, especially those in science and technology. Public libraries should consult with community groups and technology enthusiasts. However, these individuals must not view the library as Santa Claus, and planners have a responsibility to be on the lookout for requests that look more like letters to Santa than reasonable recommendations. As I write, I am thinking of one technician who caused no end of trouble to his library. He alternately expounded on the wonders of state-of-the-art equipment and the frustrations he had to endure with stupid library users. The library director never understood why the technician thought the library should purchase cutting-edge technology when he obviously considered library users incapable of using it.

Planning for Broadband Capacity

Most libraries are finding that both their staffs and their customers are plunging ahead, discovering new applications and resources almost daily. Network infrastructures are hard-pressed to keep up. Services include licensed databases, audio content like podcasts and audiobooks, digital reference, homework resources, e-books, and enhanced integrated library systems (ILSs). Public libraries are succeeding in luring large numbers of teens by providing gaming activities, but they often find themselves unprepared for the heavy volume of network traffic. The Internet 2.0 environment is also using more of the library's bandwidth.

You've probably been hearing the term *broadband* often, whether at library conferences or in the media, but what exactly does it mean? Broadband might simply be defined as a signaling method that can handle a relatively wide range or band of radio frequencies. The Federal Communications Commission has adopted a five-tiered definition of broadband that is rather technical but important when it comes to providing the communications capacity your new library will need. The five tiers are

Less than 768 Kbps ("first generation data")

768 Kbps to 1.5 Mbps ("basic broadband")

1.5 Mbps to 3 Mbps

3 Mbps to 6 Mbps

6 Mbps and above

These measurements are performed in both directions, in other words, upload and download, since the online world has become so much more interactive. This definition is based on residential access to the Internet and is not always the most useful tool for public buildings like libraries.

Many factors can affect a library's bandwidth, especially network architecture. This includes routers, video memory, hubs, workstations, and RAM memory. Network load also affects speed and capacity. Congestion points slow the system down. They can result from a variety of different staff and public computing functions, including streaming, Voice over Internet Protocol (VoIP), and the library's ILS trying to transmit information simultaneously.

Heavy Traffic

When determining the bandwidth capacity you will need, it is critical to accurately analyze the network load. What services and resources would you like to make available to your users and staff? Carefully review your current networked services and then consider how you'd like to expand them in the new library. Also consider different technical innovations on the horizon and how they might impact network load. A technology consultant or an engineer on your project team can help you translate the usage you identify into an estimate of your bandwidth needs. You might also request help from your telecommunications provider, your ILS vendor, your library consortium, or your city or county telecommunications staff.

It's a good idea to give some thought to what comes first. What are your highest priorities? When might an interruption in a service like the ILS or

Marshall (Mich.) Public Schools, Marshall High School Library Media Center, Kingscott Associates Inc., kingscott.com. Photo: Kingscott Associates Inc.

e-mail make it difficult or impossible for the library to function? Depending on your library's philosophy and policies, user access to social networking sites might occupy a lower priority. Consider all your network services in order to establish priorities. Again, you will need a technology professional to translate these conclusions into technical terms like port number and protocols. The idea is to determine what comes first. What network traffic gets a green light, and what must wait its turn?

If you are depending on your network for telephone service (VoIP), you will need to assign it a high priority to ensure an acceptable level of service. If it takes too long for data packets to travel back and forth in a two-way transmission, the delay could result in an unacceptable level of service. Services like VoIP automatically require a high priority. Backups and software updates must also have a high priority, although they can usually run during off-library hours.

Typical Library Usage

It is extremely difficult to correctly estimate the amount of bandwidth needed for each library service, but it is possible to follow some general guidelines. Every library makes extensive use of e-mail, for example, and the average size of an e-mail is 2 to 5 kb. It is not impossible to estimate the number of e-mail messages that library staff and users will send in an hour or a day or even a month. If VoIP is used extensively for the library's telephone needs, you can estimate that the average VoIP call with compression is roughly 30 kb. Broadband use, however, varies considerably with the library's busy and slow periods, and thoughtful scheduling can considerably reduce network congestion. Libraries can even make arrangements with their telecommunications providers for increased bandwidth during peak usage periods.

Computers for Staff

When choosing hardware for staff workstations, perhaps the most important consideration is compatibility with the computers in the rest of the library. Here, however, are a few additional guidelines to use when making your selections:

Consider choosing PCs unless your environment (like an art school) is dominated by Macs. Software and technical assistance are usually more widely available for PCs.

Avoid dumb terminals or nonstandard computers. A PC is more flexible, and replacement parts are more readily available.

In your RFPs, specify that computers should come with Microsoft Office and other desired software preloaded.

Network all staff computers.

Purchase as much RAM memory as you can afford, since multitasking saves time and adds functionality.

Select software that supports the full American Library Association character set for display, input/update, and printing.

Steering Clear of "Bleeding-Edge" Technology

If you are a frequent reader of computer magazines, you have already discovered that many pages are filled with enthusiastic descriptions of the next generation of computer technology. Usually some new and amazing breakthrough is described as the way of the future and the obvious direction in which technology will advance. However, if for some reason you should be leafing through last year's back issues, you would find similar articles describing innovations that in the short space of a year have had their brief moment of fame and then quickly become dinosaurs on the computer landscape.

No one, not even the most highly trained computer engineers, can predict the equipment that will become next year's standard. This means that you can't extend the useful life of your equipment by betting on technology that isn't here yet. If it's not fully developed and widely accepted, it's not for you.

If you've been around a while, you probably can count at least half a dozen trendy new technologies that turned out to be a waste of money. In the past, you could usually banish these disasters to the top shelf of the storage closet without any dire consequences. However, today's serious automation error can cost thousands or even hundreds of thousands of dollars and permanently affect your library's ability to function effectively. You will want to wait until the last possible moment to make computer decisions while keeping an eagle eye on technological developments. Nevertheless, your selections must be based on current, not future, technology. No library has the financial or human resources to take chances on "bleeding-edge" technology.

Also bear in mind that a recently introduced computer model selling for $2,000 today may cost roughly $1,500 in six months, $1,000 next year, and perhaps even $500–$600 a little further down the line. I met a librarian who is the ultimate bargain hunter. She always waits until she can buy off-the-shelf systems, including flat-screen monitors, at rock-bottom prices. She does her homework, consults back issues of computer magazines, and makes sure the model got great reviews. Then she buys a lot of equipment at one time to simplify maintenance. However, before she parts with any money, she first checks the TechSoup website (www.techsoup.org). TechSoup Stock is an online product-donation service that connects both libraries and nonprofits with technology donations from more than twenty-five leading corporate and nonprofit technology partners. The program distributes donated and deeply discounted technology products to eligible nonprofits and public libraries, charging an administrative fee that is typically 4 to 20 percent of retail prices. Microsoft, Adobe, Symantec, Cisco, and Intuit software are all available. Although my library acquaintance cannot always find exactly what she wants, she has acquired a sizable portion of the software on her library network from this excellent source.

I asked if buying these slightly older computers didn't slow the network. She replied that these computers are new when they arrive in the library; they've never been used and they're functioning just as they were intended. However, library computers don't enjoy long lives. They get harder use than computers in almost any other environment. Her penny-pinching strategy allows her to replace library computers more frequently than if she paid double or triple the price. That means the network need not be slowed down by computers past their prime, machines that have taken a beating and accumulated damaged files, registry problems, and dozens of other annoying glitches.

RFID Systems in Libraries

One of the more controversial issues facing libraries is whether or not to implement library automation systems based on the use of radio frequency identification tags, or RFIDs, as they are usually called. Initially RFID technology was used for tracking shipments and ensuring that merchandise in transit reached its intended destination. Tags were attached to shipping containers, making it possible to locate shipments and reduce losses. For example, retail chains like Walmart, Target, and Albertsons required their suppliers to use radio tags on containers or pallets so that any given shipment could be tracked while it was in transit, when it reached a warehouse, and finally when it arrived at the retail store. RFID installations gradually expanded to include individual items of merchandise. However, they have been condemned by some privacy advocates because they have the potential to "keep track" not only of the materials to which they are affixed but also of the individuals who purchase them.

RFID technology found its way to the library market in the late 1990s and is currently in use in many libraries. The big difference between library use and most commercial applications, however, is that libraries use RFID at the item level, not at the container level. In other words, the tags are attached directly to books and other materials. When used in retail, RFID tags are affixed in such a way that they can be easily removed after items are purchased. Once they've been scanned by the right device, tags can also become "inert." Some can simply be torn off, either by the consumer or at point of sale.

The way in which libraries currently use RFIDs is called "asset tracking." In other words, a library software application keeps track of materials that are checked out and checked in. *Asset tagging and identification* is another term for these functions and includes library shelving and inventory control. In these applications RFID tags replace bar codes. Like a bar code, they are scanned or read again and again, so they must always be readable. They are not intended to be turned off or torn off. The concern over privacy arises, to some extent, from this difference. Although RFID tags are still too expensive for many retail applications, they are more cost-effective for libraries, since we circulate the same materials again and again.

How Tags Work

RFID tags are about one inch square and can be attached to books in much the same way as any paper label. The tags emit radio signals that can be interpreted by RFID readers as information about a book or other item. It is, therefore, possible to inventory a shelf in seconds or an entire stack range in just a few minutes. Checkout can be accomplished without even opening a book.

The tags in use in libraries consist of very small radio receivers, each with a microchip. The microchips usually store only a small amount of information, often a number similar to a bar code number, which is programmed into the chip just once. However, it is possible to store considerably more information in some chips, and newer "read-write" chips allow information to be added or deleted any number of times. More correctly called "transponders," current tags can hold as much as 1,024 bits, with greater capacity coming soon, so it would be possible to store more information if staff time and equipment were available. Since tags can be as small as a grain of rice or as large as two inches, RFIDs can be used on both books and smaller media items like CDs.

Most RFID tags, including those used in libraries, are what are called passive. In other words, they lack a power source and so are unable to transmit a signal. They depend for power on the radio signal sent by the reader. Active tags have their own miniature power source and can not only communicate with the tag reader but also, to a limited extent, function as tiny computers.

Privacy Issues

The original standard for RFID technology (ISO 15693) was developed specifically for use with containers and was intended for supply chain applications like keeping track of inventory in a warehouse. Privacy issues were not a consideration. The newer standard, ISO 18000, was designed for item-level tagging and addresses some privacy concerns. Library applications using the earlier ISO 15693 standards are still being sold by a few vendors and should be avoided. When choosing an RFID implementation, library planners should not assume that product designers have fully addressed privacy issues. Because the chief market for the technology is in retail where privacy issues are more easily dealt with, vendors may not be willing to expend the money needed to make the technology privacy-friendly in libraries. It is important to ask probing questions about standards and the ways that library applications differ from commercial ones.

The privacy issues posed by RFIDs can be divided into two broad issues: "tracking" and "hotlisting." *Tracking* refers to the ability of someone with a tag reader to track the movements not only of library materials but also of individuals carrying them. Tracking focuses not on the item but on the individual. In other words, RFIDs can make surveillance possible, even when the observer has no interest in the content of books and other library materials. As long as library customers are carrying tagged items, or keeping them in their cars, there may be a way in which their movements can be tracked. Multiple readings can be correlated to produce a clear picture of someone's comings and goings. *Hotlisting* is a term used for building a database of materials with their RFID tag numbers. Once the database has been created, it becomes theoretically possible to use unauthorized readers to find out exactly who is checking out which items.

Reading Chips

Tags communicate on different radio frequencies. Most library tags operate on a high frequency (13.56 MHz) and have a range from roughly 16 to 39 inches. However, in other applications like passport control, RFID chips can be read from

15 to 20 feet away. Currently, library tags contain data that remain unchanged until the item is removed from the collection. Like bar code labels, they may accidentally remain attached long after they are discarded, given away, or sold by the Friends of the Library.

Library planners should be aware that RFID applications can become an emotional issue for local residents who view it as yet another privacy invasion by "Big Brother." A national controversy has been brewing over the use of RFID chips in passports, passport cards, and enhanced driver's licenses. Americans now need one of these forms of identification to travel to Canada, Mexico, Bermuda, or the Caribbean. RFID readers will radio queries to the tags, which will in turn return data—in this case, an identification number that lets customs agents retrieve information from a government database. These data will include biographical information, photos, and the results of terrorist and criminal background checks.

Research findings concerning the security and privacy of the system are mixed, causing some public alarm. For example, a study of the RFID fare cards for the public-transit systems of Boston, London, and other cities found major security flaws. In the case of passports, chip readers that are commonly used for other purposes such as inventory control can be used as is or easily modified to read passport RFID chips. Although citizens might feel that the risks posed by RFID chips in passports are outweighed by the need to combat terrorism, they may not feel the same way about RFID technology deployed to facilitate library clerical tasks. In his article "Technology, Privacy, Confidentiality, and Security," Walt Crawford wrote: "If your library proceeds with a new technology that does affect privacy and confidentiality, and you haven't addressed those issues in advance, there's a good chance someone else will address them for you."[1]

Library Policy Statements

A number of library conferences have considered various aspects of RFID implementation. The American Library Association (ALA) has been especially active in seeking out answers, while numerous vendors have shown their wares at the ALA's annual and midwinter conferences. On June 27, 2006, the ALA's Intellectual Freedom Committee adopted a set of privacy and confidentiality guidelines for the use of RFIDs in libraries. The following are some of the more important points:

> Use the RFID selection and procurement process as an opportunity to educate library users about RFID technology. . . . A transparent selection process allows a library to publicize its reasons for wanting to implement an RFID system while listening to its users.

> Consider selecting an "opt-in" system that allows library users who wish to use or carry an RFID-enabled borrower card to do so while allowing others to choose an alternative method to borrow materials.

> Ensure that institutional privacy policies and practices addressing notice, access, use, disclosure, retention, enforcement, security, and disposal of records are reflected in the configuration of the RFID system.

Delete personally identifiable information (PII) collected by RFID systems, just as libraries take reasonable steps to remove PII from aggregated, summary data.

Notify the public about the library's use of RFID technology. Disclose any changes in the library's privacy policies that result from the adoption of an RFID system.

Assure that all library staff continue to receive training on privacy issues, especially regarding those issues that arise due to the implementation and use of RFID technology.

Librarians should continue their long-standing commitment to securing bibliographic and patron databases from unauthorized access and use. [They should] use the most secure connection possible for all communications with the Integrated Library Systems to prevent unauthorized monitoring and access to personally identifiable information.

Protect the data on RFID tags by the most secure means available, including encryption.

Limit the bibliographic information stored on a tag to a unique identifier for the item (e.g., bar code number, record number, etc.). Use the security bit on the tag if it is applicable to your implementation Block the public from searching the catalog by whatever unique identifier is used on RFID tags to avoid linking a specific item to information about its content.

Train staff not to release information about an item's unique identifier in response to blind or casual inquiries. Store no personally identifiable information on any RFID tag. Limit the information stored on RFID-enabled borrower cards to a unique identifier.[2]

HIGH-TECH SPACES

Although sophisticated electronic equipment is finding its way into every corner of the modern library, certain areas deserve special consideration. Technology-equipped classrooms, meeting rooms, and conference rooms are now standard in new libraries and have quite different requirements from the islands of individual workstations found in most other areas. Traditionally, library instruction has been integral to the mission of academic and school libraries; therefore, instruction spaces have been included in most library plans.

With the omnipresence of computers, however, all libraries, no matter what clientele they serve, need space to teach basic computer skills and database-searching techniques. Libraries have a special responsibility to serve the underserved, and this includes customers who lack the resources to maintain their own personal computers. We may imagine that everyone in our society possesses good computer skills, but this isn't necessarily the case. As the number of computers in libraries increases, so does the need for instruction in using these resources effectively and efficiently.

As you plan special spaces like "smart" or electronic classrooms, you will need to consider recent innovations such as satellite uplinks and microwave transmitters that allow librarians and users to bring together television, the Internet, and the full range of telecommunications technologies. Our users have come to expect these technological marvels, so they must be considered when designing information facilities.

Of special concern is the problem of noise in an electronic classroom. In a roomful of computers, the sound that we normally think of as unobtrusive "white noise" from a single computer can become almost deafening when multiplied by a factor of twenty-five or thirty. Make sure the architect has considered potential noise problems and investigated special acoustical wall materials.

Other Considerations

A related concern is heat, which also usually goes unnoticed with a single computer. However, the heat generated by a single computer is significant. When that heat is multiplied by the number of computers in the classroom, it can easily exceed the capability of most HVAC systems. Also, don't forget that teaching spaces have unique requirements for lighting, furniture, ergonomics, and power, and, of course, computer equipment. Of special concern when viewing a film or an Internet presentation are viewing angles, the distance of the viewer from the image, screen size, light level, workstation requirements, and classroom space configurations.

If possible, spaces should be designed so that they can be used as computer labs and can also accommodate seminars and meetings. Consider computer desks that allow monitors to be recessed below the surface with glass panels in the work surface so that equipment does not obscure sight lines with a speaker or instructor. Be careful, however, that furniture is not custom-built around the proportions of today's computer equipment, because the size and shape of computers has changed radically in just a very few years and probably will do so again in the future. Having two seating areas—one for computers and one for meetings—is another alternative. This makes it possible to see the speaker or the projection screen without having to peer between computers.

Both classrooms and meeting facilities have some requirements in common. For example, both need storage space for equipment, and both usually require projectors mounted in the ceiling with easy-to-reach controls located near the speaker or instructor. Both may also require flexibility that allows a gathering to break up into collaborative work or discussion groups. This might be achieved by the use of movable partitions. Furthermore, both will need some degree of soundproofing.

Conditions that are especially conducive to learning don't just happen, and many spaces intended for this purpose just don't work. Of course, budget constraints must be considered, but wall surfaces and finishes, mechanical equipment, media systems, projection booths, media equipment, and even the lecturer's workstation and lectern are points for discussion when planning such spaces.

Telecommunications and Teleconferencing

Although a number of librarians quoted in this book think they might have been happier with less high-tech ingenuity in some of their building systems, telecommunications is the one area where they almost universally wish they had more. Extensive telecommunications facilities are essential, and many newer libraries provide distance education classrooms and teleconferencing centers. In fact, most libraries should be equipped to provide expanded voice, data, and video services throughout the building.

Changes in the telecommunications arena are affecting libraries even more than most other organizations, and keeping up with them can be an overwhelming task. For the librarian involved in a building project, telecommunications pose some unique problems. Whereas you can assume that your HVAC system is not unlike thousands of others, and both your architect and contractor can be expected to have a firm grasp on other essential information, this is not necessarily the case with telecommunications. Depending on your location and the particular firms involved in your building, it is entirely possible that your building professionals have never worked on a project as sophisticated as yours. They may need your help.

In contrast to your role in selecting heating/cooling equipment, which may be confined simply to an occasional reality check, the buck really stops with you when it comes to telecommunications. To at least some extent, it's up to you to decide whether your building professionals are prepared for their task. Do they possess the expertise to design and construct the infrastructure that will support your computer network, telephone system, and multimedia information delivery system? Perhaps even more important, do they really believe the library needs this kind of sophisticated technology? Naturally, you cannot become an instant engineer, but it will be necessary for you to become more knowledgeable about this subject than about most other construction matters.

A Working Telecommunications Plan

Give consideration to the special needs of each area. For instance, consider equipping conference rooms for teleconferencing, and bear in mind the increased use of voice, video, and data communications for meetings. While you're planning the telephone system, remember that in-house or campus phones are an important security precaution. They should be readily accessible on all floors and in every wing of the library. Not only are they essential for communicating with security guards and other emergency personnel, but they can extend reference services to areas where no service desk is available.

All areas of the library should be designed to support multiple voice and data configurations. As emphasized before, never imagine that the way you plan to be using a space on opening day is the way it will be used in the years to come. Your library's needs will change—probably much sooner than you imagine. Communications outlets should be almost as numerous as electrical outlets. The following are some general guidelines for achieving a satisfactory level of connectivity:

Equip all offices with a minimum of two telephone outlets. They should be located on opposite walls and preferably near electrical outlets. Install multiple communication jacks (one per seventy-five square feet) in larger offices and suites. A good rule of thumb is to be sure you have no fewer than one telephone outlet at every other electrical outlet.

Provide a switch-activated power outlet at the front of rooms with projection and other multimedia equipment, as well as additional power outlets and video jacks in conference rooms, lounges, collaborative studies rooms, meeting rooms, and other areas where groups of staff or users gather.

Configure conference rooms for audio and/or video teleconferencing with acoustic material on the walls and additional power, data, and lighting controls.

Equip instruction rooms and meeting rooms with outlet boxes containing power, signal/control, and communication connections. The librarian providing instruction must be able to obtain, review, display, and distribute information in whatever medium is appropriate. Make it possible for librarians, instructors, and speakers to cue up all needed media, including TV monitor/receivers and DVD players, PCs, and even thirty-five-millimeter slides.

Assume that several pieces of equipment will be needed for the same presentation, and also bear in mind that we are going through a transitional period. Presenters will have different levels of technical expertise. Some may be accustomed to media formats that have largely been replaced.

Install communication jacks at fixed intervals around the wall (a minimum of one per wall) and linked to the speaker's location. Locate video drops or outlets so that the display and lighting system provides optimal viewing.

Provide enough public-address system speakers so announcements can be heard in every area of the library, but in such a way that users working near the speakers are not blasted with sound.

TIP

Be sure you have complete plans for any buried conduit. These plans tend to disappear shortly after the building is completed, and you don't want workers digging up your parking lots looking for buried cable.

Space for Telecommunications Equipment

If you have the luxury of planning a new building or addition, you will be able to include spaces created just for telecommunications equipment. If your building will be linked to others on your campus or within your governmental unit, you may need an inter-building distribution system consisting of the utility tunnel, conduit, manholes, and/or direct buried cable. You will not want to dig up the same area every few years to add conduit, so every effort should be made to plan for future construction sites. Manholes or utility vaults should allow the conduit to enter the building with no more than two 90-degree bends.

If you are renovating a building, it is wise to make the sacrifice and allocate adequate spaces for equipment and pathways even if you must borrow from other library functions. In many existing buildings, you will find telecommunications equipment jammed into janitors' closets and other spaces that are not suitable for housing sensitive electronic components. Such environments can cause equipment failure and can limit access to the services users need, as well as endanger the people who must maintain the equipment.

The spaces you need for telecommunications equipment include facilities to bring cable into the building and to house specialized equipment. Ideally, larger libraries will include a service entrance, a central equipment room, and distribution closets.

Video Teleconferencing Facility

Although it is not an absolute necessity, most public and academic libraries should probably consider creating a conference room or classroom where groups of individuals separated by distance can meet with one another. There are probably many groups in your community that need to communicate but for whom a face-to-face meeting would be difficult. For example, a group of citizens want to meet with their state government representative, or the chapters of a service organization located in different towns need to get together to plan an event. Of course, distance learning is extremely popular in higher education, but there are really no limits to the different uses to which a teleconferencing facility can be put.

Audio facilities have been available for many years, but video teleconferencing has tended to be limited to larger institutions with professional technicians in attendance. However, plummeting equipment costs and standardized equipment have made video teleconferencing an option for even modest libraries, courthouses, and branch business enterprises like banks. Now may be the time to consider a video teleconferencing facility to meet a variety of community needs. For example, smaller businesses in your service area may need help getting started or assistance in dealing with an especially difficult problem. Your video teleconferencing equipment can put them in touch with a wide variety of services offered by the Small Business Administration. Their staffs can meet with colleagues from other businesses that have gone through similar growing pains. Since hospitals and many medical clinics may have a teleconferencing facility, your customers may also be able to consult with a distant specialist when a face-to-face consultation might require overnight travel. Finally, library organizations can meet without the inconvenience and library disruption that might otherwise result. Branch library staff members can meet with the central library staff, and harried library directors can be in two places at once. Of course, to be effective, there must be another teleconferencing facility at the other end of the line. In the last few years, however, equipment costs have declined, and most people can usually find some facility to which they have access.

The main benefit of teleconferencing is that a group of people can hear the same information at the same time. Of course, this is possible with a conference telephone call, but much more information is communicated when people can see one another. Groups that share a concern can meet without having to be in the same physical location, so participants save time and fuel costs. It often means that people can participate in a discussion when their opinions and solutions would otherwise have been left out.

How It Works

Equipment specifications are, of course, changing rapidly, but basically video teleconferencing involves the compression of digital audio and video streams of real-time data. This compression depends on what is called a codec, a name which stands for coder/decoder. These data are broken up into binary components (1s and 0s), which are sent across networks in the form of packets and decoded at the other end. Your facility will need video input, such as a video camera or webcam. Video output requires a television, projector, or computer monitor. Microphones supply the audio input and speakers produce output. Data depend on your telephone network or the Internet. Since videoconferencing is becoming so popular, you will be able to choose between a wide range of systems. If you choose a dedicated system, you will need a console containing all of the required necessities for teleconferencing, including a control computer, an electrical interface, software, and sometimes additional hardware. Portable systems may have all-in-one fixed cameras, microphones, and speakers.

However, libraries often choose a desktop system in which various components are added to a personal computer. You can then choose from a wide range of cameras and microphones. Unfortunately, despite improvements, technical failures do happen. The joint Rotary meeting may end unexpectedly when the picture disappears or the audio becomes garbled, but such crises are no longer frequent.

Many companies are getting into the act and offer web teleconferencing services. In fact, it is sometimes very difficult to understand exactly what the vendors provide and whether their services actually meet your needs. It's a good idea to contact other libraries or businesses that you know to be experienced teleconferencers. ACT Teleconferencing is a web-based teleconferencing firm that provides the ability to send spreadsheets or other files, provide audio and video content, and apply various levels of security to the conference. The Conference Depot emphasizes a variety of assistance to businesses. Meeting One is yet another company providing services, but your choice should probably be based on talks with happy customers in your area.

OTHER KEY TECHNICAL AREAS

As the name implies, a service entrance is a room in which outside cable connects to the building's internal telecommunications backbone. The entrance must provide sufficient space and structural elements to support the installation of a variety of cables and devices. Typical fittings include splice containers, cable termination mountings, and electrical protectors. The service entrance should be located on the lowest level of the library and within fifty feet of an outside wall. It should allow direct access to the entrance conduit, the point at which feeder conduits enter the building. The service entrance should also be close to the equipment room. Service personnel should be able to enter the room directly from a central hallway, not through another room.

Central Equipment Room

Although architects and contractors use a variety of terms to designate this area, a space should be reserved for the telecommunications equipment room. It should be a central space used to house equipment that may serve devices throughout the building. Examples of equipment include video distribution equipment, Centrex or PBX switching nodes, local area network hubs, and network routers.

The room should preferably be located near the service entrance. It should be designed with future expansion in mind. Like the service entrance, the equipment room should not be subject to flooding or other hazards. It should be away from electrical power supply transformers, motors, generators, elevator equipment, and other sources of electrical interference.

A fully functional air-handling system is essential for controlling temperature and humidity affecting the sensitive electronic components housed here. These components generate an amazing amount of heat all day every day, and they can suffer extensive damage if not kept at a constant cool temperature. Although some library systems are shut down for periods of time—during the night, on weekends, or during break periods in the case of academic libraries— it is essential that the air-handling system for your equipment room provide positive airflow and cooling even during these downtimes. This may mean the installation of a small stand-alone cooling system designed just for this purpose. To ensure uninterrupted cooling, the unit should be connected to the building's backup power generation system. Ideally, the normal operating temperature should be between 64 and 75 degrees or normal room temperature.

Telecommunications equipment is much smaller than in the past and will probably continue to shrink. For this reason, it is hard to state with authority exactly how large your equipment spaces should be. Talk with the electrical engineer assigned to your project, and you might even wish to contact the systems administrator in a recently built library. Always remember that you are part of a wonderful fellowship of librarians, and both they and their staffs are accustomed to sharing information.

Be sure that your equipment storage room has adequate ceiling space to accommodate water pipes and air-conditioning ducts. Do not use false ceilings, and to protect the room from flooding, do not position drainage pipes directly over the room. Any accidental leaking should be directed around or outside the room. Nevertheless, make sure a floor drain is installed in the middle of the floor as a fail-safe backup measure.

Like the service entrance, walls should be covered with ¾-inch A-C plywood and painted with fire-retardant paint. To protect the room from fire, install a fire sprinkler system and link it to the equipment electrical panel so that power can be disconnected automatically if the sprinkler system is activated.

Distribution Closets

Once again, terminology may differ, and some architects and contractors still refer to distribution closets as telephone closets. Distribution rooms or closets, however, are spaces that support the cabling and equipment necessary to transmit data. As the name implies, they are small spaces, usually about five by eight feet in size. You will need at least one distribution closet on each floor. They should be stacked one above the other and centrally located within the building so that the distance from the room to the most distant user locations is roughly the same.

ELECTRICAL SERVICE

A building's basic electrical system consists of transformers, generators, circuit breakers, wiring, outlets, and transfer switches. Other components of the system may be transient voltage surge suppressors, power factor correctors, and power-conditioning equipment. Because your building will be brimful of computers and other electronic equipment, it presents special challenges to electrical contractors. With the advent of new systems furniture with partitions that can be reconfigured over and over again, permanent walls are even less in evidence than in the past. Therefore, you cannot limit the installation of electrical outlets to walls alone. One solution is a grid of recessed electrical floor outlets underneath carpet, which can provide power almost anywhere in the building.

"Clean" Power

Harmonic currents or distorted electrical waves (electrical interference) generated by large electrical equipment like HVAC blowers and chillers can cause transformers and wiring to heat and burn. They can also cause computers that have "switch-mode" power supplies to fail. Since computers are an important part of a library, a distinction must be made between clean and dirty power. PCs need power that is clean enough to do away with the little disturbances that affect distributed computer equipment. Dirty power creates many such disturbances, even though it may be perfectly adequate for most of the library's electrical needs.

It is important that power-conditioning equipment be installed to ensure clean power to operate computers throughout your building. Proper grounding is also important, since grounds can return electrical noise to its source. Grounding also provides a zero-voltage reference to safeguard sensitive equipment. This is important because just a few volts of electrical noise can interfere with computers' low-voltage logic signals. Computer equipment not only needs special treatment, but it also creates problems for other equipment by generating its own electrical "noise." This means that you must pay special attention to segregating it with grounding and double-sized neutral wires so that the noises don't affect the entire system.

Choosing an Electrical Contractor

Again, you may not have a lot of influence when it comes to selecting an electrical contractor for your project, but this is an area of specialization that is not understood by many people. Because the government agencies that award contracts know little about libraries, they may have no idea of the kind of expertise that will be required. The kinds of skills needed to wire a typical home are very different from those needed for a sophisticated library. Be sure that your electrical contractor is experienced with large-scale projects. This is not the place to cut corners and hire the low bidder who lacks experience with a variety of sophisticated, high-tech buildings having heavy power and data requirements. Although discussions with an electrical contractor may resemble a conversation in a foreign language, the responses (as best as you can interpret them) will give you some idea of whether your electrical contractor knows the business.

You might ask the contractor, for example, whether cables will be placed together in wire trays. This is a bad practice; a separate conduit should be used for each circuit. Another important issue is whether an experienced electrical testing firm will inspect the electrical system, test circuit breakers, and use thermal-scan equipment to find "hot spots" due to bad connections or faulty equipment. These inspections are in addition to the ones required by your local government authority and are usually at the discretion of the electrical contractor. Once again, this is a pretty reliable indicator of whether you're dealing with a real professional, because the inspection is a vitally important precaution. Electrical wiring has changed drastically in recent years, and you want to be sure that your electrical contractor has been keeping up with all the new ways of delivering power.

In this chapter we've attempted to cover a variety of technical issues about which you will need some knowledge. However, as you've probably noticed, practically every chapter includes some discussion of technology. Increasingly, every aspect of library planning is integrally linked to modern technology. In the next chapter, we'll be discussing security, and once again technology will be front and center. As librarians, our challenge is to find ways to adapt a wide variety of different technological innovations to the needs of our customers. Unless technology works for them, it doesn't work at all.

NOTES

1. Walt Crawford, "Technology, Privacy, Confidentiality, and Security," *Library Technology Reports* 41, no. 2 (March–April 2005): 24.
2. American Library Association, RFID in Libraries: Privacy and Confidentiality Guidelines, www.ala.org/Template.cfm?Section=otherpolicies&Template=/ContentManagement/ContentDisplay.cfm&ContentID=130851.

RFID RESOURCES

American Library Association. "Resolution on Radio Frequency Identification (RFID) Technology and Privacy Principles." www.ala.org/ala/aboutala/offices/oif/statementspols/ifresolutions/rfidresolution.cfm.

Ayre, Lori Bowen. "Position Paper: RFID and Libraries." The Galecia Group. August 19, 2004. www.galecia.com/included/docs/position_rfid_permission.pdf.

Boss, Richard W. "RFID Technology for Libraries." Public Library Association (PLA) Tech Notes. www.ala.org/ala/mgrps/divs/pla/plapublications/platechnotes/ rfidtechnology.cfm.

Dvorak, John C. "RFID: Tagged, You're It!" PCMAG.com. www.pcmag.com/print_ article2/0,1217,a=154915,00.asp.

Eden, John M. "When Big Brother Privatizes: Commercial Surveillance, the Privacy Act of 1974, and the Future of RFID." *Duke Law and Technology Review* 20 (2005). www.law.duke.edu/journals/dltr/articles/2005dltr0020.html.

Electronic Frontier Foundation. "Privacy Risks of Radio Frequency Identification 'Tagging' of Library Books: Comments to the San Francisco Library Commission." October 1, 2003. www.eff.org/Privacy/Surveillance/RFID/20031002_sfpl_ comments.php.

Garfinkel, Simon L. "RFID Privacy: An Overview of Problems and Proposed Solutions." *Security and Privacy* 3, no. 3 (May–June 2005): 34–43.

_____. "The Trouble with RFID." *The Nation.* February 3, 2004. www.thenation.com/ doc/20040216/garfinkel.

Juels, A., D. Molnar, and D. Wagner. "Security and Privacy Issues in E-Passports." IEEE SecureComm. 2005. www.cs.berkeley.edu/~dmolnar/papers/papers.html.

Kobelev, Oleg. "Big Brother on a Tiny Chip: Ushering in the Age of Global Surveillance through the Use of Radio Frequency Identification Technology and the Need for Legislative Response." *North Carolina Journal of Law and Technology* 6, no. 2 (Spring 2005): 325–42. http://jolt.unc.edu/abstracts/volume-6/ncjltech/p325.

Molnar, David, and David Wagner. "Privacy and Security in Library RFID Issues, Practices and Architectures." CCS'04. October 25–29, 2004. Washington, DC. www.cs.berkeley.edu/~dmolnar/library.pdf.

"The ROI of Privacy Invasion." RFID Connections. January 2004. www.aimglobal.org/ technologies/rfid/resources/articles/jan04/0401-roispy.htm.

Schneider, Karen G. "RFID and Libraries: Both Sides of the Chip." California Library Association Intellectual Freedom Committee. www.ala.org/ala/aboutala/offices/ oif/ifissues/rfidbothsideschip.pdf.

Zetter, Kim. "RFID: To Tag or Not to Tag." *Wired News.* August 9, 2005. http://www .wired.com/politics/security/news/2005/08/68271.

Security and Safety in Today's World

Library security is unfortunately becoming a major cause of concern among librarians. Although libraries are certainly not hotbeds of crime and violence, they do provide unique opportunities for the criminal elements of society. Therefore, the personal safety of our customers and staff must be an important consideration when planning a new building. Because libraries are among the most public of public buildings and are often the only buildings open during evening and weekend hours, they tend to attract people who have no place else to go. In itself, this is not a problem, but without careful planning, it can lead to some dangerous situations.

DANGER FROM MANY DIRECTIONS

Too often for comfort, we encounter a story of sensational library violence like the Columbine High School Library tragedy, the Sacramento Public Library staff members who were gunned down by a mentally deranged man, or the eighteen Salt Lake City patrons and staff members who were taken hostage by another disturbed person. Such dramatic events are rare, but lesser crimes have become uncomfortably frequent. Patrons often seek out remote nooks and crannies because they are well wsuited to reading and study, but such areas are extremely difficult to monitor. With small library staffs responsible for large areas, purse snatchers, book thieves, and exhibitionists may have what amounts to a golden opportunity.

Safety, however, is not simply a matter of protecting people and property from criminal activity. Mother Nature, in the form of tornadoes, hurricanes, or floods, can be even more destructive, and preparing for these and other natural disasters must be an integral part of your planning process. Depending on the terrain and the part of the country, your building professionals will evaluate these threats differently, but all should take seriously the possibility of fire. Whether the work of nature, arsonists, or careless patrons, fires are far more common than other major types of disasters. In addition, the building itself may contain materials that are hazardous to library staff and visitors. Chemicals like formaldehyde, an integral part of the manufacturing process, can cause serious illness if problems are not addressed.

DESIGNED-IN SECURITY

As discussed in previous chapters, the choice of the library's site can have a major impact on building security; so, too, can the basic design of the building. Think back to the old Carnegie libraries. With their central rotundas and clear sight lines into stack areas, they permitted good control of large areas. Of course, such monumental architecture does not appeal to today's customers, but you can arrange stacks and other furnishings in such a way that you don't create secret hideaways. Avoid creating poorly lit areas and make sure it is relatively easy to change lights throughout the building. (One librarian complained that the maintenance staff had not changed hard-to-get-at bulbs above a stairway since his library first opened.)

A Comprehensive Plan

As you plan for a secure environment, think about how staff will be stationed around the building. Try to position them in spots where they can see what's going on, but be careful that you don't isolate them. A lone office on the top floor can serve as a magnet for petty thieves or worse. Some areas may require surveillance cameras, but even highly visible "dummy" cameras can discourage potential troublemakers. While I was visiting libraries, interviewing librarians, and collecting information for my two books on the customer-driven library, I discovered that although most libraries are larger than they were a decade ago, the number of staff members actually working in public areas has shrunk.[1] This is due in part to shrinking staff size, but perhaps more important, it represents an attitude shift.

Traditional reference service required a number of staff members stationed at public service desks. Larger libraries often had several subject-oriented reference or other service desks as well as a central reference area. With the arrival of computers in libraries, there arose a belief that the public no longer needed reference assistance. What they need now is help with computers, and computers are usually clustered near one another. Increasingly, therefore, librarians and other staff members, though theoretically assigned to public services, spend much of their day in offices or cubicles. They may actually spend no more than two hours a day assisting the public.

Rethinking Staff Roles

Whatever the reasons, it became clear to me that there are many parts of the library so far from service desks that customers are entirely on their own. No staff member would be aware of a disturbance, none could hear a scream, children could be molested, and sneak thieves could go unnoticed. As you're planning the library, look at every area from both the customer and the miscreant's point of view. If you were a customer, would you feel safe there? How would you summon help? Would you be seen and heard if someone accosted you? Then think about what might make the area attractive to a thief or child molester. Is it possible to move staff members into unsupervised areas? Computers have largely eliminated the necessity for backroom workstations. Would you need much more than a small service desk equipped with a computer, telephone, lockable desk, and filing drawers to make staff members productive? If necessary, you might even add some glass-walled offices, but whatever choices you make, put customer needs first.

Security Equipment

It is well worth the effort to devote some time to learning about today's high-tech security systems, including security cameras, electronically accessed entryways, and motion detectors. Although these don't take the place of observant human beings, they can increase security in many areas. Nevertheless, some library buildings are a lot easier to secure than others because of inherent design features. Security must be a consideration from the very beginning of the planning process.

When making plans for building security or selecting surveillance equipment, be sure to involve your staff, at least a few customers, and the people who will be charged with protecting your facility. If you are building a college or university library, your campus security head would be a logical choice to include in the planning process. In a public library, you might ask your city or county police chief to appoint someone to work with you. These experts have an excellent idea of what works and what doesn't. Depending on the circumstances, they can save you a surprising amount of money on unnecessary high-tech equipment, while pointing out unsecured entryways or design features that are especially vulnerable to vandalism.

Components

Although your library probably can do without many of the bells and whistles that go into high-end surveillance systems, it's important to know something about the basic components. The function of what are usually called contacts and sensors is to detect something that is not right, in other words, some change from the norm, on the assumption that the change may herald the arrival of an intruder. The following are some examples:

Motion detectors. Common types of motion detectors include ultrasonic, microwave, photoelectric, and passive infrared detectors. Ultrasonic and microwave detectors are somewhat similar in that they transmit a signal (ultrasonic or microwave) and receive the reflected signal on its return trip. Movement causes an increase or decrease in the frequency of the signal, thus setting off an alarm. Microwave motion detectors are somewhat more effective than ultrasonic ones because they can penetrate most interior walls. Photoelectric motion detectors transmit beams of light. When the beam is interrupted and does not reach the receiver, an alarm is set off. They are extremely effective, but they do require a space where nothing blocks the line of sight between the transmitter and the receiver.

Passive infrared motion detectors. These differ from the sensors above in that they do not transmit energy; they detect it. Heat energy is given off by human bodies, and so movement of the heat source can trigger an alarm. Since these detectors don't send out a signal or beam, they are an extremely economical solution. In addition, there are a number of somewhat specialized detectors. For example, there are floor mats that, when placed under rugs, trigger an alarm when the weight of a human body causes a slight movement in the floor.

Vibration detectors. Any time an intruder attempts to enter a building through a window, vibrations are naturally set off. Vibration detectors trigger alarms when someone attempts to break the glass.

Audio discriminators. Sound such as breaking glass is another indicator that an intruder is on the premises. Also known as acoustical or sound detectors, these devices can be placed on window frames, walls, or ceilings. They are tuned to the specific frequencies associated with intrusions, and they trigger alarms when sounds of that frequency are detected. Unfortunately, they are prone to false alarms because a lot of innocent noises may have similar frequencies.

Glass breakage detectors. If yours is a library with a lot of windows, you may want to consider something that sends out an alarm when the glass is broken. Acrylic, polycarbonate sheets can serve this purpose, as well as wire glass. Vibration detectors and audio discriminators can also be used with glass.

Window and door contacts. When a door or window is opened, a magnet mounted on it causes a switch mounted on the frame to open, thus triggering an alarm. Different types of contacts can be chosen to deal with different situations. Since this is an inexpensive and highly effective technology, it is a good idea to install contacts on all doors and windows that are accessible to intruders.

Window screens. Special wire can be woven into window screens to trigger alarms if it is cut. This can be very convenient in that it allows windows to remain open after the security system is armed.

Sophisticated Systems Can't Do It All

Take a good look at your design team and the individual members charged with designing your building security. Modern computer-monitored systems are becoming so sophisticated and complicated that it really takes an expert to design an effective system. Consider whether the planners seem to understand the kind of security problems you're likely to have or they're just parroting the information provided by the equipment vendor. Security professionals will tell you that you can spend a lot of money and not achieve your security goals.

On the other hand, a less expensive system can achieve more effective surveillance. For example, no matter how expensive and elaborate the system, obvious entrance and exit routes are sometimes forgotten. Since you (and often your architects and contractors) have limited experience with crime, it may not dawn on anyone that the equipment storage room is accessible through the suspended ceiling from the room next door. Try to get all the free professional advice you possibly can, and if there isn't enough good free advice available, be prepared to pay a security consultant.

Practical Precautions

Plan on centralizing all financial transactions at one desk and invest in a safe (the kind with a slot so the staff members closing the library at night needn't know the combination). You will want to arrange to empty the safe daily and keep money at the desk to the minimum needed to carry out regular library functions, make change, and handle refunds. Most libraries need two safes. In addition to the one for everyday transactions, one should be fireproof and used to protect valuable objects. Both safes should be large enough and heavy enough to discourage theft.

TIP

Be careful of "nooks and crannies" for reading areas. When trying to clear out a library, these are great places for patrons to hide and can be especially dangerous for short-staffed libraries. In addition to these security precautions, carefully consider the placement of vending machines since these are often broken into. Also look into copy cards instead of coin-operated photocopiers, computer printing stations, and microfiche printers. Make sure, however, that these precautions don't inconvenience your customers and that weekend visitors don't encounter a library where card-dispensing machines are broken and no one can make change for the vending machines.

An Integrated Security Plan

As you develop a security plan for your new building, think in terms of a total system. Security involves personnel, facilities, communication, and electronic systems. Your objective is to make the thought of committing a crime as unattractive as possible. Potential wrongdoers are looking for opportunities in isolated locations where they can come and go freely and where a criminal act can be completed quickly and easily. To thwart their machinations, you will need to take a multipronged approach that includes all of the following.

Control Access

Fences and intrusion-detection systems can help control access to the library, but the building's layout can be even more important. Design the building in a way that restricts public access to staff and storage areas.

Enhance Visibility

Position staff workstations where staff can best see what's going on. Make good use of glass partitions. You will probably need to hire security guards, at least for certain hours, but you can reduce the need for security personnel simply by positioning staff workstations effectively. Windows can also inhibit theft, vandalism, and improper behavior. The idea is to make people believe they will be seen if they do something wrong. Outside the building, plan the landscaping to minimize hiding places and use exterior lighting to illuminate other places of concealment.

Increase the Probability of Detection

Delay can sometimes be as effective as prevention. Thieves and vandals don't want to be caught, and any delay increases the probability of their being discovered. If a criminal act looks like it will be difficult and time-consuming, it may not seem worth the effort. If such delaying hindrances do not dissuade the criminal entirely, they may at least provide time for security forces to arrive.

Remove the Appearance of Opportunities

Bear in mind that criminals do not always know what is worth stealing. They may cause considerable damage breaking into a cash register or vending machine that holds only a few dollars. Look at your building as an "outsider" might. Where might money or valuables be stored? You might find yourself protecting—or, to use the industry term, "hardening"—areas that in themselves don't really need protection to prevent expensive vandalism. Announce the presence of security measures with signs, highly visible locks, and other obvious security additions.

Consider Hiring a Consultant or Security Engineer

If funds are available in your budget, you might hire a security engineer to evaluate risks, assess terrain features, and select appropriate security hardware and equipment. Working with the engineer or other security professionals, set up an organized plan that identifies all the issues that must be considered. The plan should cover everything, including site selection, perimeter barriers, exterior lighting, facility layout, and access control.

Selecting Security Systems

As the new building takes up more and more of your time, it's easy to lose track of what is really happening in the library. You may find yourself comparing the features of various security systems with little thought to how they would really function in your unique library environment. The following are some basic considerations to keep firmly in mind when you're confronted with a supersalesman or a gaggle of security bells and whistles.

Ease of Use

While you're listening to the architect or vendor describe a space-age, super high-tech security systems, stop a moment and ask whether you and your employees will really be able to use it on a day-to-day basis. If the library staff will have a hard time figuring out how to use the system, they are very likely to disable it or find other ways of preventing it from doing its job. If the system gives false alarms repeatedly, you will grow angry. Your staff, who probably know less about the system than you do, will have even shorter fuses.

Obsolescence and Cost

Another important question to ask is how soon the system will become obsolete. How long has the vendor been selling this particular system? If it's too old, your system will be obsolete before your building is completed. If it's too new, you're taking a chance on a system that may not have all the quirks out of it. How stable is the vendor? Is the company likely to be around ten years from now? If so, will it be committed to maintaining your geriatric system? Security is one of those high-tech industries that is in a constant state of flux. However, the costs associated with purchasing, installing, and learning to use a new security system are great enough that you must be prepared to live with your system for a good many years. Consider the hidden costs of the system. For example, how much additional electrical capacity and extra wiring will be needed to accommodate the new system? How much will it cost? Remember to add this amount to the equipment, installation, and maintenance costs when comparing the costs of various systems.

Serviceability

Does the vendor you're considering rely on a third-party company to service its systems? If the answer is yes, which it often is, you will want to ask similar questions about that service company. Is service locally available, or will you have to pay expensive travel charges? Does the company promise service within a certain number of hours or days? When your system goes down, you will need help quickly. Now's the time to find out what you can expect.

Training

What kind of training does the vendor provide? If the library staff never fully master the system, you've wasted a lot of money. An hour's walk-through and a voluminous, incomprehensible manual do not constitute adequate training.

Simplicity

The more magnetic locks, security gates, card-accessed closets, motion detectors, vibration detectors, cameras, monitors, and other controls there are, the more confusing the system becomes. Don't allow yourself to get carried away. Just remember all those passwords you've forgotten, those keys you've misplaced, and the instruction manuals that have disappeared over the years. How much information can you reasonably expect to pass on as library staff members come and go?

Planning Doors and Locks

If most of the projects designed by your architects are office or classroom buildings, you may be surprised to find that the first round of drawings include far too many interior and exterior doors. It may take some time to convince them that you need only one public entrance, a loading dock, and the minimum number of emergency exits required by code. They may also be unaware that it's very easy to get into a library with its long hours and open access. Our problems are a little like those of grocery or computer store managers, who must take precautions against thieves getting away with merchandise.

Before your project is complete, you will have uttered dozens of oaths (minced and otherwise) at the multiplicity of doors and locks you must contend with. When you talked about library spaces, architects may have understood you to mean "rooms" complete with walls and doors. Since most library spaces will be available to customers when the library is open, there's little need for separate lockable rooms. However, that still leaves more doors and hence more locks than you really want to deal with. The number can run into the hundreds. In the case of each door, you must answer a complicated set of questions and make decisions about whether the lock is needed.

> Does the door in question require a lock? If the answer is yes, then on which side must you insert a key? Inside and outside are not always self-evident.

> Should the door lock automatically or remain unlocked until staff remember to relock it? Self-locking doors may be a sensible security measure or the bane of your busy staff's existence.

> Should you be able to lock the door without a key by punching in a button on the knob or latch? These are not usually appropriate for public areas where children can create pandemonium by locking themselves into restroom cubicles, broom closets, and study rooms.

> Should there be an alarm for the door? If so, should the alarm be turned off when the library is open, or will it require its own keypad to activate and deactivate?

> Does the hardware on the door comply with your local fire code? Will hardware like a barrier or panic bar deter thieves from running off with valuable equipment while still serving as an emergency exit in case of fire?

> How should stairwell exits and entrances be planned? Determining the best door hardware for stairwells can be particularly confusing. In case of fire, patrons should be able to enter any stairwell on any floor. However, the same stairwell that opens into a public stack area on one floor may lead into a rare book room, media storage space, or staff processing area at other levels. Therefore, you will want to safeguard these areas, possibly allowing the public to exit the stairwell only on certain floors.

> Will all your auxiliary locking devices like barrier bars, slide bolts, and padlocks violate fire codes? If such devices require that patrons have special skills or prior knowledge in order to exit, they could be trapped in the event of fire. One good solution to the problem is a dead bolt mechanism with a fifteen-second delay. Although that may not seem like much time, it does serve as an effective deterrent.

Do you want to use keys on all lockable doors? In some cases, a lost key will compromise security and require expensive rekeying. Increasingly, electronic access card readers are being installed wherever it's important to restrict access. Such systems may be a good choice, but they can be both expensive and temperamental. Here are some issues that should be considered before you rush to install card readers throughout the library: (1) type of door (single or double); (2) "tailgating" (what happens when someone without a card enters behind a cardholder); (3) ice that can keep the magnetic lock from functioning properly.

Although it's an exhausting process, the best way to secure the building effectively is probably to make a list of all the doors. Identify them from the floor plan and consider who will use them, whether they will protect anything of value, and whether they could allow an intruder to leave the building unobserved. You might want to develop a form to make the review process easier. Such a form could identify each door, possibly with a number that corresponds to a location on the blueprint. It should also indicate the rooms on each side of the door, when and why the door would be kept locked, and which side allows people to exit in case of fire. If the door should lock automatically, indicate this as well.

Staff Input

Involve your staff in a physical or virtual tour of the library, imagining each door (complete with hardware) through which they pass. Ask them to pretend that they're burglars attempting to escape with a laptop computer, or staff members carrying a precarious load of books from one area of the library to another. It's a good idea to involve your staff in your lock-and-key quandaries from the very beginning, since several heads are better than one. However, you will probably want to consult with a locksmith long before any firm decisions must be made. Give yourself time to change your mind frequently before placing hardware orders. It is all but inevitable that you will make some mistakes, but preplanning will keep them to a minimum and prevent a full-blown nightmare on opening day.

FIRE SAFETY

Planning for fire safety is not just a simple matter of requesting sufficient sprinklers and fire extinguishers. Fire safety requires an integrated approach to protection, and these preventive measures must be orchestrated in such a way that they permit the detection of and rapid response to fires that may break out anywhere on the premises. Every building system is involved. For example, the telecommunications system should provide for direct fire department notification, and the HVAC system should be programmed to shut down some operations and start up others. It is essential that a fire be detected at the earliest possible stage and that library staff members be alerted immediately, enabling them to evacuate the building without injury or loss of life.

Sprinkler Systems

If you have been a librarian for any length of time, you're probably aware of the arguments that have raged over the years about the best method of protecting the library from fire. To sprinkle or not to sprinkle became the big question. Libraries and archives have experimented with almost every new system available, usually with mixed results. For example, fire-retardant gases were in vogue for a number of years, and gas-flooding systems may still be the best choice in certain situations. However, many gases are harmful to the environment, depleting ozone levels and contributing to global warming. Some gases produce thermal decomposition products that are corrosive or toxic. They may even cause certain cardiac reactions if used in sufficient concentrations to extinguish a fire. Since fire-retardant gases are also expensive and the ongoing costs can be high (especially when false alarms cause discharges), they are no longer a frequent choice for library installations.

Early water sprinkler systems doused large areas when staff members burned their toast and set off smoke alarms. The technological improvements of recent years have finally provided a fairly satisfactory product. However, librarians, by this point, have become gun-shy, and architects may have a very limited understanding of library needs. Though the thought of introducing water into a library is the stuff of nightmares, modern automatic sprinklers are probably the most important component of a good fire management system. Such systems are not without problems. Librarians still worry about the potential for inadvertent operation—as with burned toast incidents. The most important question, though, is how the damage due to water release compares with the damage to the library building and the danger to patrons and materials if sprinklers are not installed.

Wet Pipe Systems

Sprinkler systems can generally be divided into three broad categories: wet pipe, dry pipe, and pre-action systems. The wet pipe system is perhaps the simplest of the three and in recent years has become known for reliability. Since wet pipe systems have the smallest number of components, they tend to malfunction somewhat less often than the other systems. Because a sprinkler system often gathers dust for years before it is needed and library maintenance schedules are often years behind, reliability is especially important. Wet pipe systems are also relatively low in cost, requiring less time and expertise to install as well as fewer service calls. Following a false alarm or even a real fire, wet pipe sprinkler systems need less time and labor to restore—simply replace the fused sprinklers and turn the water supply back on. These systems are not, however, a good choice for subfreezing environments.

Dry Pipe Systems

In a dry pipe sprinkler system, pipes are not filled with water. Instead, they contain pressurized air or nitrogen that holds a valve in a closed position. When a fire occurs, the heated air escapes, and the dry pipe valve releases, allowing water to enter the pipe. Dry pipe systems offer protection in spaces such as unheated warehouses where freezing is possible. Some library and museum professionals think dry pipe systems better protect water-sensitive areas from leaks, but this has not turned out to be a significant concern. Since dry pipe systems are more complex, they require additional control equipment and more maintenance and so can be less reliable. In addition, they do not offer the design flexibility of wet pipe systems and take up to sixty seconds longer to respond to a fire. Unless the system is completely drained and dried after use, sprinklers may corrode, causing them to malfunction.

Pre-action Systems

The pre-action sprinkler system, the third type in common use, is like the dry pipe system in that water is not kept in the pipes. It is held in check by an electrically operated valve called a pre-action valve. To release water, both the pre-action valve must operate and the sprinkler heads must fuse, thus providing greater protection against accidental discharges than with the wet pipe system. This means that smoke or dust that is not the result of fire may cause an alarm to sound, but water will not flow.

DISASTER PREVENTION AND PREPAREDNESS

Although the threat of fire affects all libraries, natural disasters tend to single out libraries in specific areas of the country. One library may be situated near an earthquake fault; another is located in a coastal area regularly visited by hurricanes. The structural adaptations that should be incorporated into the plans of each of these libraries are quite different but equally important if the libraries are to continue to serve the needs of their users for years to come. Disaster prevention and preparedness should, therefore, be an integral part of your planning process.

Flooding

If at all possible, don't build your library in a floodplain. If you are not successful in this campaign, then be certain that a flood wall is included in the plans. Ask if a back valve will be installed to prevent water from backing up into your building. This ingenious gadget works because the pressure of water backup in pipes closes it. If a soggy basement is a distinct possibility, an automatic sump pump in a recessed area of the floor can expel water before your flood bears any resemblance to Noah's. If you live near the coast, you may need to plan for flooding from the ocean during heavy storms or hurricanes, and you will need some sort of protective structure between your building and the ocean. Tidal surges are another problem and may require openings at lower elevations so the water can run out through the building.

Water-Resistant Materials

If flooding has been a problem in your area, it's a good idea to identify construction materials that will best withstand the elements. When flooding occurs, it is almost inevitable that water will get into walls, floors, and other structural systems. Some building materials are more resistant to moisture, water, flooding, and mold than other materials. Discuss potential problems with your design team and your contractor. Ask if they will be selecting materials that can withstand floodwaters for three days or more without significant damage. Of course, it may not be possible to select all materials based on these criteria, but your building professionals will have many choices available to them.

Will It Dry?

The design and construction of the library building should allow the structure, including wall and floor cavities or systems, to drain and dry after waters recede. Water can move through very small cracks to enter cavities or building systems. Therefore, both the water and the vapors that it creates must be able to escape in at least one direction so the structure can dry. Even better, the design can allow water to escape in two directions. Of course, librarians are not usually involved in the selection of construction materials, but they can make it clear to the design team that they are concerned about the problem. They can also inquire about selection criteria. Materials chosen should

- resist water damage or be water-tolerant
- be easy to clean
- permit wall and floor systems to drain and dry
- resist mold growth
- resist transporting water or moisture to adjacent materials
- remain stable when exposed to water
- maintain their strength and stiffness after exposure to water

After the water has been drained from the building, cleanup will be easier if water-resistant and drainable materials are in place. Materials should not only be easy to clean but also able to withstand disinfectants. Materials containing cellulose such as paper, wallboard, and natural fiber fabrics are more likely to develop mold than synthetic materials. Hard surfaces such as metal are easier to clean than porous surfaces such as ceiling tile, wallboard, or upholstered furnishings. Always remember that moisture trapped inside must have a way to get out or the building will not dry. Damage will continue to increase until moisture has been removed.

If flooding is an issue of special concern to your library planners, you might check with local or area building officials or perhaps a floodplain manager to learn more about building requirements. Become familiar with National Flood Insurance Program regulations as well as local and state requirements.

Earthquakes

Earthquakes are a concern for more libraries than we usually imagine. Even small tremors that local residents may not notice may damage walls and foundations. If earthquakes are a source of concern in your region, you should know that seismic building codes exist to protect against loss of life. However, they may not really prevent or even minimize building damage. A number of factors may make a building more vulnerable to earthquake damage. These include

- precast, pre-tensioned, or post-tensioned concrete
- tilt-up designs with weakly connected load-bearing members
- timber framing with severe irregularities
- first floors without adequate support

However, site selection has a lot to do with the likelihood that your building will be damaged in an earthquake. Choose a site where there is no man-made fill, in other words, where land has not been filled in or a streambed covered over. You may remember the San Francisco Loma Prieta earthquake of 1989, when much of the damage centered on filled-in areas of the city—large, sandy, man-made landfills along the San Francisco Bay waterfront. However, there was evidence that even in San Francisco, buildings constructed on piles stood up much better than their neighbors.

If you build on a hillside, look for rock close to the surface and make sure there is no evidence of rock having slid down in the past. Avoid a filled-in swamp, perhaps the worst place to locate a building. Many buildings fall off their foundation in a major quake. Roofs also separate from walls because they are not properly tied to them. All parts of the building should be bolted or connected so that the building behaves as one object, not several. Experts also consider diagonal bracing important, and the upper floors should not be constructed as separate buildings sitting on the floor below. These recommendations do not apply to very tall buildings like skyscrapers, which must be flexible. However, libraries are rarely more than two or three stories, so tightness should be a byword. Practically every aspect of building design matters when it comes to reducing earthquake damage. For example, flexible pipe fittings will help avoid gas or water leaks. Flexible fittings also resist breakage.

These are just a few recommendations, but your building professionals must be fully aware of earthquake hazards in your area and prepared with the latest information. This is one argument for using local architects, engineers, and builders. Occasionally, the planners on a large public building project want to make a splash and hire a nationally or even internationally known architectural firm. If your area is especially prone to earthquakes, hurricanes, or other natural disasters, this may not be a good decision. If a firm is not accustomed to designing buildings for situations like yours, less trendy locals may be better choices.

Hurricanes and Tornadoes

During a hurricane, winds can rush in and destroy everything inside the building, so storm shutters can be useful for protecting windows. A track at the top and bottom of windows and doors or recessed in concrete slabs at their bases allows the shutters to be slipped into place quickly. Electronic shutters similar to garage doors can be used to roll down and protect the main door and windows.

Storm-resistant windows that offer protection from flying projectiles are another good idea, as are recessed windows that can deflect the impact of flying objects. Bracing installed behind doors is still another option.

Tying It All Together

Like earthquake damage, risk depends to a considerable extent on how well a building is tied together. A weak link can breach the "envelope" of the structure. It's important that the building act as a unit and not have many vulnerable pieces. The foundation in a high-risk area should support a lot of pressure, so concrete footings should be made bigger than average to keep the library building from becoming detached from the ground. The concrete used should have a higher-than-normal compressive strength, as high as 4,000 pounds per square inch. Steel columns should also be designed for higher stresses.

Tornadoes can occur almost anywhere, although there are areas known as tornado corridors. Experts recommend fewer windows if tornadoes are a particular problem in your locale. It is essential to keep the wind from getting inside the building. Of course, windows are important to you and your users, so eliminating them is not really an option. Instead, they can be reduced in size and inset to keep debris from hitting them. Storm windows also give additional strength to deflect debris.

In hurricane- and tornado-susceptible areas, be sure your roof is well connected to the rest of the building since it can fly off, exposing the building to interior damage. If a door opens out, it is less likely to be blown open. Where fire codes permit, something as simple as a doorstop can keep doors in place, protecting the building from interior damage. In your building design, be sure to include safe places where staff and users can wait out the danger. A safe room should have several walls between you and the outside. Since innocent objects turn into unguided missiles when they are hurled by the wind, a safe room should not have any windows. The floor, walls, and ceilings of safe rooms should be fastened together with metal ties, and the floor plate should be securely fastened to the foundation.

SICK BUILDING SYNDROME

Although the above sections deal with natural disasters, modern man has created some new problems that can be almost as daunting as hurricanes and tornadoes. In recent years, we've been hearing a lot about sick building syndrome. Since the term has been embraced by the media, its definition has become extremely flexible. However, the EPA has defined sick building syndrome as a constellation of "situations in which building occupants experience acute health and comfort effects that appear to be linked to time spent in a building, but no specific illness . . . can be identified."[2] In other words, a building is defined as sick when a significant number of the occupants of a building suffer increased medical problems that are especially severe during the hours they spend at work. Such problems may result from breathing in particles, mainly petroleum-based chemicals emitted by construction materials, cleaning compounds, office equipment, and office furnishings, particularly carpeting.

Sick building syndrome tends to affect new buildings—bright, shiny, seemingly well-built structures that their occupants have been waiting impatiently to occupy. In fact, the World Health Organization found that polluted air may reside in one-third of all new and remodeled buildings. The energy crisis of 1974 was responsible for a new emphasis on energy-efficient buildings. Later, the determination to reduce dependence on foreign oil resulted in major reductions in the amount of fresh air designed to circulate through buildings' ventilation systems. This goal also resulted in the development of modern insulation materials that are almost too efficient at holding this recirculated air inside the building.

Most people are familiar with Legionnaires' disease, which has spread through HVAC systems in some hotels. This is an illness caused by sick buildings. Hotels, however, are not the only buildings subject to the malady. A new courthouse in Martin County, Florida, had to be immediately renovated at more than twice the cost of the original building. The cause was mold and mildew allowed to thrive in the ventilation system. Such a disaster to your new library building could ring the death knell to your hopes and dreams.

Henderson County (N.C.) Library, Etowah Branch Library, Craig Gaulden and Davis, cgdarch.com. Photo: Michelle Gunning/Sling Shot Imaging.

Symptoms

What are the symptoms of sick building syndrome? Although the problem affects different individuals in different ways, here are some of the most common symptoms reported by employees:

headaches	eye and skin irritations
physical and mental fatigue	dizziness
respiratory infections and allergy flare-ups	forgetfulness
breathing difficulties	nausea
depression	nosebleeds
cold symptoms (runny nose, bronchitis, sore throat)	drowsiness
	rashes

If such symptoms are ignored, the toxins responsible can weaken the body's immune system, leading to many more serious health problems related to the liver, kidneys, and central nervous system.

Causes

Sick building syndrome is caused by an extraordinarily wide variety of culprits, but the HVAC system is a frequent offender. For example, poor ventilation systems that have leaks or that trap stale air, as well as systems that do not circulate sufficient quantities of air, may be at fault. Air ducts harboring dust, mold, bacteria, and mildew are another frequent problem. As pointed out earlier, when humidity levels are not adequately controlled, mold spores and mildew can collect and circulate through the ventilation system. Sometimes the problem is not with the system itself but rather with the human beings responsible for its maintenance. For example, poor housekeeping may allow dust to build up on ventilation filters, or, in misguided attempts to economize, engineers may set systems too low to allow adequate amounts of air to be circulated.

In other situations, the system may not permit sufficient human intervention. The absence of individual manual controls or a dependence on computers rather than human beings to respond to temperature, humidity, and ventilation problems may be at the root of the problem. Inadequate filtration of airborne particles is another frequent problem.

In addition to problems related to the HVAC system, there are a large number of other potential conditions that produce illness:

- ◆ radon or asbestos present in the building
- ◆ urea-formaldehyde foam used as insulation
- ◆ pesticide chemicals that are not adequately ventilated from the building
- ◆ cleaning agents containing hazardous chemicals
- ◆ airtight buildings that can't "breathe" and so entrap indoor air pollutants
- ◆ high levels of hydrocarbons and carbon dioxide

Precautions

The cost of a sick building in terms of delay, repairs, staff absences, and medical costs is astronomical. What can you do to prevent sick building syndrome? Your efforts should begin with your initial discussions with the design team and continue throughout your tenancy of the building. The problem does not end when the workers leave and you open for business. Attention to the problem is required day in and day out, and a good motto to tack up over your office door might be "Eternal Vigilance." The following are just a few important precautions, many of which lie within your control:

Be sure your HVAC system can control humidity independent of temperature.

Provide local environmental control.

Use high-quality materials like rubberized asphalt membrane.

Install copper flashing around window openings to prevent leakage.

Keep green plants around. They give off oxygen and absorb harmful impurities in the air.

Balance airflow throughout the building.

Select windows that can be opened for ventilation.

Install ceiling fans.

Use nontoxic paints.

Install carpeting made of natural fibers.

Use tacks, not glue, to keep carpeting in place.

Select office furniture that is covered or made of nontoxic materials.

Place copiers near windows to ensure that ozone is directed outside.

Place ventilation ducts on or near the ceiling.

Increase the use of outdoor air. An adequate HVAC system should be able to meet the standards of ASHRAE. These standards specify the exchange of between fifteen and sixty cubic feet of outside air per minute per occupant.[3]

Inadequate Fresh Air

Modern HVAC technology has given us very sophisticated energy-recovery systems. They are capable of returning exhausted heat and humidity back into the building's ventilation in the winter. In the summer, cool air is returned. This can mean a savings of up to 75 percent in heating and air-conditioning costs. In other words, the system will recover 75 percent of the energy expended. These systems also allow you to reduce the size of your air-conditioning equipment, further cutting costs. Even though the system is capable of such savings, you really don't want to have such large quantities of used and even contaminated air circulating through your building. Outdoor air is essential for a healthy building and for healthy occupants of a building. Fresh air needs to circulate throughout an entire building, not just a few areas.

Your building may require a control system to monitor and control air distribution. Such equipment includes sensors that can detect contaminant levels. Not one but a series of air filters is also important for reducing contaminants. Some experts recommend 30 percent pre-filters for large air particulates, followed by 90 percent final filters for fine particulates. Both filters should provide antimicrobial treatments to inhibit and control the growth of organisms that the filters catch. Good filters make good sense economically, since high-efficiency filtration will mean reduced cleaning of ductwork and other system components.

Temporary Quarters

Making our library buildings safe and secure for staff and customers is an important consideration in any library building and one that sometimes fails to get the attention it deserves. I recently had occasion to observe a (thankfully) temporary move to a makeshift building while the library was being renovated. The temporary library building was probably built during the early 1960s and was completely lacking in windows. Because it was the property of a fraternal order whose members had been gradually dying off, it had not really been used for many years. For a year and a half both staff members and customers were miserable. Reports of headaches, sore throats, and a wide variety of afflictions circulated. Various efforts were made to remove mold and other toxins, especially from the HVAC system, but of course it was not possible to make major building modifications.

Fortunately, the seemingly endless ordeal finally did end and the new library building was greeted with even more appreciation than might otherwise have been the case. However, the experience made me realize how very important it is to have a safe, healthy, and comfortable library building. Virtual libraries are wonderful, but we are not virtual people. Flesh-and-blood creatures that we are, we are all acutely aware of our environments. In the next chapter, we will talk more about the library environment and its impact on its customers.

NOTES

1. Jeannette A. Woodward, *Creating the Customer-Driven Library: Building on the Bookstore Model* (Chicago: American Library Association, 2005); and Jeannette A. Woodward, *Creating the Customer-Driven Academic Library* (Chicago: American Library Association, 2009).
2. U.S. Environmental Protection Agency, Office of Air and Radiation, "Indoor Air Facts No. 4" (April 1998), www.epa.gov/iedweb00/pub/sbs.html.
3. American Society of Heating, Refrigerating, and Air-Conditioning Engineers, Guideline for Commissioning of HVAC Systems (ASHRAE Standards, 1-1989).

SICK BUILDING RESOURCES

Bluyssen, Philomena M. *The Indoor Environment Handbook: How to Make Buildings Healthy and Comfortable.* London and Sterling, VA: Earthscan, 2009.

Fisanick, Christina. *Eco-Architecture.* Farmington Hills, MI: Greenhaven, 2008.

Godish, Thad. *Sick Buildings: Definition, Diagnosis, and Mitigation.* Boca Raton, FL: Lewis, 1995.

Millar, Myrna, and Heather Millar. *Sick Buildings and Sick Schools.* Vancouver, BC: NICO Environmental Health Strategies, 1999.

U.S. Department of Energy, Office of Scientific and Technical Information. "Indoor Environmental Quality and Ventilation in U.S. Office Buildings: A View of Current Issues." 2005. www.osti.gov/servlets/purl/10118623-fuDw7H/webviewable/.

Widdicombe, Richard. "The Complicated Symptoms of Sick Buildings." *Public Library Quarterly* 25, nos. 3–4 (2007): 113–25.

Creating Customer-Friendly Spaces

It's Not Just Decor

8

In the decade since the first edition of this book was published, a great deal has transpired in the library world, not all of it positive. In fact, some libraries even find themselves in peril. Although public libraries are threatened by the current economic crisis, academic and special library use has been negatively affected by the increasing availability of electronic resources. If our customers can obtain most of the information they are seeking from the comfort of home or the local coffee shop, why should they come to the library?

In general, public libraries have been more successful at attracting customers, since they offer a wider variety of resources that can compete effectively with the Internet. However, most successful libraries have discovered that something more is needed. Customers will not spend time in an unpleasant environment if they don't have to. To be successful in the twenty-first century, libraries must appeal to the five senses. The way the library looks, the way it smells, the way it sounds, and the way it feels all contribute to the success or failure of its mission.

A WELCOMING ENVIRONMENT

I once thought that decor should be left to decorators and designers. Since board members, university presidents, and the Friends of the Library have strong feelings about interior design and complain loudly about the color of the upholstery, why should the librarian get mired in such petty details? Why not turn such decisions over to decorators and let them take the rap? Then I began to notice all the libraries with white paint, gray cubicles, gray carpet, and more gray carpet that calls itself wall covering. Such a scheme solved a multitude of problems.

It was practical, reduced maintenance costs, eliminated the need to match or coordinate colors, reduced the work of design professionals, and invited little argument or criticism. There was only one difficulty: who would ever want to spend time in such a building?

Bonding with the Library

As we know, it takes time for customers to develop a relationship with their library. Most people have no idea of the plethora of services available there. If you were to question your regulars, you would discover that they continue to be surprised as they discover yet another resource or service that meets their needs and makes their lives more satisfying. If, on their first visit to the library, they encountered the look and feel of a hospital, state office building, or courthouse, if they sat on uncomfortable chairs, or wandered through cavernous, confusing, and unattractive spaces, they would have no incentive to return. Only some strong motivation would bring them back a second time, and since libraries increasingly compete with the Internet and glitzy chain bookstores, such motivation might be absent.

Librarians are not trained as interior designers, but they know better than anyone else the kind of atmosphere in which their customers thrive. They know that library users are looking for a warm, comfortable, and aesthetically pleasing place to be. They are looking for entertaining books and cozy chairs where they can get away from the pressures of high-octane lifestyles. They look for solid tables where they can spread out their books and papers, as well as electrical outlets to accommodate their laptop computers. They are also looking for a certain atmosphere that has multiple components: appealing shapes and colors, sunlit windows, quiet nooks away from busy aisles and heavy footfalls, as well as the absence of unpleasant smells.

In short, they are seeking the comforts of home with the resources and services that only a library can provide. Designers who specify gray-carpeted walls do so because they fail to understand this basic need. Library directors who approve the purchase of several hundred identical chairs without even testing them on real customers (who come in a wide variety of shapes and sizes) are much more at fault, since they should know their customers far better than any design professional.

The Librarian's Role

My research and consulting practice has taken me to many libraries, and I have gradually developed a list of requirements that are nonnegotiable. In other words, designers should be encouraged to use their talents as they see fit, but they must be guided by the library's mission as interpreted by the librarians. Here are some basic principles around which any design must be created.

> Individuals have varying needs. A successful library must provide different kinds of spaces, different furniture choices, different color combinations, and different lighting conditions to meet a cross-section of these

San Jose (Calif.) Public Library, Willow Glen Branch, Krong Design, krongdesign.com.
Photo: Bernard Andre Photography.

needs. True, it is never possible to make everyone happy, but one chair does not fit all.

A library must relate to its environment. A cozy rainy-day retreat may be unappreciated in the desert Southwest, and a wall of windows looking out on a cold, dark winter scene may be equally undesirable.

A customer should be able to comfortably spend two or more hours using the library's resources or preparing for class. If you wouldn't enjoy spending your own time in such a space, then customers would also avoid it. Customers need not be especially comfortable when visiting the post office. They need only send off their packages and depart for pleasanter surroundings. Library customers may sit in the same chair for several hours. Few enjoy working in the middle of large, cavernous spaces, and no one is willing to be jostled and thumped by passersby.

Practical considerations like long-wearing materials are very important, but they must be balanced with human considerations like appearance and comfort.

The library must be designed for its customers first, with the library staff, the custodial staff, or other stakeholders taking up the rear. Staff spaces are much smaller and less complicated than they once were. With buildingwide wireless network access, staff can be stationed almost anywhere and remain productive. With superfast shared or outsourced cataloging and processing, large spaces are no longer needed for backroom operations.

Because of your experience, you are well aware of the role that each chair and computer desk and display unit must play in supporting the services of a new library. However, you know your customers too, and you know that a cheerful, attractive building is important to them. Librarians across the country report that adding an up-to-date, even trendy, interior space can cause flagging attendance and circulation statistics to soar. Circulation figures may go steadily downward as the library building gets older and seedier. When the same collection, services, and staff are moved into their new quarters, usage skyrockets. Most people are very aware of their surroundings and want to be in a bright, clean, welcoming environment with a harmonious color scheme.

Stakeholders with Conflicting Agendas

It is probably safe to say that few things irritate our compatriots more than the whole subject of decor. On almost every building project, there is someone in a position of authority who considers herself the ultimate arbiter of taste. Most people are content to leave the HVAC system to the professionals, but you will probably find that your board, administrators, and local residents will all have strong opinions when it comes to the subject of interior design.

Although the furnishings and floor coverings in a library serve an important practical function, their purpose can easily be forgotten by those project participants who want the new library to make a statement; that is, they are far more concerned with the way the library looks than with the materials and services it provides. This same failure to focus on function comes into play when selecting flooring materials and wall coverings. For example, it would be nice to match the floor covering to the blue in the upholstery pattern, but it is far more important that the chosen surface does not send patrons skating perilously across the entryway when it becomes wet. Someone—maybe a trustee, college president's wife, or library board member—who knows nothing about the functions of a library will happily sabotage your efforts and inflict all manner of horrors on your users as long as the results are *tres chic*.

The Common Denominator of Comfort

Unless you are willing to purchase lavender computers with raspberry printers and spend your every moment refereeing battles between tasteful factions, you are going to have to come to grips with the problem of differing tastes. While you were worrying about high-pressure exterior lighting, wireless routers, and dry pipe sprinklers, you were probably left blissfully alone. However, the instant the words *color, style,* or *fashion* are publicly uttered, you will be besieged with opinions. Everyone is a self-styled expert. Unfortunately, you will never find two people in total agreement on the subject. Taste is highly subjective, depending on culture, social affiliation, age, eyesight, and dozens of other variables. Fortunately, there is a "flip side" to this situation. If you were to take those very same people on a field trip and surround them with different spaces, different lighting conditions, and even different colors, they would have surprisingly similar reactions. In other words, human beings who are members of the same culture tend to find comfort in similar environments, while their personal creative urges may clash sharply with one another.

Important Decisions

There are some decisions that don't really matter and others that are vitally important; don't get the two categories mixed up. For example, furniture must be designed for living, breathing human beings. There's nothing wrong with attractive chairs, but first and foremost, they must be comfortable and withstand heavy use. Library users will be sitting on them for hours at a time, and I doubt that your staff includes a chiropractor. Decisions about fabric and wood stain are best delegated to an experienced, reliable decorating professional who understands your goals and can present choices to your planning group. Be careful, however, that this individual is well grounded in reality or you will be dealing with yet another disruptive trendsetter. You will want to be sure that any chairs under consideration are sized for different body types, are "sit-able" for long hours of study, and are strong enough to stand up to the wear and tear of a real library setting.

Be generous in delegating decorating decisions. You really don't want to pick the color of the restroom walls, but you do want a library that welcomes your customers. There are probably any number of color schemes, fabric choices, and furniture styles that will achieve your goals. Set the parameters yourself and let others choose between acceptable alternatives.

Many contemporary color schemes would meet with the approval of your users, but in a few years they will tire of them. Think about how you feel when you enter an avocado-and-gold building reminiscent of the 1970s. Having endured just such a library complete with shag carpet, I'm convinced that nothing makes a building look old and depressing like yesterday's colors. Therefore, you will want to be certain you can get rid of them when they are no longer au courant. This means that accent walls are fine, but furniture intended to last for thirty years should not be rainbow-hued.

HIRING AN INTERIOR DESIGNER

TALE

We had an egotistical interior designer who insisted that everything match, whether it was functional or not. Make sure you have a decorator who puts function first.

Interior decorators or designers can possess a surprising assortment of practical skills and perform many useful services. Those experienced with dealing with demanding clients have mastered the role of referee, keeping your fashionistas under control, presenting a choice of color palettes, and limiting choices to reasonable alternatives. The designer is a professional whose judgment carries weight. It can't be just any designer, however. As the tale above illustrates, decorators can be almost as disconnected as architects. They can be quite as narrow-minded as any interfering trustee and may exhibit terrifying tunnel vision when they are obsessed with creating their elegant masterpiece. It is hard to coexist peacefully with someone who wants to hide the copy machines because they are not aesthetically pleasing.

Interior Designers Are Professionals

On the other hand, a designer does more than just take the blame for unpopular color choices. If you are fortunate enough to have one involved in your project, you may have access to a wealth of practical advice not only about decor but also about the efficient use of space and flexible floor plans. A good designer is even aware of relevant building codes, fire and life-safety requirements, and accessibility guidelines.

Despite stereotypes, they do not usually begin by choosing paint or carpet colors. Instead, they develop a program—a comprehensive list of specifics based on library functions. They make note of the number and size of workstations, conference rooms, service desks, and storage areas, considering practical and aesthetic requirements. Some interior designers are part of the design-build team and may develop preliminary layouts of the space, loosely blocking in public study areas, book stacks, work areas, and traffic patterns. Such design professionals can be very helpful. You might think of them as interior architects who select appropriate materials, fixtures, and furniture to achieve the best integration of aesthetics, efficiency, and cost-effectiveness.

If you will be working with a decorator, be sure to have the following information available. (This is yet another of your written handouts.)

number of square feet planned for each function and how you see it being used

library organization chart with staff positions, including titles and functions as well as department relationships

adjacency requirements—who needs access to what areas

furniture and equipment requirements for each function

electrical, acoustic, lighting, and other requirements

Be sure your decorator is sensitive to your region and its architectural traditions. One need not be slavishly "Santa Fe" in the Southwest, for instance, but a color scheme appropriate for a New York skyscraper will be unlikely to travel well.

SELECTING FLOORING MATERIALS

The floor coverings and surfaces selected for a library or archive should not simply be left to planning professionals. These materials will have far more impact on the library's ability to function effectively than any architect realizes, and one size does not fit all. Each area must be considered separately, and most buildings require different materials for different purposes, such as restrooms, entryways, meeting rooms, and so on.

Advantages of Carpet

Consider carpeted areas, for example. Patrons like to walk on carpet, especially on cold, biting days. Staff members who must be on their feet during much of the day find that carpet reduces leg pain and other discomforts. Valuable printed materials, however, are endangered by the dust and other pollutants that inevitably come from carpets. No matter how frequently it is cleaned, a carpet is a comfy home to all sorts of creepy, crawly things that may peacefully coexist with people but not with paper. There are, indeed, types of carpets that release fewer pollutants into the air than other types, but where rare and valuable collections are the priority, carpets really cannot be considered safe.

One library I visited was carpeted with thousands of yards of broadloom, laid down everywhere except in staff spaces, where tile and cement reigned supreme. The choice was unintentionally cruel. Staff members spend eight or more hours a day in the library and have every right to be comfortable. Walking through the technical services departments of some libraries, I'm reminded of the uncomfortable servants' halls of yesterday. Yours may be a repository in which the collection is considered too precious and fragile to tolerate any carpeting at all. However, if you are planning to use carpeting in public spaces, it is almost always appropriate for offices and workrooms as well.

Hard Surfaces

So considering these factors, where will you use carpeting, and where are other materials more appropriate? Look carefully at your present library building.

When patrons enter through the front door in sodden raincoats and muddy boots, those first sloppy steps should not be taken on carpet. What is needed is a surface that is easy to clean and does not become slippery when wet. The best choice is probably some type of slip-resistant tile.

If your elevator doors open into a carpeted area, you may live in fear of mishaps caused by book trucks and constant foot traffic that gradually scuffs up the carpet edge, leaving it exposed and dangerous. The difficulty encountered when rolling book trucks through the library will give you a fairly good idea of the obstacles experienced by users in wheelchairs who must navigate thresholds, high-pile carpeting, and barriers created by the transition from one surface to another. Restroom flooring presents additional maintenance considerations. You probably have seen restroom tile that always looks dirty because dirt becomes lodged in grout crevices and is difficult to remove. What about stairs? Carpeting can make them less treacherous, but it will receive heavy wear. Carpeting with rubber treads may be a good choice. Carpet tile would be a poor one, since tiles coming unglued represent accidents just waiting to happen.

The Right Choice

One of the most important considerations is the nature of your collection. If you have large archival or rare print collections, then you may wish to keep carpeting to a minimum. You may even need a separate ventilation or air-handling system to keep carpet pollution away from collections. In fact, if this is a major consideration, you may wish to forgo carpeting altogether. This is a rather radical position, however, since other options are somewhat limited. Vinyl tile tends to give a "cafeteria" look to a space. Ceramic tile, reminiscent of the Southwest, can be lovely, but it is hard, slippery, and agonizing for anyone pushing book trucks. Hardwood floors are usually well beyond the budgets of most libraries and, depending on the product, may not hold up well under heavy foot traffic.

Consider the Collection and the Customers

You might think about where your library or archive can be placed on a continuum, with concerns for patron comfort at one end and concerns for preservation at the other. At one end might be a repository where the preservation of the collection is the prime consideration and patron use is confined to one or more small reading rooms. In such a facility, carpet might be totally absent. One of several excellent modern sealants might be applied to the cement floors in place of tile. That way, there are no cracks in which dirt can breed. Book trucks can roll smoothly over such a surface too, but staff will find it far from cozy.

At the other end of the continuum, you might find a public library branch with lots of programs, children's activities, and an easily replaced popular collection. Here, you would choose floor coverings based on programming needs and patron preferences. Young children are constantly falling down and need a soft surface on which to land. They may be quite noisy, and hard surfaces serve to echo and magnify the hubbub. Since the collection will not be around long enough that you need concern yourself with preservation issues, carpet is clearly the best choice.

Carpet Tiles

Carpet tiles are a very attractive option when you have large numbers of voice, data, and electrical outlets installed in the floor. Although carpet tiles can cost 30 to 50 percent more than broadloom carpeting, carpet tiles make it much easier to add computers and media equipment than broadloom. It's also easier to replace tile in heavy traffic areas without turning it into a major project. Ultimately, when you consider the long-term cost of having to replace either carpet tile or broadloom, the cost is about the same.

Whether you choose carpet tiles or broadloom, it's a good idea to purchase more than you need and store the leftovers for future use. Some areas wear much faster than others, and you may find yourself replacing certain relatively small sections more often than you will purchase new carpeting for the whole library. Furthermore, it may be hard to match small sections with new carpet because dye lots vary considerably, and manufacturers frequently discontinue textures, colors, and patterns.

Static Electricity

Since the modern library has so much money invested in computers, it is important that they remain in good working order for as long as possible. Static electricity is produced by walking across carpeting. It builds up gradually until finally when patrons touch something metal, they notice a slight (or somewhat more severe) shock. Static electricity poses a much greater hazard in dry climates and during the winter months, when heating systems remove most of the humidity from the air. Not only is it annoying and a little painful, but it can cause serious damage to delicate electronic equipment. For example, static can cause printers to spew out unwanted toner, burn out tiny spots in a monitor screen, and interfere with the computer's functioning so that frequent rebooting is necessary.

Over the last few years, the practice of treating carpeting with an antistatic solution has become common, and many of the static problems have been alleviated. Furthermore, some newer varieties of carpet effectively reduce static electricity. Nevertheless, it is necessary to remain on guard against static and exercise restraint in selecting carpeting for electrical and equipment closets, as well as in areas where servers or other hard-to-replace equipment is kept. It's a good idea to require that library technicians wear antistatic wrist straps whenever they work on the inside of a piece of electronic equipment; in addition, you may want to attach grounding devices to the equipment.

Aesthetics and the Hard, Cruel World

Attractive flooring materials can add a great deal to the ambience of a library, but aesthetics should not be the most important consideration when making selections. First and foremost, consider safety. In addition, you will want to consider

TALE

The beautiful blue-green carpet started developing runs in the children's department two weeks after the grand reopening.

how well the materials will wear over time. The following are some things to think about when you compare various flooring materials.

Is there a safe "transition" area in front of the elevator to prevent patrons from tripping over the edge of carpeting and injuring themselves?

What happens to the flooring material you're considering when it gets wet? Does it become dangerously slick? (Marble, for example, becomes positively treacherous.)

How difficult is the flooring material to clean?

Is the floor sloped?

How much traffic do you expect in a particular area? (Carpeting will not long survive in your central lobby area.)

Will ugly black marks or permanent indentations result when you move stacks and other heavy pieces of furniture?

What are the product's antistatic qualities?

Does the carpeting comply with fire regulations in your area?

For how long is the flooring material guaranteed?

Will you be rolling book trucks through an area? (They can make a terrible racket on ceramic tile and should not be rolled across studded resilient flooring.)

Have you given special consideration to high-risk areas like ramps, stairs, and potential wet or damp areas?

Have you planned a "runoff" area at the entrance where patrons can clean their shoes?

Are your stair landings safe, slip-proof, and equipped with color strips to call attention to different levels?

Other Flooring Materials

For those areas where carpeting is not a good choice, you and your team will have a variety of other materials from which to choose. The following sections provide a brief overview of the general categories and classifications. This is definitely one of those topics that will require long hours leafing through manufacturers' catalogs, but before anyone gets carried away by an aesthetically pleasing material, take time to learn a little about industry specifications and standards.

Resilient Flooring

The term *resilient flooring* usually includes

vinyl tile and sheet flooring

vinyl composition tile

linoleum tile and sheet flooring

rubber tile and sheet flooring

cork tile and sheet flooring

Librarians are sometimes surprised that commercial resilient flooring does not have an easy-to-clean urethane surface like residential vinyl floors do. The increased traffic of a public area makes such a surface impractical, although it may be perfectly satisfactory for home use. Unlike the no-wax floor in a kitchen, resilient flooring materials for a library need to be polished regularly. Installation also takes longer than in residential applications because the adhesive used to install commercial flooring must set up properly before heavy equipment can be moved across it. If it hasn't set, adhesive displacement can result in unattractive dents that your contractor will never be able to remove. If it is essential to bring in heavy objects, place sheets of plywood or underlayment over the flooring to spread the weight.

If a resilient floor covering is installed over a concrete slab, take moisture and pH tests, since the vinyl acts as a moisture barrier. Since most adhesives used are water-based, moisture can be trapped in the concrete slab, making it impossible for the adhesive to set up properly. Then adhesive can ooze up between tiles, or tiles can pop loose.

Ceramic Tile

Ceramic tile has been in use for thousands of years. It is a mixture of different clays and other minerals that have been shaped and fired at high temperatures. The higher the temperature, the harder the tile. This "hard body," sometimes called "bisque," is given a glazed wear layer or left untreated. A glaze is actually glass that is fused to the bisque by intense heat. The fewer air pockets in the clay, the denser and thus stronger the bisque. The ceramic tile industry measures density by the amount of water the tile absorbs. Nonvitreous tiles are those that absorb 7 percent or more of their weight in water; semivitreous tiles absorb between 3 percent and 7 percent water. Vitreous tile absorbs 0.5 percent to 3 percent water; and impervious tiles are the densest and strongest, absorbing between 0 percent and 0.5 percent of their weight in water. These distinctions are extremely important when deciding which types of tiles are most suited to a particular installation. In general, when you're given a choice, you will probably find that denser tiles are the best choice.

Another common choice is between glazed and unglazed tile. Unglazed tiles, like porcelains and quarry tiles, are baked pieces of clay in which the color runs through the entire clay body. Unglazed tiles are usually thicker and denser than glazed tiles. Although color selections for unglazed tile may be limited by the colors of the clay, it is usually an excellent choice for areas where there is a lot of wear and tear.

The Porcelain Enamel Institute has developed a system to rate the durability of each type of tile. The following is a very abbreviated outline of the system:

Group I: This category includes tiles that are suitable only for residential bathrooms. They cannot stand up to the wear that characterizes public buildings.

Group II: This category is also appropriate only for residential installation.

Group III: These are tiles suited for commercial areas that experience light traffic, such as offices and reception areas.

Group IV: Tile in this category is appropriate for medium commercial and light institutional applications.

Group IV+: This is the category that, in most cases, you will want to choose for the new library. Tile in group IV+ is suitable for heavy traffic and wet areas where safety is a major concern. It can also be used for walkways and building entrances.

Monocottura technology is a ceramic technology that is in common use today; this Italian word means "single-fired." That is, the tile is shaped, glazed, and fired in one step, thus speeding up production and reducing costs. The process can produce tiles in less than one hour compared with days in the past. The result is a denser body and harder glaze. In addition, tiles produced with this method have a flat back that makes them easier to install than tiles produced with older processes.

Laminate Flooring

Most librarians are familiar with laminates like Formica used in countertops, but they don't think of it as flooring material. A good way to define a laminate floor is an interlocking tongue-and-groove flooring system that floats on top of the subfloor (a concrete slab, an existing vinyl floor, or a hardwood floor). This means that the new floor is not attached to the floor underneath. A bead of water-resistant glue placed between the tongue and grooves of every plank holds planks together and seals the edges from moisture. Before the floor is installed, a polyurethane padding is placed over the subfloor to prevent glue from sticking to the subfloor. The laminated material is composed of a hard-core material, with a laminated printed layer and backing secured to the core. The sandwich of materials is saturated in a resin called "melamine" in much the way that Formica countertops are produced. Of course, the amount of resin applied must be much greater to produce a flooring material that resists wear and tear. The result is a floor that can work well in certain library areas.

Hardwood Floors

Because of escalating costs and environmental concerns, hardwood floors are becoming an infrequent choice for libraries. However, hardwood floors are still the preferred option when a touch of luxury is needed, such as in a boardroom or rare book reading room. Solid wood floors use planks that are one complete piece of solid wood from top to bottom. Most often, they are ¾ or $5/16$ inch thick and 2¼ or 1½ inches wide. One of the most serious problems experienced with this type of flooring is its reaction to moisture. Winter heating dries the wood, making it contract or leaving gaps between the boards. Summer humidity will cause the wood to expand and cup.

Oak is perhaps the most common hardwood floor. Unfinished solid oak comes in several different qualities:

- ◆ clear (no visual blemishes or knots; extremely expensive)
- ◆ select (some small knots; very little dark graining)
- ◆ better (similar to select but slightly less desirable)
- ◆ #1 common (more knots and more dark graining)
- ◆ #2 common (even more knots)

Engineered is a term that refers to laminated boards that have two, three, or five layers of wood laminated together. They range in thickness from ¼ to $9/16$ inch and in width from 2¼ to 7 inches. The process involves cross-graining (in other words, the grain of each layer is perpendicular to that of the layer above and the one below), so it is more stable and less affected by moisture than solid planks. Because wood always expands in one direction, solid planks expand across their width, not their length. By changing the direction of wood graining, it is possible to greatly reduce expansion and contraction. Parquet was once the ultimate in luxury floors, but today parquet is often an engineered floor, usually composed of 12-by-12-inch squares. The term *long strip* means an engineered floor characterized by extra-long planks (usually 84 inches) and separated "sliced cut" slats that are glued together to produce the face of each plank.

The planks of most solid wood floors are sawed from the tree trunk, cutting through the tree's circular growth rings. In an engineered floor, veneers are cut with sharp knives as the trunk is spun in a circle, producing a much larger, aesthetically pleasing surface area. When the veneer has dried, it is laminated to other layers to make wood flooring planks.

WALLS SET THE MOOD

Walls are, of course, integral to the structure of the building and serve a variety of essential functions. In addition, however, they also provide an unparalleled opportunity to alter the look and feel of the building—most important, the image it presents to your users. As you're considering the look and feel of interior spaces, remember that modern computer environments can seem coldly dehumanized. Wall treatments can be your most important ally when it comes to creating the kind of welcoming environment you envision, and paint, plaster, and wood paneling as well as paper and cloth wall coverings can enliven any interior. For example, you may wish to incorporate some soft, homey wall coverings into both public and staff spaces and use colors and textures that are pleasing and restful. Flooring materials and textiles as well as wall coverings can provide a unifying background and complement the library's architecture for a warm, restful image.

Advantages of Drywall

Although colorful, highly textured wall coverings can be extremely effective in small areas, it is best to be sparing in your use of these materials. Painted drywall is much less expensive than other materials, and it can be repainted again and again with whatever colors are in vogue. Paint may be your most valuable weapon in your war to keep the building from looking antiquated and boring. A splash of bright color or a striking design may create exactly the kind of ambience you are going for, but don't get carried away.

Wall Coverings

The majority of the flexible wall coverings sold for commercial applications in the United States are of fabric-backed vinyl construction. The rest include coated paper, textiles, solid sheet vinyl with paper backing, and grass cloths. Wall coverings are especially useful in retrofitting older structures in order to hide cracked walls or unsightly wiring installations.

Wall coverings are divided into two basic types: type I includes wall covering weights of 15 ounces and under, while type II includes up to 22-ounce weights. To a large extent, the weight of the wall covering is a good indicator of quality and depth of texture and finish, as well as a predictor of performance. Some wall coverings are available unbacked for light duty. Such materials are not usually appropriate for libraries, however. A good polyester backing is usually essential for good performance and durability. Be sure that the wall coverings chosen are free of solvents, biocides, and stabilizers that damage the environment and produce allergic reactions. Off-gassing and volatile organic content emissions from some adhesives used during installation are another source of pollution and sick building symptoms.

Long-Lasting Materials

It is inevitable that your library walls will be the recipients of considerable deliberate and accidental abuse, whether from college freshmen or from children with crayons, who look at your walls as a vast canvas on which they can exercise their creativity. High-abuse areas may require using coatings of Teflon, Scotchgard, or acrylics to resist stains. If the wall covering is in an area that receives direct sunlight, investigate the product's color-retention properties.

If you are asked to look at samples of wall coverings being considered, be sure that you see the samples under the same conditions as those in the new library. Determine whether each will be viewed under natural or artificial lighting conditions. Try to identify the type of artificial lighting that will be used in a particular space for which you are selecting the wall covering and find a similar environment in which to view the sample.

San Diego County Library, Encinitas Community Library, Manuel Oncina Architects, oncinaarc.com.
Photo: Melissa Jacobs.

SELECTING LIBRARY FURNISHINGS

When you begin thinking about furniture for your new building, consider the activities that will be conducted within the building. Imagine what your patrons will be doing. Get out of your office and look around. Then consider the opportunities the new facility will offer for expanding your services and resources and picture your patrons using those resources. You might even create an inventory of activities that will take place in the library.

Even though the future is unknowable, try to imagine what patrons will be doing in the library ten or twenty years from now. Consider preparing a written, area-by-area activity description for the whole building. Once you have a complete list, translate these activities into equipment and furniture selections. Some libraries have begun their planning with just such a list of activities. They have first identified the furniture and equipment to support the activities and then wrapped them in walls and spaces until they have a building.

Whether you're working with a decorator or selecting furnishings yourself, look for correct ergonomics, comfort, durability, safety, looks, and value. No one of these factors can be ignored or given priority over the others. Providing a warm, welcoming environment is as important as choosing study carrels that can survive the abuse endured by high-use facilities. Chair design and construction must minimize both the danger to the patron and the damage to furniture when a clever kiddie decides to impress his friends by pivoting on one chair leg. The process of selecting furniture and furnishings for a library or media center varies with each library's individual requirements.

Learn from Your Library

Begin by talking with staff from all library departments about their furniture needs. Discuss how patrons use and abuse existing library chairs and tables. If you have children's and young adult sections, are the sizes and shapes appropriate for the different age groups? Were the chairs in your adult reading room really built for adults, or do they seem sized more for children? Remember that five-foot-tall women and 250-pound men will be using your resources. How well does your existing furniture meet their needs?

Next consider colors, fabrics, and finishes that can unify and add interest to library spaces. As you talk with decorators and others, consider that people have very strong likes and dislikes. You're going for a look that many people will find pleasant and attractive, not a decorator showcase.

Furniture Construction

Find a way to see any furniture line that is under serious consideration. Visit local libraries or ask for samples of chairs or other smaller pieces. Analyze their construction to decide which kinds of furniture will last longest. Furnishings must last a long time, and almost any librarian in a new building will tell you that much furniture construction is remarkably shoddy.

Look for signs of good craftsmanship. For example, the well joints on file drawers and steel desks should have double-sided walls for strength and stability. Sometimes the company with the big name is living off its reputation, and you can find better values from number two or three. High-end knockoffs for chairs and desks can be as well made or even superior to the brand-name equivalents. Some of the better library furniture vendors are Buckstaff, Worden Company, Luxor, Gressco, Fleetwood, and Virco. However, the marketplace is changing constantly. It is also a good idea to look further and consider where you can use less specialized and often less expensive office and computer furnishings.

Look for surfaces that resist fading and moisture, especially if the furniture will be in direct sunlight. Stay in close contact with your designer and be sure she has samples of colors and finishes. There are many different finishes called "oak," "warm oak," "sunny oak," or some similar meaningless name, and every one of them clashes with all the others. Unless your contractor has samples and understands that wood finishes must be coordinated, the woodwork, doors, and furnishings will all be at odds with one another.

Cleaning and Maintenance Issues

If, like Harry Potter, you were to don your cloak of invisibility and follow the custodial staff around your library, you'd probably discover that their carts are equipped with two squirt bottles, sometimes referred to as "blue juice" and "red juice." Every offending surface is zapped with the contents of one squirt bottle or the other. Blue juice is the milder of the two concoctions, while red juice is intended for heavy-duty jobs. Both are industrial strength, however, and can disintegrate delicate surfaces. After years of frustration, I have finally concluded that nothing should be purchased for the library that cannot be safely "juiced."

I've witnessed the demise of too many lovely study tables to take any further chances. Not only do I require that every wood surface be protected with polyurethane, but I get nervous if I can even feel the grain of the wood.

Custom Furniture Issues

As you've discovered when shopping for personal needs, any item created for a specialized market usually costs more than similar mass-marketed equivalents. This is definitely the case with library furniture. You may be able to get better buys with standard office furniture if it fits your needs. Even consumer products can occasionally be good buys if they're built for the kind of wear and tear you can expect in a public environment.

Think hard about what you gain with specially designed library furniture. Compare catalogs aimed at a variety of different markets, like tables produced

TALES

We told the architects what kinds of office furniture we needed, but not specific brands or models, and left it to them to get what we needed. That was a mistake. Based on our descriptions, they selected desks, filing cabinets, chairs, lockers, and so on that they thought were what we wanted but weren't, and then put together a bid package. Based on the bids, orders were placed. Fortunately, I happened to find out about one piece that I knew was totally wrong. When I looked at the entire order, I was dismayed to discover that we were spending tens of thousands of dollars more than we needed to in order to buy furniture that would not meet our needs.

A major factor in promoting respect (among 2,400 students) may be the high quality that was designed into the building.

for restaurants, schools, and offices. You'll discover that the size of the market affects price, as does the perceived affluence of the buyer. For example, prices escalate noticeably when furnishings are intended for use in a hospital or doctor's office.

Custom Design Woes

Although the number of pieces should be kept to a minimum, nearly every library has some built-in furnishings that must be custom-built. These might be counters, service desks, oak bookcases in the boardroom, or any of a number of special-function structures that you simply can't buy off the shelf. These units tend to be fraught with even more than your daily quota of problems because you and your architects must create them. When you choose a piece of furniture or equipment from a library catalog, you can have at least some assurance that the manufacturer understands (more or less) library needs. This is emphatically not the case with a custom furniture builder. Since you're always reinventing the wheel, communication between you and your furniture builder is especially important.

Service Desks

If reasonably acceptable service desks are available from library furniture vendors, buy them. Whatever else is wrong with them, they have been standardized over the years to meet most library needs. Their heights are standard, their knee-holes are standard, and their book-drop slots are at the right height to accommodate book bins. Most are modular and can be arranged in a variety of different configurations. In addition, no matter how astronomical their prices, they usually end up being cheaper than their custom-made equivalents.

You may, however, require custom-millwork service desks because they must fit into oddly shaped spaces or because the architect insists that off-the-shelf units will not be compatible with the rest of the building. If so, plan to spend hours in other libraries measuring and remeasuring their service desks. Don't stop at measuring height and breadth; also measure how much space is available for drawers, knees, shelves, and so on. The functionality of service desks really matters and deserves substantial planning. If you'd rather not spend the time yourself, appoint a small committee with representatives from your library's circulation and reference desks. They would probably be delighted to right some of the wrongs they have been living with.

Desk Height

Every so often, a battle erupts on one of the online library discussion groups about the height of the reference desk. One school of thought holds that the desk should be at table height to encourage reference interviews and permit staff member and patron to sit comfortably across from one another. The other school holds that the desk should actually be a high counter behind which staff either stand or sit on stools. This faction contends that the high desk is more visible and that most questions do not require a sit-down reference interview. Amid all the

TALE

Make sure you see shop drawings of workroom cabinetry, and so on. Shop drawings are typically sent by the subcontractor to the architect for approval. The owner is often left out of the loop. We received cabinets that were not what we asked for as a result, and there was a considerable time delay while cabinets were remade to our original specifications.

philosophical and psychological arguments, you might remember that librarians will more readily take their turn at the desk if they are comfortable. Few methods of torture have been invented to equal an hour or so perched on one of those high swivel stools that provide no real support for dangling feet. If you decide on the lower desk height, locate both desk and chairs out of the way of foot traffic. The idea is to provide the opportunity for a relaxing exchange between librarian and customer, not cause a traffic jam.

Circulation Desks

Although the circulation desk is an integral part of our library lives, our minds tend to go blank when we begin planning these important workstations. In a sense, they are the hub of the library—a sort of action central that can contribute to the library's efficiency or cause endless problems. The following are some of the many items that may need to be accommodated at the desk:

- computers
- computer printers
- fax machines
- bar code scanners
- RFID readers
- book detection sensitizers/ desensitizers
- lights and light switches
- substantial counter space to accommodate several customers and staff
- key box and checkout system
- equipment storage

- stationary and mobile files
- security video equipment
- media shelves
- telephones
- cash registers
- credit card charging machines
- depressible book-return bins
- public-address system components
- reserve collections
- panic buttons
- fire alarm pulls

Detailed Specifications

If you're sending out RFPs for custom furniture, be sure that the requirements are extremely specific. This is one area where you definitely do not want the low bid unless quality standards are assured. Bid specifications should include all the necessary information for the furnishings, as well as bonds and installation requirements. When the bids come back, make sure you are comparing apples with apples. Use a spreadsheet to create a table of prices and features. If a vendor hasn't been specific enough, ask for more information. Don't give serious consideration to any vendors until you have complete information about their products.

Once contracts have been awarded, make arrangements to review any alternate finish materials and to approve mock-ups, if available. Remember that delivery must be timed precisely, and you will need solid assurances that the vendor can deliver the furnishings on schedule. You will not want furniture around while construction is still going on, since it is almost impossible to store the large quantities needed and it will be subject to loss and vandalism. Similarly, a completed building is almost useless until the furniture arrives. Library furniture usually arrives looking like a vast Erector set. Installation must be carefully coordinated and integrated into your project schedule. You will want installers to begin their work as soon as possible without getting in the way of construction workers.

Wiring Issues and Library Furnishings

Whether your furniture is custom-made or selected from a catalog, it must accommodate the plethora of computers that are an integral part of any new library. You may occasionally feel as if you're designing the entire building around the special requirements of electronic equipment, but in doing so, you are also serving your users. Computer workstations not only require large amounts of clean, conditioned power, but the cables for that power pose other challenges as well. Even though recent systems furniture and library carrels may appear to be well designed, you can end up with the same old spaghetti of electrical cable configurations that characterized your old library. The following are some basic points to consider when selecting and installing computer workstations:

Select workstations that permit easy installation of cable and have ample space for cable storage. Electricians should be able to separate and store cables by function.

Store cables in channels to eliminate excessive clutter.

Select workstations that don't require wiring to be accessed from behind panel base plates, thus requiring the workstation to be disassembled when equipment is replaced.

Be sure outlets are located conveniently, preferably at desk height, not below work surfaces or behind storage units.

Select workstations that allow users to plug into electrical receptacles and phone/data junction boxes located within the wire-access cavity.

Locate cable-access cutouts on all work surfaces to allow electronic equipment to connect above and below the work surface without requiring special grommets.

Encourage electricians to store "goof loops" (extra wire) in workstations to avoid rewiring when changes are made or equipment is added.

Be sure workstations use lay-in cable management rather than conventional string-through methods. This makes future changes easier and protects wires from damage.

User Workstations

More and more reading and stack areas in a modern library are equipped with computer workstations for public use. As you select computer furniture, you will naturally be looking for work surfaces large enough to accommodate the equipment. You will be looking at the size and positioning of shelves, provisions for the cable jungle bulging out behind any PC, and all the other considerations described previously. What you may not consider, however, is what the patron is doing at the computer workstation in addition to using the computer. Students require space for notes, pens, and textbooks. Women need a safe place for their purses, and many readers carry books and magazines from other areas of the library. All of these encumbrances require space on the work surface.

If you walk through many computer areas, you will see personal possessions piled on the floor or notebooks perilously balanced on student laps. A computer workstation should accommodate all the same paraphernalia that patrons have always needed for their library activities, in addition to providing space for equipment. The space traditionally allotted to a reader is not sufficient for a computer-equipped workstation. The exact size will vary depending on your equipment. For example, more work space is available to the user if tower-case computers are installed below the work surface, and more space will be needed if workstations include printers, scanners, or other peripherals. However, a good width for computer-equipped study carrels is five feet, allowing space for books, equipment, data ports, power outlets, and locks where appropriate. Multipurpose tables should also be spacious, with data and power provided at every seating space.

Staff Workstations

When designing staff spaces, consider the wide variety of tasks that are performed in a library. As much as possible, build in flexibility with adjustable chair and work surface heights. Many library tasks are highly repetitive, so take care to minimize strain. Consider the following suggestions when selecting furniture and equipment for staff spaces:

The ideal work surface can be adjusted from 22 to 45 inches high, although normal desk height is 26 to 28 inches.

People with back injuries may find it more comfortable to work and use equipment while standing, so provide a few workstations at the appropriate height.

Several people may use the same workstation, since libraries are open days, nights, and weekends. Workstations need to be easily adjustable.

Adjustable levers on furniture should be readily accessible and easy to use.

Lots of space should be available for book trucks.

Ample shelving should be provided.

As you investigate specifications for the ideal staff workstation, you will encounter many differences of opinion. Such conflicting information arises from the difficulty of trying to satisfy the needs of the average staff member. Why not design staff work spaces especially for your existing staff? Of course, staffing will change with the years, but so will the equipment. Specific modifications have a lot to do with the age of staff, whether they wear glasses, and other considerations. Ask the library staff to conduct experiments, with one person viewing a screen at the most comfortable height and distance while another staff member measures.

Compact-Shelving Issues

Although electronic resources are becoming numerous in libraries, print collections continue to be important. Early in the planning stages, you will want to decide whether you will install compact shelving now or possibly at some time in the future. The decision needs to be made now rather than later because compact shelving requires significantly higher loading capacity than regular shelving. Although a capacity of 150 pounds per square foot live load is adequate for many stack areas, compact shelving requires about 300 pounds per square foot.

Since the additional cost of shelving and installation can mount up (a few dollars per square foot), you may wish to designate certain lower floors for this purpose. On the other hand, it is possible to designate a section or a quadrant on all levels within which the floors will be reinforced and additional load-bearing columns installed. Chicago's Harold Washington Library chose to accommodate heavy floor loads on several floors at the ends of the building to provide more flexibility when reorganizing the collection in the future.

If funds are tight, you may just elect to pour a thicker slab for the ground floor, as long as your subsoil can support the weight of fully loaded shelving. Just be very certain that your soil has been tested and found to be satisfactory. Horror stories abound about ill-fated buildings that begin sinking into the earth soon after the contractor departed. If you are not planning to install compact shelving now, be sure that the floor-to-ceiling height is sufficient to take into account both the shelving itself and the track assemblies needed.

It's a sad fact that light is considerably reduced by fully loaded compact-shelving units. In fact, light from ceiling fixtures may not shine directly into aisles even if you have given careful attention to stack lighting. It is worth the additional cost to specify that lighting fixtures be attached to moving shelves. Most manufacturers of newer compact systems can provide such fixtures.

All compact-shelving manufacturers are not equal. A number of librarians complain that they were forced to use the vendor who came in with the low bid even though the product was less than satisfactory. If compact shelving is in your future, spend some time researching the alternatives. If you decide that some types are unacceptable, put it in writing. Be certain that the RFP provides solid grounds to reject unacceptable vendors.

Ergonomics Issues

One way of defining ergonomics is "the study of the human body at work." Although the Industrial Revolution and World War II contributed to our understanding of the way human beings interact with machines, it is only in recent years that we've become aware of the dangers of bad ergonomics, such as

TIPS AND TALES

We wrote the specifications for a Spacesaver compact-shelving system. The general contractor, overseeing this construction as a subsystem, opened the bids and awarded the contract to a competing bid that was all of $200 under the Spacesaver bid. As library director, I learned of this after the contract had already been signed by the general contractor. Our university facilities planner, overseeing the project for the university, also was not consulted by the general contractor before the contract was awarded and signed. Surprise!

Recently on my mailing lists there have been comments about the pros and cons of automatic versus manual-crank compact shelving. All I can say about this is that you get what you pay for. I talked to many librarians and archivists and interviewed several compact-shelving manufacturers. I recommended Spacesaver. The director balked because of the higher price, bid it out, went with the lowest bidder, and now we live with the results.

We decided to go with manual-crank compact shelving since it is in a staff-only area. From what I've read, I think that's good. I was concerned, however, if for instance, we hire a disabled librarian—the aisles are not wide enough, he or she would have to get a wheelchair over the lip up onto the platform, and so on.

Be sure you have the weight load specs for compact shelving.

---

repetitive stress injuries. With the move in recent years from blue-collar to white-collar jobs, emphasis has moved from factories to offices and on the way human beings interact with computers: the new discipline called the human-computer interface.

Libraries are in a unique position in that they must consider not only staff members, who spend long hours at their computer screens, but also library patrons, who may spend nearly as many hours reading and doing research. From the staff point of view, increased use of computers has been associated with increased absenteeism, muscular discomfort, eyestrain, and reductions in job satisfaction.

Ergonomics of Computer Use

Human beings are not comfortable when they must remain frozen in one posture for a long period of time. The computer screen is seen as one of the main culprits because it requires that users work within a very restricted posture range. You can move a book or stack of papers up or down as well as to the left or to the right. You simply can't do this with a computer screen. Not only do humans come in different shapes and sizes requiring adjustments to their environment, but they must move frequently to remain comfortable. Such needs can be difficult enough to accommodate for staff members, but they become almost overwhelming when multiplied by the thousands of patrons who use the library. Ignoring ergonomic requirements can inflict considerable pain on the library community and can cause long-term disability.

When you select computer desks or tables, be sure you can place monitors, keyboards, and other input devices at heights that encourage proper posture and straight wrist positions. The correct monitor height can reduce eye and neck strain. Especially for staff working at service desks, workstations that permit both sitting and standing are desirable because they can promote improved circulation and reduce back strain.

Research has shown that workers using computer equipment more than one hour per day complain twice as often of neck and shoulder discomfort as a control group that did not use computer equipment. Computer users also reported eyestrain three times as often as the control group. When workers were permitted to participate in the selection of furniture and the development of layouts, absenteeism dropped from 4 percent to less than 1 percent, and error rates in document preparation fell from 25 percent to 11 percent even when the amount of computer use was actually increased.[1]

Eyestrain and Workstation Design

Eyestrain is becoming a frequent complaint from both staff and patrons who use the library's computers for long hours at a time. Symptoms include tired and dry eyes, difficulty focusing, and frequent headaches. The use of monitor screen filters and film coatings that reduce annoying flicker can help minimize strain, as can lowering overhead lighting levels to avoid glare and shadows. However, the combination of print and computers in libraries makes eyestrain an increasingly serious concern.

As discussed earlier, we librarians have been so concerned with raising light levels in order to penetrate shadowy stack areas that we sometimes forget that the modern library's lighting needs are much more complex than they used to be. Staff find that task lighting fixtures with adjustable, articulated arms provide focused light on whatever needs to be illuminated while reducing glare on computer screens. Window coverings can also eliminate screen glare, and computer screens can be positioned in such a way that they don't catch reflections from uncovered windows. Background and character colors with a high level of contrast can also be helpful.

Distance is the key consideration when positioning computer monitors. When we read or look at an object near at hand, the ciliary muscle in the eye changes the shape of the lens. Then the lens bends light rays in such a way that they strike the retina at a single point and produce a sharp image in the brain. The image is blurred if this point is too far in front of or behind the retina. When the eyes are resting and looking at nothing (sometimes called "staring into space"), they are actually focusing an average of about 31½ inches away. The closer the position of the monitor approximates this resting distance, the less eyestrain. With age, the lens changes, and this ideal point gets farther and farther away.

Viewing Angle

When we read a book, we direct our eyes downward, which just happens to be an excellent way of increasing our ability to accommodate a wider range of distances. In other words, we can read an open book on an elbow-height horizontal surface more easily than we can read the same information if presented vertically at the same distance from the eye. In fact, people prefer to look downward at an average angle of 29 degrees below the normal computer-work position, and the closer the object, the farther down people want to look. A downward gaze also reduces the need for head movement.

Still another cause of pain is "neck tilt," especially when it is increased to 30 to 45 degrees. Ideally, a forward neck posture of 15 degrees is considered best. Although this may not always be possible with user workstations, it is desirable to at least provide separate surfaces to support the keyboard and monitor. Where possible, the screen should be at a level where the user looks slightly down to the center of the screen. As you're positioning monitors, bear in mind that anyone who wears bifocals probably needs the visual display screen as low as possible, since they very likely read through the bottom part of the lens.

Because most of your patrons are not experienced computer users, it is desirable to reduce the distance between the keyboard and display screen, since they will probably move their eyes constantly between keyboard and screen to make sure they are pressing the correct keys. In the past, you might assume that the people who regularly used typewriters had been formally taught (often in high school or business school) to type correctly. This meant not only learning keystrokes but also correct posture and hand positions. Now most people who type on a computer have no formal training, so patrons may feel more discomfort after an hour at a computer than yesterday's typists experienced after several hours at a typewriter.

Physiology and Workstation Design

One study of performance conducted on employees of the State Farm Insurance Company showed as much as a 15 percent increase in productivity with ergonomically designed workstations and seating.[2] A study of back discomfort by the Norwegian State Institute found that back-related absenteeism was halved after improvements to workstation layout and seating.[3] Years ago, it was decided that a standard height of 29 inches for working desk height and 26 inches for typewriters met the physical requirements of the "average" individual.

Women and Stress Injuries

Although chairs may be adjustable, these fixed heights mean that shorter-than-average individuals must raise their chair to reach a comfortable working position at a too-high work surface and either leave their legs hanging with their feet off the floor or endure discomfort from pressure under the thigh where it presses against the chair. Since many nerve endings and veins pass through this part of the leg, such a position forces the user to sit forward in the chair to avoid discomfort, leaving the back without support.

Since desk heights were determined before large numbers of women joined the workforce, the "average" individual was really an average male. It is, therefore, more often women who fall victim to repetitive stress injuries. Taller people are also affected, however, when the work surface is too low, causing them to slouch with a curved spine and their knees near or approaching the chin level. When a tall person sits in a chair, the chair will tilt back, so the sitter must then sit forward away from the back support. This may cause back pain, fatigue, or aggravated tension.

Ergonomically Correct Chairs

What do people do in libraries? They sit! Of course, that's not the only thing they do, but seating is certainly an important consideration when designing a library. Therefore, ergonomically correct chairs are especially important. When staff or users are working in front of a computer screen, their body parts (back, thighs, elbows, and legs) should be at right angles with their feet solidly planted on the floor. Chairs should support the natural S-shape of their spines. When they are reading or writing, it is easier on their backs if the chair seats can follow their body movements forward to prevent pressure on their thighs and the leg arteries.

When selecting chairs, look for resilient padding that reduces contact stress on hips and thighs and provides even weight distribution. Look for adjustable height, sliding seat depth, back supports, and adjustable backward and forward tilt, as well as height- and weight-adjustable arm supports. Ideally, users should be able to sit back in their chairs with their thighs parallel to the floor and their weight evenly distributed across the chair. Sitting straight upright may look healthy and alert, but it rotates the pelvis backward, thus straightening the lordosis (curvature) that is natural to the spine. A chair that reclines somewhat is better for reading text from a monitor, while leaning forward is more appropriate for paper copy and other work involving fine detail. In the case of library staff work areas, integrated library software, e-mail, web browsers, and other networked communications programs eliminate much of the walking from the workday, resulting in dangerous semi-immobility.

Drawbacks of Executive Chairs

Choose chairs with recessed or sloping arms rather than chairs with high and prominent arms, because high arms prevent users from being properly positioned at their desks. Armless chairs, however, are usually an even better choice, especially at angled workstations. Historically, typists never had chairs with arms, but somehow we've come to see chair arms as a status symbol. The exalted boss had a "papa bear"–sized executive chair with fixed arms that distinguished his work space from that of the lowly typist. It is hard to accept the fact that the typist had the better deal. Footrests can be helpful for maintaining proper back posture, and some even include a back-and-forth rocking motion that exercises the feet, ankles, and legs.

The renowned architect Mies van der Rohe once described a chair as more difficult to construct than a skyscraper. The people who will use your library come in all shapes and sizes. No matter where they choose to sit, whether at a computer terminal, television screen, table, or study carrel, they should be able to find a convenient chair where they can sit comfortably for several hours. Few people are willing to stand for more than a few minutes, yet libraries frequently equip stacks, reference collections, and OPAC stations without a chair or stool in sight.

Possibly it is because patrons once walked from drawer to drawer while using the old card catalogs that librarians fail to realize how uncomfortable their customers become when using modern online catalogs. A customer may spend half an hour or more at an OPAC station marking records, printing bibliographies, and accessing resources at remote libraries. Surely we don't want to discourage them from taking their time with the catalog to narrow their search to precisely the materials they really need. The modern trend toward fully functional personal computers located throughout the library is gradually solving the OPAC problem, but the number of users uncomfortably camped out on the carpet in stack and reference areas has not declined. Chairs are essential for most library activities.

Chairs for Real People

Be sure your designer or architect knows that you want to test any chair under consideration. Ask for sample chairs from vendors and have your library staff test them. Ideally, chairs should be passed around so staff can sit on them for several hours at a time. Among the things they should be looking for are

> separate chair seat pan and back if the chair is adjustable
>
> concave seat
>
> solid foam cushioning that holds its shape
>
> "waterfall" edge that's rounded so circulation will not be restricted in the back of the thigh
>
> seats wide enough to accommodate a variety of people shapes (seats that for most people extend at least one inch from the hips on either side)
>
> armrests that don't prevent users from getting close enough to the work surface
>
> appropriate height (low enough so women's feet reach the floor and high enough to allow older users to rise without difficulty)

Repetitive Stress and Workstation Design

When most people think of repetitive strain injuries (RSIs), the first thing that comes to mind is carpal tunnel syndrome or possibly tendonitis. Many of us have friends and associates who are suffering from some condition that causes pain in the wrists or fingers. Workers with hands bent away from a straight hand in line with the wrist position are prime candidates for an RSI. Bending or arching the hand can stretch or compress tendons, ligaments, and nerves.

A common problem with computer keyboards is that they are too high, so users are forced to raise their arms. If shorter people must raise their arms from the shoulders to support the weight of both the upper and lower arm, they strain the muscles across the top of the shoulders and at the base of the neck. Ideally, the keyboard should be at the same level as the elbow when users drop their arms to their sides while sitting. This allows them to work in a comfortable sitting posture, with their forearms at right angles to their bodies and parallel to the floor. Keyboards that are too high cause people to drop their wrists or palms onto the surface that supports the keyboard to relieve their discomfort.

Of course, your first concern must be library staff who, unlike patrons, cannot get up and leave if they are uncomfortable. However, senior genealogists, students writing papers, or any number of other avid patrons can easily log more consecutive hours in the library than a staff member. The needs of all these people should not be ignored. If workstations allow all keyboards to be adjustable, the home row of keys can be adjusted to elbow height, making possible a straight hand in line with the wrist position that can be maintained without shrugging.

By this point, you and your planning group have made most of the decisions that go into designing a functional and attractive library building. The next step is to turn those plans into brick and mortar.

NOTES

1. "Deploying an Effective Ergonomics Process: Part 1: Risk Management," *Ergo Advisor* (Spring 1998).
2. M. Franz Schneider, *Ergonomics and Economics* (Calgary, AB: Allscan Distributors, 1999), available at www.allscan.ca/ergo/ergoecon.htm.
3. Ibid.

RESOURCES

Bridger, R. S. *Introduction to Ergonomics.* 3rd ed. Boca Raton, FL: CRC, 2009.

Brown, Carol R. *Interior Design for Libraries: Drawing on Function and Appeal.* Chicago: American Library Association, 2002.

_____. *Planning Library Interiors: The Selection of Furnishings for the 21st Century.* Phoenix, AZ: Oryx, 1995.

Davidson, Mary Alice. *2007 Library Buying Decisions Series: Vol. I, Furnishings.* Bethesda, MD: LYPonline.com, 2007.

Foa, Linda. *Furniture for the Workplace.* New York: Architecture and Interior Design Library, 1992.

Marras, William S., and Waldemar Karwowski. *The Occupational Ergonomics Handbook: Interventions, Controls, and Applications in Occupational Ergonomics.* 2nd ed. Boca Raton, FL: CRC/Taylor and Francis, 2006.

McKeown, Céline. *Office Ergonomics: Practical Applications.* Boca Raton, FL: CRC, 2008.

Woodward, Jeannette A. *Creating the Customer-Driven Academic Library.* Chicago: American Library Association, 2009.

_____. *Creating the Customer-Driven Library: Building on the Bookstore Model.* Chicago: American Library Association, 2005.

RESOURCE ORGANIZATIONS

American Society of Interior Designers (ASID)
608 Massachusetts Ave. NE
Washington, DC 20002-6006
(800) 610-2743
www.interiors.org

American Society of Testing and Materials
Committee on Resilient Floor Coverings
100 Barr Harbor Dr.
West Conshohocken, PA 19428-2959
(206) 822-2423

International Interior Design Assn. (IIDA)
341 Merchandise Mart
Chicago, IL 60654-1104
(312) 467-1950
(312) 467-0779 (fax)
www.iida.com

Surviving Construction

9

At this point, let's imagine that plans have at last been finalized, funds have been raised, and ground has been broken. The contractor is on the site, equipped with the largest, loudest machinery you've ever seen. You feel as if you and the library staff have survived enough crises, pitched battles, and misunderstandings to last a lifetime, but you have more "adventures" ahead. Eventually, your library building will emerge from the clutter and chaos, interior partitions will be in place, and it will begin to feel as if the library may soon be a reality.

CHANGE ORDERS

Since this is probably your first library construction project, you're still a neophyte when it comes to reading blueprints. No matter how diligently you study the plans, you will almost inevitably fail to recognize problems that your contractor will insist are clearly indicated. There are also a number of vital necessities that the architects solemnly promised to include but somehow forgot. This means that as construction on the new library progresses, change orders will become the scourge of your existence. You will discover that assumptions any ten-year-old could be expected to take for granted have eluded your building professionals. To be honest, it is sometimes your own fault for having failed to ask enough questions or spend sufficient time digesting the information you've been given. Change orders almost always cost money unless you can clearly establish that you made your needs known in advance (usually in writing) and your request was ignored.

Santa Rosa Junior College, Petaluma,
California, Herold Mahoney Library,
TLCD Architecture, tlcd.com.
Photo: Technical Imagery Studios.

There is probably no way of avoiding change orders altogether, but they can usually be minimized. In addition, better written documentation of your requirements may mean that the library need not pay for all change orders. Don't trust yourself to catch every problem. Ask the library staff to review floor plans and imagine themselves performing their usual tasks in the new spaces. Request extra copies of the blueprints, but be prepared to pay for them. The relatively minor cost of extra sets of plans will be more than repaid by savings on change orders later. Ask staff to think about the locations of closets, positioning of light switches, and placement of doors. Each person could be made responsible for identifying potential problems in his or her assigned area.

Getting the Numbers Right

Libraries rarely cost precisely what we expect. Since there are thousands of variables (e.g., the price of steel, the condition of the soil, labor disputes), numbers will keep changing throughout the life of the project. The problem is that library boards, government agencies, and newspapers and other media outlets, as well as taxpayers, have all been told that the library will cost a given sum. Sometimes that number is specified in a sales tax resolution or bond election. The city council or the county commission has been assured that this amount will be needed and no more.

Politicians get elected by promising to control costs and save the taxpayers' money. If they have not been prepared for cost increases or have not approved any additional funds in advance, there's a good chance that the library may be blamed for fiscal irresponsibility. When I write "library," read "library director." Of course, the library board has the final word in monetary decisions, but it is often assumed that the library director is the one responsible. Newspapers may be willing to run upbeat articles extolling the wonderful new library on page 10, but you can bet that the story accusing "library officials" of fiscal mismanagement will be right there on the front page.

Many librarians have discovered that no one on the project is really keeping track of each and every unanticipated cost. Even a project watchdog or manager hired by the library may be unclear about who's paying for a change order. The contract itself may not clearly spell out which costs are fixed and which can be adjusted by the contractor. For example, a limited selection of wall treatments or flooring materials might be included in the contract, but so-called premium selections cost extra.

Cost Overages

Because library directors' reputations can be irreparably damaged by such misunderstandings, it's in their interest to become the best source of accurate information. Unfortunately, this means becoming something of a broken record, asking again and again "Will this cost extra?" "Will this increase the cost to the library?" Each time it becomes clear that something must be done differently or that more materials or labor will be needed, you will need to find out who's paying for it. It's best to expect that contractors will interpret contractual clauses in the way that's most advantageous to themselves. That means you will need to practically commit to memory the relevant sections. Fuzzy phrases should be discussed and clarified in written communication.

Who Approves Financial Commitments?

In the first chapter, we discussed the need to start out with a clear understanding between the library director and the library board or university administration. In the case of public libraries, the same goes for an understanding between library participants and local government officials. Among the most contentious subjects is the authority to make financial commitments. Again and again, it will be learned that something will cost more than anticipated. Must the increase be officially approved? Can it be authorized by the library director without board input? Can it be authorized by the library board without city or county input? Is the library director authorized to make monetary commitments up to but not exceeding a given amount? For smaller cost increases, it is usually possible to spend a little more on one thing and cut back on another. Eventually, however, such changes will put a project over budget. Neither local government agencies nor taxpayers react well to unexpected cost overruns, so it is essential that a plan be in place to sound early warning bells.

When you were a child, you probably played the game "musical chairs." Each time the music stopped everyone rushed to take a seat, but one person was left standing without a chair. When building projects go over budget, everyone rushes to escape blame. While the library board and government agencies maneuver to protect themselves, the one person left standing is often the library director. No one is so intimately involved in the project or so publicly visible.

Preparing for Conflict

Occasionally, even with the most efficient project management, there is simply no way to complete a library building under budget. If the worst happens, library directors should realize that they could be left, to mix my metaphors, holding the bag. To protect themselves, they should be able to produce a variety of written documents, including correspondence with local officials, minutes of library board and city council meetings, and other evidence that procedures were followed, officials kept informed, and expenditures authorized by the appropriate persons. I emphasize the word *written* here because casual conversations provide little support. When bureaucrats' jobs are at stake, they may conveniently forget that they were made aware of problems or unofficially agreed to changes.

Precise Numbers Are Essential

Since contractors are probably keeping track of additional charges on spreadsheets, it's a good idea for library directors to maintain project spreadsheets of their own that include as much description as needed to clarify each and every unexpected expenditure. At frequent intervals, compare your figures with your contractor's and reconcile any differences. Ask your project manager for input, and you may even want to be sure that other building professionals agree with your understanding. Once you're sure that your figures are correct, share them with your board and other oversight groups when it's appropriate to do so. In my experience, building professionals tend to overlook a variety of costs when the money will not be going directly to their firm. This occurs less frequently with the design-build delivery system when architects, engineers, and contractors all work under the umbrella of the same business entity. However, the problem is never completely absent.

If it looks as if the project will go over budget, begin taking action immediately. Find out what your options are. What chance is there that additional funding will be approved? How might the project be pared down without doing major damage to the future library program? Then decide how best to present this information to those

Carnegie Library of Pittsburgh, Hill District Library, Pfaffmann and Associates.
Photo: Marc Soracco Photography.

who must make the final decision. Since you knew from the start that your building might cost more than expected, you should have a plan in the back of your head to deal with this eventuality. Of course, you want to believe that every inch of space is vital and must not be sacrificed. However, to survive the ordeal with a minimum of conflict and with your reputation intact, concessions need to be made. You will need to see the project as the public might. What will really matter to them?

THE SPECIAL PITFALLS OF A RENOVATION

If you are renovating an older library rather than building from scratch and you're planning to keep the library open during construction, you can expect a pretty harrowing experience. You will be living with constant banging, clanging, and confusion. You and your staff will be asked to vacate areas crammed with books and equipment with less than twenty-four hours' warning. You may knock down and reassemble the same stack sections three or four times during construction. Although surviving such an ordeal is difficult, you can at least minimize the disruption.

Coexisting with Construction

Whether you're renovating or enlarging a space, be very sure that the architects and contractor fully understand the expanded electrical needs of a modern library and have given due consideration to the source of the additional electrical power. To provide for the additional power needed while construction is under way, a new breaker panel should probably be added even before the project begins. It is not uncommon for a project to come to a screeching halt while change orders are filed for the new panel.

To minimize other problems, here are some other things to consider if you are renovating an existing facility.

Work should be planned in phases and, when possible, during low activity times to minimize disruptions to patrons and staff.

Cleanliness is vital. It may be necessary to install temporary drywall partitions in work areas to reduce noise, dust, and dirt as well as to keep people out of the hard hat area.

Be careful that the project does not grow out of control. Renovation was probably chosen over new construction because of cost. You will inevitably find more and more that needs renovating, but you have a budget to think about. If funding is really flexible, then maybe a new building or at least a new addition would have been a better choice.

Don't start confusing frills with functionality.

TIPS AND TALES

Contractors don't always (or perhaps usually) build what's on the blueprints. I've met a number who couldn't read them—they just build what they think is needed, or easiest, regardless of what the architect designs. This leads to light switches in the wrong place, plumbing running through vaults, open sewer pipes in offices and vaults, air-conditioning fan-coil units draining onto shelving, and ductwork penetrating vaults rather than being routed around them. The costs go up and up as you find them after signing off.

"To engineer is human," and humans make lots of mistakes. Be sure to encourage both architect and contractor to communicate with you frequently, discussing any potential problems they have identified. If you can catch the problem early, a change order may not be needed. Hiring a watchdog early in the project can also help to anticipate difficulties and make needed adjustments before they require tearing out walls and ductwork or making other expensive changes.

Don't assume that people will inform you of changes. Keep your nose in the action, even if people try to play political games with you. Keep asking questions, and verify what has changed or not changed over time. Sometimes those in charge will "OK" what they think is a relatively minor change and not bother to check with you.

Make sure you know what the deadline for "free" changes is. At some point in time, any changes made cost a lot of money.

Be a "hands-on" owner during the construction, so you can check each day to see if things are getting done the way they should—even if you have a construction manager on the project. The manager will make sure you are getting done on time and budget what you requested, but you may need to make adjustments. If you don't look, you will never know!

Keeping your eyes open helps a lot. I encountered two men standing in a hallway with a set of blueprints looking at the ceiling outside the film vault at an institution where I used to work. When I questioned them, it turned out they were running new ductwork for a group of rooms occupied by a different department. They were discussing cutting holes in the walls of the refrigerated vault and running the ductwork through the vault into the next building. They planned to do this work in the middle of the night when no one was around so as not to disturb anyone. This would have destroyed the environmental integrity of the vault. When I suggested that there might be a better way, we examined the plans and discovered that we could route it through the ceilings of a general office, avoiding the vault entirely.

You need to go over every detail of every plan. Architects "forget" the necessities to make their overall plan work. This means measuring and remeasuring, counting wall sockets, checking door openings, keeping track of plumbing lines, researching fire-control systems, checking sight lines for staff who oversee public areas, and so on.

The finished measurements of rooms are smaller than sizes shown on plans. This can make a difference when planning the size of work tables and the placement of furniture.

Know your building. I stopped a contractor from installing compact shelving over a service tunnel because I knew the tunnel was there and it wasn't on the plans he was supplied. I also discovered that a contractor had led a hazardous waste fume duct into the building's cold air return rather than to a chemical waste duct because I examined all of the building plans. It sounds like we had a terrible time, but I found the whole thing (for the time I was involved) to be rather interesting. It has taught me to keep a close eye on projects that are being handled by others outside the library.

Don't do a little here and a little there. Renovation is disruptive, so you will want to concentrate on the neediest areas.

Be sure that the carpet and wall coverings specified by interior designers are readily available. Insist they avoid custom choices that can cause delay. You certainly don't want to have to operate the library on a cement floor, clear everything out of the space, lay carpet, and bring everything back. Besides, custom selections can cost up to 50 percent more than standard styles.

Remaining Open for Business

Closing your library during renovations places a heavy burden on your user community. No matter how nerve-racking, it's often better to stay open while construction is under way. A temporary library building solves some problems but creates others. Go over the pros and cons with your building professionals. Compare the costs. For example, if you remain open during construction, scheduling subcontractors will be much more expensive. Instead of doing all the electrical work at once, your electrical contractor may need to divide the work into several phases, scheduling each phase when staff and customers are not occupying the space. This is surprisingly costly.

On the other hand, a temporary move would mean finding, renting, and possibly remodeling another facility, as well as moving furniture, equipment, and materials back and forth. You and your library staff will need to identify all the costs of a temporary move yourselves. Then ask your building professionals to estimate the additional cost of renovating the building in phases, working around the needs of library staff and customers. Don't forget the additional safety precautions that will be needed with large numbers of people spending time at the construction site. Also consider the extra work involved for the library staff and the disruption of library operations. Compare the two estimates and make your decision.

How Much Disruption?

If you decide to remain in the library building, which services must continue to function throughout the period? Which collections must be available? How can you maintain convenient and safe access to the library? Be sure your contractor understands your priorities and the need for minimal disruption of power and water. Work together to find ways to avoid excessive noise, vibration, fumes, dust, and debris. You may have some difficulty getting your building professionals to see the library operation through the eyes of the staff and users. They may imagine that the inconveniences will be much less intrusive than turns out to be the case. They are accustomed to working in environments in which noise is not as great a problem as in a library environment. Reading and study are not activities that can take place in the presence of constant loud noise. It is important that the architects and contractors be honest and identify the true scope of the renovation and its impact on library activities.

One reason that disruption is so extensive is that building professionals cannot assess the existing situation without opening spaces in walls and ceilings to examine structural, mechanical, electrical, and plumbing systems. Exploratory demolition may seem unnecessarily disruptive, but early investigative work is essential. It is far better to uncover hidden conditions as soon as possible and solve problems early in the design process rather than later, when surprises result in expensive remedial work.

Library Services and the Project Schedule

How will your contractor sequence the project schedule? Will crews be working horizontally floor by floor, vertically, or randomly as space becomes available? Discuss these plans at length. Don't be taken by surprise each time you are asked to vacate a space. Try to look at the library as a builder might. Plumbing, for instance, might be done vertically with plumbing risers and floor penetrations, while other segments include horizontally adjacent spaces.

Tactfully encourage your builder to spend time on a phasing study to help avoid problems, such as running piping or ducts through an area that has already been renovated or performing disruptive work near occupied areas. A good phasing study is in the contractor's interest as well as yours, since an accurate schedule minimizes delays and costly change orders as well as allowing subcontractors to submit more accurate bids.

Try to identify the most frequently used areas in the library and request that, when possible, your contractor schedule work on those areas during low-traffic periods. In an academic library, summer is an excellent time but is not always convenient for the contractor. You can probably win more compromises if you and your staff vacate areas on time with a minimum of grumping. Ideally, only one wing or area should be under construction at a time, but such a plan may be unrealistic.

The safety of your staff and users is your most important consideration during this grueling period. Construction is a dangerous activity, and you should work with your contractor to ensure that your facility remains a safe place throughout the project. For example, emergency exits must be maintained, and construction activity must be segregated from patron areas with barriers and signage. Unusually disruptive activities (like turning off all the electricity) should be specially scheduled.

Avoiding Crises

There will probably be times when you have no alternative but to close the library. These times, for example, when water, electricity, natural gas, and other utilities are connected, should be kept to a minimum with careful planning. Get into the habit of having brief chats with your contractors. Make the chats as upbeat as possible so they don't start avoiding you. Communication is possibly the most important ingredient in a successful project. Communicate what you learn to your staff and customers through meetings, e-mail, newsletters, signs, and notices. Customers will be forewarned and can schedule their visits at the most opportune times.

Ask about subcontractor activity and how it will affect the library's operation. Sometimes your general contractor has the best intentions in the world, but somehow subcontractors don't get the word. Be prepared to lose data, power, or water unexpectedly. Such crises will probably occur sooner rather than later, so a contingency plan for dealing with the consequences is essential.

Temporary Quarters

After weighing various options, you may decide that it is not possible to continue to provide library services while construction activities are taking place. In a smaller building, for example, there may be no way to separate the construction from library-occupied areas, and the entire building may become a hard hat area. It may be that library activities can comfortably coexist with the construction of a new wing, but this may be impossible when extra floors are being added. Each project is different, of course, but major renovations are unlikely to be completed in less than a year. Your challenge will be to find a way to function as normally as possible during this period and to close your doors for the briefest time possible. University students obviously must have access to their library's collection, and public libraries will be under considerable pressure from their boards and borrowers to do business as usual.

Just as boards and administrators approach a building project with little understanding of how libraries work, they may also have unrealistic ideas of what constitutes adequate temporary quarters. Many facilities will not make satisfactory ad hoc libraries, and the cost of even minimal refitting of them is usually greater than most people imagine. You will probably need every bit of tact and negotiating skill you possess to reach consensus on an acceptable facility.

Be sure you are prepared well ahead of time with a list of minimal requirements for a facility. Use your online discussion groups to identify a network of colleagues who have superintended a move to temporary quarters. Consider whether it might be possible to hire a library consultant specifically for the task of identifying a suitable facility. Be sure you have access to information about such vital matters as the floor's live-load capacity. Proposed temporary facilities are often old, and technical information may have been lost along the way. If in doubt, hire an engineer to make sure the building can accommodate not only the weight of book stacks but the data and power needs of a library.

Vacant Facilities

I have noticed one category of temporary library buildings that were originally built during the 1960s and 1970s. In many cases, they have been empty

TALES

We had a provision in our contract that the builders would have to give us thirty days' notice any time they wanted something moved. The minute they fell behind, this provision went out the door, and it was our entire fault if something didn't get moved quickly enough for them to work.

As the project began, the campus facilities planner predicted that only two departments of the library would face the double disruption of moving to temporary or transitional quarters during the expansion and remodeling. In the end, eleven of the thirteen library departments had to operate out of temporary locations before moving into permanent locations.

or little used for a number of years, but they're not quite decrepit enough to be torn down. In our town, the choice was the old American Legion hall. Since membership had been dwindling over many years, the building had not been properly maintained. Furnace and air conditioner filters were not changed, moisture seeped in under the roof shingles, and routine cleaning and maintenance tasks were not performed.

The absence of windows in structures of the period meant that little outside air ever entered the building. Dirt and mold gradually invaded practically every nook and cranny. Superficially, however, the building looked sturdy enough, and it was not until library staff began experiencing the symptoms of sick building syndrome that anyone realized the building was toxic. The big problem, of course, was that very little money was available to deal with the multitude of problems. HVAC equipment and ductwork would have been replaced if this were the library's permanent home. A new roof was desperately needed, but there were no funds for that either. One "Band-Aid" solution after another was tried. Maintenance staff worked overtime, and every inch was cleaned and cleaned again until the building reeked of disinfectant. Yet the allergies and illnesses persisted.

Planning a Temporary Move

An excellent source of information on managing a move to temporary quarters is the Education Resources Information Center document "Planning and Strategy for Setting Up and Operating Academic Libraries in Temporary Quarters: Experiences of Two Northeast Colleges."[1] The libraries of both Skidmore College and Lyndon State College moved temporarily to gymnasiums on their respective college campuses. In both cases, the new space was much smaller than what had been available in their library buildings. The staffs of both libraries were forced to cope with very stressful conditions before they could at last move into their expanded and refurbished buildings. Although the two staffs went about their Herculean tasks in somewhat different ways, the following is a general outline of the procedure they recommend.

1. Measure the stack areas, work spaces, and seating areas to determine the minimum space needed for each function in the temporary facility. Bear in mind that you will need to function with a very limited collection and very little work space. However, if the library shrinks beyond a certain size, there is little point to remaining open.

2. Ascertain that the live load of the floor in the temporary facility is at least 150 pounds per square foot.

3. Create a preliminary stack layout, ideally using computer-aided-design software.

4. Calculate the total shelf space available in the temporary facility by taking into consideration the maximum number of stacks and shelves that can be accommodated in the space.

5. Subtract the total shelf space available in the temporary facility from the total linear shelf space in the library to determine how many books will need to be placed in storage. This must be done precisely or you will end up having to transport part of the collection twice.

6. Lay out spaces for circulation, reference, patron seating, technical services, and the other areas that must be accommodated. If the architect is not available, create preliminary layouts for spaces using computer-aided-design software.

7. Identify any areas where you can squeeze out space by moving stacks closer together or doubling up on staff spaces. Stack areas will probably not be wheelchair-accessible in the temporary location. You may wish to consider closing the stacks or identifying ways in which you can more effectively serve the needs of users in wheelchairs.

8. Design areas in such a way that furniture such as stack units and file cabinets can substitute for walls and can be used to control access. You will probably need to use the temporary space more or less as is and will be unable to construct or tear down walls.

9. Determine where additional power outlets and phone and data jacks must be installed. Keep these to a minimum, since they will be temporary and may use up funds needed for more urgent matters.

10. Decide upon a method for identifying books for storage.

11. Determine how much seating space is absolutely necessary. Remember that other spaces are available for reading and study. You will probably need to sacrifice seating space for collections.

12. Consider using a larger portion of the acquisitions budget for online resources to make up for unavailable printed materials.

13. Prioritize services and decide which ones will continue to be available throughout the transition period. For example, service to outside groups may need to be restricted.

> **TIP**
>
> Be ready with figures if a city council, manager, or county commissioner wants the library to move into an old building that doesn't have the proper foundation to hold the weight of books.

SIGNAGE SYSTEMS

Whether you are spending your last weeks and months in the old building or camped out in temporary quarters, construction workers are rapidly (you hope) approaching the completion of the job. Once the new building or addition has achieved its final shape and the interior partitions are in place, it's time for you and your staff to start thinking about signs. Since the building and its environs are still a hard hat area, this will very likely mean increased stress for both you and your contractor.

Signs are custom-made for your particular library. Earlier in the project, you should have prepared a general list of the kinds of signs that would be needed. You looked at signage in other libraries and compared samples from different vendors, settling on one that offered quality at a reasonable price. Since larger vendors can provide a signage consultant (whose services will be truly invaluable), use the opportunity to master Signage 101 while you're waiting for your building to take shape. However, there is no way you can anticipate precisely what will be needed until you're actually inside the building.

Walk the Talk

Blueprints cannot really tell you what is visible from what angle. It inevitably turns out that a sign that looked great on the floor plan is actually hidden from view by a column, stairway, or ceiling fixture. Visitors may approach from an unexpected direction. Until you can walk the length and breadth of the space, you cannot know for sure which signs are needed and precisely where they should be mounted. On the other hand, if you delay ordering signs until the contractor gives the all clear, your patrons, instead of exclaiming about the wonders of the new building, will be wailing in frustration as they unsuccessfully search for the restrooms or the DVD section.

Imagine for a moment your newly opened library. Your first users enter through the pristine front door, proceed into the lobby area, and look around. What now? How will you make it clear that the periodicals are straight ahead and to the right, that the computer commons is behind the reference area, and that the literature books are on the second floor? "Signs," you answer quickly.

Effective Signs

But just as you utter the word, an image of your present library pops into your head. Signs are plastered everywhere; some are professionally produced, but many are homemade and dog-eared. The thought of all those beautiful new walls marred by ugly signs is too painful to contemplate. Why must we provide signs anyway, argue some librarians (and architects). Nobody ever looks at them. Patrons ask directions to the restrooms when signs are in plain view.

Just remember what you know about information-seeking behavior. Your users respond differently to visual stimuli, but most find simple, clearly worded signs helpful. However, color blindness, spatial perception, and many other factors all influence the effectiveness of your signage. How will you provide enough signage without cluttering up the place? How will you design signs that harmonize with the decor yet stand out sufficiently to be noticed? How will you decide which areas your users will find on their own without difficulty and which will require several signs at different points to keep them from becoming confused?

Organized Approach

A systematic approach to signage allows you to communicate information effectively to your users. Usually called a signage system, an effective plan demands a careful analysis of your users' needs. It forces you and the library staff to adopt standardized terminology, always calling a location by the same name. It is only after you know what you want to say and where you want to say it that you're ready to consider layout, color, and other design elements. The appropriate use of signs can considerably reduce the number of simple directional questions asked at service desks, as well as make users aware of the full range of library services and resources available to them.

A complete signage system can include changeable floor signs, hanging and wall-mounted directional signs, room-identification signs, and point-of-use instructional signs where appropriate. The hallmark of a really good system, however, is its ability to respond to the user's need to progress from general to specific information and provide directional information at decision points where choices must be made. Your challenge is to identify the best means of displaying information at precisely the point of need, taking into consideration all the unique challenges posed by your building design. Not only will you be using signage to overcome them, but you can even make them work to your customers' advantage.

Working with your vendor, draw up a "sign schedule," a detailed, sign-by-sign list keyed to locations in the building. A professional sign designer provided by your vendor can render invaluable assistance in deciding upon graphic standards like typography, colors, layout, and other characteristics. Take advantage of the design features of the new building that lend themselves especially well to signage. Although your old library will be physically quite different from the new one, you can still gather information about the behavior and needs of your users.

You can also keep track of the most frequently asked directional questions and conduct on-site tests to be sure that proposed solutions actually work. Nevertheless, no matter how careful you are, you are bound to make some mistakes. Be sure that you reevaluate signs after opening to decide whether they should be relocated or additional signs should be purchased.

Signage 101

The task of designing a signage system is fraught with potential problems, but the following suggestions will help you avoid many of the most common ones.

Use durable materials that can stand up to long-term use but allow for changing needs as the library grows.

Retain information on the vendor and on the style, colors, and materials of the signs to make sure new signs will be compatible with existing ones.

Use symbols and terminology that users have become accustomed to in other public spaces such as airports and hospitals.

When using specialized library terminology, develop a "controlled vocabulary" of library terms. Don't, for example, refer to magazines on one sign and periodicals on another.

Select the most readily understandable names for rooms and services. For example, the term *checkout* means more than *circulation* to most users.

Place building directories in lobby areas and near elevators. Be sure directories have modular lettering that can be changed easily when locations change.

List library resources, areas, and services shown in relation to a building map and provide additional information closer to the destination.

Provide self-guided tours in print, on your website, or on tape, keyed to locations on the building directory.

It is helpful when users can identify areas from a distance, so large signs with few words or oversized graphics are effective to mark large areas. Signs marking facilities for handicapped users should be visible from a considerable distance.

Provide signs to identify specific library tools. Display "how-to" information beside important resources like OPAC catalogs, specialized computer equipment, databases, and print reference sources. Present such basic information clearly and in as few words as possible. Use signage to reinforce library instruction or to provide simplified explanations of various library procedures.

Use the sign system's graphic elements on bulletin boards, suggestion/response boards, and fliers. Bulletin boards in high-traffic areas can be very effective for posting current information.

Keep regulatory signs to a minimum, but clearly communicate smoking, food/beverage, noise, copyright, and security policies.

Provide signs for fire exit routes, emergency procedures, meeting room capacities, and other information required by law.

Provide changeable signs to notify users of temporary conditions, library hours, and special events.

The Signage System Schedule

If you've ever had the job of designing a signage system, you'll realize that it is far from an easy task. General plans for the system should be included as part of the overall library building design, and the basic components should be developed as part of the interior design and space-planning process. Get bids from sign vendors early in the construction process. You need not provide the actual wording, and you need only estimate the number and size of the signs needed. As mentioned earlier, until you can actually walk through the building and approach each area from different directions, you will not be able to decide on the exact wording and placement of signs. Even then, unless you are clairvoyant, you cannot possibly imagine every wrong turn your users are likely to make until you actually move into the new facility.

Perhaps the best solution may be to divide your project into two stages, leaving funds in your budget to purchase additional signs from your vendor after you have had a chance to live in the building for a while. You might also insert a provision in the signage contract that allows you to make limited changes after you've had a chance to observe your customers' reactions. It may even be a good idea to withhold some money until you're satisfied, although this may be impossible if all capital funding disappears in a puff of smoke on a given day.

Planning for Change

Even if you somehow manage to open your library with the right signs in the right places, this blissful state will not long continue. Libraries are changing at an astounding pace. We librarians seem to spend half our work lives moving things around. One area may begin its existence as a listening area, then be converted to a space for young adults, and ultimately become a computer lab. Somehow your signage must keep up with these transformations. Changeable elements are needed to keep pace with your changing floor plan. Modular signs with panels that slide in and out are useful for this purpose. Individual letters that slide in and out can be handy, or they can be extremely frustrating if your more creative patrons make a habit of rearranging the letters. When you're considering purchasing signage components from a vendor, ask your staff to take on the roles of troublesome patrons and see how difficult it is to disassemble modular signs.

Easily Updated Signs

Directories will probably be the most expensive signs you purchase. Most directories include floor plans for each level and indicate the collections and rooms in each area. For example, the word *literature* may be screen-printed on the floor plan in the northwest corner of the second floor. When you reorganize and move the science collection into this area, the directory will become obsolete. Since the library is unlikely to have funds to replace the directory, it is likely to remain as it is, misleading users who are seeking the literature collection.

Rather than include complete location names, why not label the floor plan with a series of numbers or letters? To the side of the floor plan, include a space where you can insert modular (changeable) letters that spell out the location names. Take a look at the directories in your local shopping mall. Theirs are probably far more elaborate than you can afford, but they have the same problem of accommodating change. Think of how many stores come and go in a short period of time. Because directories use up so much of your signage budget, you may even want to try to find an alternative to the professionally produced cabinet-type models. I have seen very attractive directories that were made from a sheet of Masonite imaginatively designed by a local sign painter. Locations were indicated with letters or numbers as suggested above. However, the actual names were listed on a small modular sign that was adjacent or attached to the large Masonite one.

Sign vendors seem to go out of business with disturbing rapidity. This can become a major problem when your modular signage components are unique and cannot be used with components supplied by another vendor. Some incompatibility is probably inevitable, but think twice if you hear a vendor touting a "revolutionary new design."

Modular Systems

Invest in modular signage components to display the call numbers at the end of stack ranges, since nothing looks worse than typed or handwritten index cards, even if they are displayed in small metal frames. Before you contract with a vendor, request samples of its products so that you can see how tamper resistant they are. You will discover that an enterprising child or college student can deface or dismantle poorly designed ones with a minimum of effort. The words can be rearranged to spell out messages you don't want to inadvertently communicate to your users. Since these systems are made up of thousands of little pieces, be sure that someone in the library is in charge of storing the components in an organized manner and "editing" signs as needed.

Temporary Signs

Much of the sign clutter in your present library results from the need for temporary signs explaining policies, advertising events, or associated with displays. Fortunately, color ink-jet and laser printers do an excellent job of creating professional-looking, spur-of-the-moment signs. The problem is that they quickly become dog-eared and dirty if tacked or taped to your walls. A wonderful solution is a wall-mounted, window-type sign that most vendors keep in stock. These consist of frames, usually color-coordinated with your other signs, that surround an 8½-by-11-inch glass or plastic window. The frames may be large or small and come with screen-printed library logos or text like "Coming Attractions." They may be either portable or permanently mounted. Quickly produced ink-jet signs can be slipped into the window, where they stay clean and protected.

Soon after you open your doors, you will find yourself at war with users who try to post their own signs. Within less than a week, you will have pieces of paper taped to your doors, windows, elevators, and on every blank wall. Although you may feel tempted to stalk through the library ripping off the offending sheets of paper, it is probably best for public relations and your own mental health to find another solution. Bulletin and message boards help keep clutter to a minimum, and tack strips also allow users to post fliers in a limited, controlled space.

Signs You May Not Need

It may be that libraries have too many signs reading "Staff Only" or "No Admittance." With recent staff downsizing, it's becoming harder and harder for customers to find someone to help them. Ask yourself (and your staff) why you really want to keep them out of a particular area. If valuable materials are lying around unsupervised, the signs make sense, but if staff just don't want to be bothered with the public, you may want to reconsider. Most of us no longer have the luxury of hermetically sealed back rooms, and I'm not sure this was ever a useful policy. Most staff members nowadays have some interaction with the public and should be available when needed. Of course, there will always be areas that must be kept closed to the public, but instead of a negatively worded sign, maybe you might have one that reads "Please knock before entering" or "This door is kept locked. Please see librarian for assistance."

NOTE

1. Garet Nelson, Laurel Stanley, David Eyman, and Peggy Seiden, "Planning and Strategy for Setting Up and Operating Academic Libraries in Temporary Quarters: Experiences of Two Northeast Colleges" (1996), Education Resources Information Center, ED 410956.

SIGNAGE RESOURCES

Bosman, Ellen, and Carol Rusinek. "Creating the User-Friendly Library by Evaluating Patron Perceptions of Signage." *RSR Reference Services Review* 25, no. 1 (1997): 71–82.

Boyd, Debra R. "Creating Signs for Multicultural Patrons." In *Multicultural Acquisitions,* ed. Karen Parrish and Bill Katz, 61–66. New York: Haworth, 1993.

Brandon, K. C. "Wayfinding in Libraries." *PNLA Quarterly* 66, no. 4 (Summer 2002): 7–8.

Johnson, C. R. "Signage and the ADA." In *Library Buildings, Equipment, and the ADA: Compliance Issues and Solutions; Proceedings of the LAMA Buildings and Equipment Section Preconference,* 48–52. Chicago: American Library Association, 1996.

Leisner, A. B. "Not Fit for Print—Are Libraries Sexist? [Library Signs]." *Against the Grain* 11, no. 3 (June 1999): 80.

Naylor, B. "Just a Minute—[Redirecting Library Users with Signage]." *Library and Information Update* 1, no. 1 (April 2002): 21.

"Orientation: Building Independence among Young Users." *School Library Media Activities Monthly* 13, no. 1 (September 1996): 34–36.

Ragsdale, Kate W., and Donald J. Kenney. *Effective Library Signage: A SPEC Kit.* Washington, DC: Association of Research Libraries, Office of Management Services, 1995.

Singer, Len, and John M. Ritz. "Wayfinding: Symbols and Signs That Send Us on Our Way; Resources in Technology." *Technology Teacher* 56, no. 3 (November 1996): 16–20.

Smitshuijzen, Edo. *Signage Design Manual.* Baden: Lars Müller, 2007.

Sommerhoff, Emilie Worthen. "Signs of the Times." *Facilities Design and Management* 18, no. 1 (January 1999): 40–44.

Moving In and Getting Settled

By this point in your project, you and the staff are probably showing signs of wear. Your tempers may be somewhat frayed, and you're thinking about joining the International Association for the Annihilation of Architects and Interior Designers. You may need to stop periodically and make yourself realize that things are really going pretty well. You've averted innumerable catastrophes, and you feel some assurance that a reasonably functional library will soon emerge.

CONSIDER THE STAFF

Remember the comment in the Tips section about keeping lots of chocolate on hand? You and your staff need plenty of TLC. Be sure you don't take your frustrations out on them, and in the midst of your agonies, don't separate yourself from their world. Of course, their usual complaints and frustrations are going to seem petty when compared with yours. However, you may not be delegating enough of the new building oversight duties to make them feel fully involved. Just because the building phase is over, there's still a lot to be done. The staff will feel much more ownership in and appreciation for the new building if they have a "piece of the action."

If you have been imagining that once moving day is over you will be able to sink back in your new color-coordinated executive chair and relax, I'm afraid I have some rather unpleasant news for you. This chapter begins with moving day, but as with the real world, it does not end there. The first year in a new building can be as stressful as the year or years leading up to the move. No new building is free from flaws, and you will probably be shocked at the number of construction mistakes you will be dealing with.

In my own library building, we dealt with so many small, unexpected restroom problems that I've lost count. For example, restroom doors were inches too short and too narrow. The contractor had simply used oversized hardware to attach doors to stalls, providing no privacy for users whatsoever. It was years before we solved the problem of poorly designed restroom sinks. After numerous "fixes," vanities were still getting waterlogged, causing them to warp and separate from the walls. Yet overall, it turned out to be a pretty good building.

MOVING DAY

Did you know that in business and industry, studies indicate that many of the staff responsible for their company relocation plans are fired, demoted, or have to take a leave of absence due to stress-related illness? If you've ever been a key player in a library move, you probably won't blink an eye at this fact of work life. Even though moving a library may be one of the most stressful experiences known to man or woman, careful planning can minimize the gray hairs and contribute to a smooth transition.

Basics of a Library Move

Every move is different, of course. You may be moving across town or merely down the hall. However, there are basic axioms applicable to most moves.

First, allow sufficient time to plan the move. Moves to libraries of less than 50,000 square feet need six months of planning; those greater than 50,000 square feet take at least twelve months. Considering that you probably have many other full-time duties, it may be necessary to begin planning even earlier.

Next, identify ways to streamline the operation. Weed the collection before the move. Get rid of old files and equipment. Decide what furniture and equipment will be left behind and what will come with you.

Establish clear goals and a concrete, step-by-step plan so you can explain what is happening to movers, construction workers, customers, vendors, and others.

TALE

We went to great effort to find a company that could provide us with cardboard boxes that were long enough to hold one full shelf of books. The plan was to have two students carrying each box. They would carry the box from the old library to the new library, which was about a block away. Other students would be loading the boxes and unloading them onto shelves. The plan seemed very well organized. Nothing would get out of order. However, by late morning we noticed that many of the carrying teams began to drop out. We called in trucks, and then, of course, the flow of boxes got all out of order. The bottom line: make sure trial runs take every possible factor into consideration.

If at all possible, hire professional library movers, even if this means additional costs associated with bringing them in from out of town. If you are unable to hire professional library movers, at least contract with an experienced, reliable local mover and work with the supervisor to develop methods for keeping boxes in order.

Assign staff to work with movers and see that boxes and shelves are clearly labeled.

Prepare Your Battle Plan

The preceding tale makes it clear that it may not be wise to depend too heavily on volunteers (or conscripted custodians) who lack the training, experience, and stick-to-it-ivity to do a professional job, but funds are often depleted by the end of the project and you may have few options. If professional library movers are out of the question, then Plan B should be a respected local moving company. If funds are unavailable for that option, consider where you can obtain trucks and strong arms without saddling the library with expensive liability issues.

Do not use library staff members as movers. Of course, you will want to protect everyone from injury, but bear in mind that the average age of a typical library staff member is considerably older than in most other occupations. Studies differ, but it's safe to assume that many or most of the people working in your library are in their fifties. This is a period when back problems are rampant. Back injuries are hugely expensive, as are lawsuits. Make it clear to staff (preferably in writing) that no one who has any concerns about his or her back should be lifting boxes. Remember that such admonitions are meaningless if there isn't a system in place for getting the job done without staff members being made to feel guilty or useless.

Alternatives to Professional Movers

If your project consists of a new addition or a renovation, your task will be much lighter than if you're moving into a brand-new building. You can still lose valuable materials and equipment if the move goes awry, but in general, a somewhat more relaxed approach is possible. By contrast, a move from one building to another on the other side of town must be planned long in advance like a military campaign. Absolutely nothing can be left to chance. It is hard to overemphasize the value of experienced library movers. If, however, professional movers are out of the question, consider how else you can get the job done. Are work crews available from a low-security prison or honor farm? What about nonprofit job programs in your community?

Just make sure that agencies carry liability insurance on their workers. Of course, your community will want to pitch in by lending their muscles and enthusiasm to the library. If the old and new library buildings are close enough for a "chain gang" of volunteers, it can be a lot of fun and a good way of increasing enthusiasm for the new library. However, you will do well to consider it more a public relations activity than a practical way of moving the library. Experienced librarians will tell you that you can move about 10,000 items with a chain of volunteers. The rest of the work will probably need to be done by paid employees. City managers and university administrators who have seen photos of smiling community members passing books along the chain may not understand that this is not a replacement for professional movers. Library moves are more difficult and complicated than most, so it is essential that you communicate this fact of library life early in the planning process.

Plan Every Detail

Whether or not you use professional movers, work out a clear, detailed plan for boxing, transporting, and reshelving the collection and give it the time and attention of the D-day landing. Meet often with library staff to plan the move and to make sure they feel personally involved. Delegate as much responsibility as possible. Set up a staff committee on moving to define issues, set priorities, identify schedule conflicts, solve problems, and disseminate information. Be sure that all the details of telephone and data lines have been worked out long before the actual move and that the lines are ready to be activated on moving day. A week in a new building with no phones is not an experience anyone would enjoy.

TIPS

After the contractor released the building, the staff supervised the loading of all the boxes onto book trucks. Then we supervised the unloading in the new area. After completing the move, we checked the physical location of the boxes on the shelves with the shelving list.

We were closed to the public for a week during the actual move, but otherwise we offered minimal service for a week on either side of the move.

Ideally, if you can close during the move, you should do it. If you have to provide service, try to keep it to a minimum during the move. Our patrons were very understanding, and we were able to keep the worst of the disruption to one week.

Don't be misled by a "move-in date"—this will definitely be shoved back at least once and probably two to three times. Once you have moved you are still not finished; you will soon discover all the "little" things left undone: scratched, dented signage that can't be read or that is in the wrong place, and so on. Contractors will be interrupting you for several weeks or months after you've moved in. Be prepared.

Temps make great book movers and are much cheaper if you have a good supervisor.

HEALTH HAZARDS OF A NEW BUILDING

As you prepare to move into your beautiful new building and begin joyously inspecting its nooks and crannies, your nose suddenly twitches and you come down to earth with a thud. The building smells! If it were not so crude, you might even say it stinks! What you smell is off-gassing from many of the construction materials used in a modern building. These include

- carpet pile releasing irritating microscopic fibers
- carpet adhesives
- carpet backing that contains styrene butadiene latex

- volatile organic compounds such as paints
- glues used to bind pressed-wood products

Paints, adhesives, and carpets all exude gases as part of the curing process. Though unpleasant, the smell is not really the problem. Paints and some adhesives may smell quite strong, but in a short while, the odor will disappear without creating any major problems. What can be far more dangerous, however, are materials having a high content of volatile organic compounds (VOCs) like bromide and formaldehyde. If curing proceeds at its own pace, most of the gases are gone by the time you move into the new building.

Unfortunately, however, many materials are covered up soon after they are applied, thus decreasing the airflow to them. Exposure to air is essential to the curing process, but in modern construction, paint that might cure in twenty-four hours under normal conditions may take several days, depending on temperature and humidity. For example, the colder the material, the longer it takes to cure. Work with your contractor to identify sources of off-gassing and decide if small schedule adjustments can help keep your staff and users healthy. If possible, run the HVAC system for at least two weeks before the move and bring lots and lots of fresh air into the building.

Select a Reasonable Move Date

Your contractor is probably under a lot of pressure to finish the job quickly and move on to another construction project. You and your board or administrators are undoubtedly contributing to the pressure because you have made your plans around specific dates. For example, the new school year is about to begin, or there's only a very small window when the movers are available. When you add to these pressure points the realization that your project will almost inevitably be behind schedule, you have a recipe for environmental illness. In those last few weeks, of course, you're anxious to move. You're in a sort of limbo, and every delay makes you more frustrated. Talk with your contractor about a realistic move date. Of course, you will still have work crews in the building, but don't try to move in the day after the carpet is laid down.

Know What You're Dealing With

At the very beginning of this book, you were encouraged—and perhaps even nagged—to collect installation instructions, operating manuals, and other printed matter on the materials and equipment used in your building. Among the most important of these are material safety data sheets. Manufacturers are usually required by law to make these available and to include information on total off-gassing and volatile components. Once your building is complete, don't lose track of these data sheets. A little research will help you interpret the information you find in them. It is also important to have this information available for use by local fire departments in case of an emergency.

Bay Shore–Brightwaters (N.Y.) Library,
Janice Davis Design, janicedavisdesign.com.
Photo: Janice Davis.

If you have extensive collections of rare books, manuscripts, or other fragile materials, some emissions could cause a reaction. PVC glue, for example, affects most plastics and can ruin paper products as well. (If you're building a repository to house a substantial collection of fragile materials, this book is not adequate to meet your needs. A problem like this one, which is usually just a small annoyance in most libraries, may have devastating consequences in an archive or rare book center.) If you have the impression that yours is an unusual situation with problems during construction that might have let excessive moisture seep into construction materials, you might want to discuss the matter with your contractor. Rental equipment is available for VOC removal that is not extremely expensive. The air in your building can be rapidly recirculated. Desiccant wheels that are coated with a VOC-absorbing material can remove most of the contaminants.

Even if construction has been uneventful and your building is curing on schedule, you might wish to hold off a while before moving in valuable materials or archival collections. In his book *Solid, Safe, Secure: Building Archives Repositories in Australia,* Ted Ling suggests that "before you start bringing records into your new building, you should allow it the opportunity to acclimatise and 'breathe.'"[1] He goes on to recommend that you keep your HVAC system operating normally for at least a couple of weeks before you move in so that any contaminants that were accumulating during the construction phase are removed.

THE SHAKEDOWN PERIOD

The first few months in a new building are by far the most trying. All kinds of unexpected things occur, and you discover dozens of problems you never anticipated. As you walk through the new building each day, you'll probably be mentally kicking yourself that you didn't think of this or that potential problem. Each space will stimulate guilt pangs or feelings of hostility toward the architects or contractors who misinterpreted or deliberately ignored your requests. Stop! Let it go! The building is finished, and although there are still many small improvements you can make, such unproductive musings can destroy your pleasure and sense of accomplishment. You've completed a truly Herculean task. The best thing you can do now is congratulate yourself and your staff and then go on to serve the needs of your users. It is not unusual to find that something that looked fine on paper really doesn't work when paper gives way to bricks and mortar. Of course, you will want to change as little as possible, but control the impulse to be defensive. You can't be right all the time. You also cannot anticipate all the reactions of your users.

Prepare for Water Damage

Over the years, I have become convinced of one particular law of nature. Any new basement will leak or flood the day after you stack boxes in it. After a burst pipe destroyed computer equipment and administrative records in my library, we decided to hold up the move of a half-million-volume storage collection until everyone was fully assured the basement was watertight. Hence, the collection was not moved for several months, during which time absolutely nothing more went wrong. Then at last, the first thousand boxes were delivered and stacked to await shelvers. Within less than twenty-four hours, water came cascading down a wall, puddling over a sizable portion of the basement.

Sooner or later, of course, you're going to have to use the basement for its intended purpose. You can't keep on waiting indefinitely for the evil below-ground gremlin to go away and leave your new building in peace. Hold off as long as possible, and then take precautions. Be sure that all boxes are up on skids or pallets. If you're installing book stacks or warehouse-type shelving, leave the bottom shelves empty. Maybe if you spoil the gremlin's fun, it will go find some other basement to beleaguer.

It's Not Over till It's Over

It seems as if everything will go wrong during your first year of operation. The roof will leak, the HVAC system will be set incorrectly, keys will not open doors, and sewage will erupt into the restrooms. Therefore, you will need to view this entire period as a construction phase. If you imagine that you will be moving into a finished building in which everything will go smoothly, you are dooming yourself and your staff to a year of misery.

The first year of operation is the time when tempers flare. Library staff members anxiously await the move to the beautiful new library, imagining that it will be like heaven. Then moving day comes and goes; staff feel as if they are running on a treadmill, trying to reestablish services, rethink procedures, placate dissatisfied users, and locate hundreds of missing items. Customers may expect the new library to open with all systems functioning perfectly and all the limitations of the old library magically gone.

By this time, the tendency of architects and contractors to blame one another for mistakes has become all but intolerable. When librarians are confronted by errors that would be obvious to a six-year-old child, no one will take responsibility.

Dealing with Conflict

Repeated incidents can create an atmosphere of resentment and hostility. Ideally, we should all realize that these conflicts are inevitable and that the best thing to do is to forgive and forget. Inevitably, the project is behind schedule. Construction crews have not finished their work, and they resent the usurpers who have taken over their building. Annoying people are telling them to wipe their shoes and lower their voices. In my own library, a worker came in with his radio on. The poor man had been repeatedly frustrated by the fussy rules of the newly arrived building occupants, and when irate staff members demanded that he work without the inspiration of his favorite radio station, it was the last straw. He snarled, turned the radio up to full volume, and stomped off.

Some of my colleagues insist that there is a basic, even primeval antagonism between librarians and construction workers. Interpersonal eruptions like the one above are not uncommon. In most cases, the building is not really ready for occupancy, and the presence of outsiders slows down and complicates every task. Treat such problems with professionalism. After all, everyone's goal is to get the building completed quickly with as few problems as possible. Count everything that does work correctly as a blessing and face the fact that this is not the norm.

The Building Coordinator

Long before you ever move in, decide how you will deal with the traumas that will soon be greeting you daily. You will be busy developing services and procedures tailored to the new building. In addition, there will be staff to hire, hordes of new customers to accommodate, emergency plans to devise, and generally enough work to keep you busy twenty-four hours a day. That means you will not have time to argue with the painters who forgot the finish coat in the meeting room or the building engineer who insists your frigid lobby is cozy warm. You will need to appoint a staff member as the official contact with contractors, engineers, security gate vendors, and all those other people who will be trooping into your building, playing loud radios, and dropping cigar butts on new carpet.

I strongly recommend that you appoint a staff member who will serve as your building coordinator. You'll need someone who's good at details, easy to get along with, and who will deal with every problem that arises, one migraine at a time. If you're the library director, don't try to do all of this yourself. You don't have the time, and besides, your nerves are already shot. Choose someone who will be charming but tenacious, who can stay on the telephone from dawn until dusk reporting leaky pipes, broken windows, wobbly chairs, defective cabling, arctic temperatures, and all the rest. Take your coordinator with you when you do the punch list and involve her in meetings with the contractor.

Give the building coordinator's name and phone number to vendors, contractors, and everyone else who will be working in the building. Just make sure that you clarify the types of decisions that require your input. For example, your coordinator may be told that something is impossible. You know from past experience that this is not the end of the conversation, and it may be necessary to find out what "impossible" really means. For example, it may simply mean that a contractor doesn't want to be bothered. Ask that they check in when they come to finish a job or make repairs. Your building paragon is going to have to be assertive but nice. A good "come hither" trick is to have a pot of coffee brewing for good little workers who make their presence known. Keep a sign-in sheet by the coffeepot for times when the building coordinator is out of the library.

MOLD

If you work in a region afflicted by high humidity, you already know all about that gooey gray stuff that poses a constant threat to your collections. Mold, however, does not require a damp environment to prosper. Even if the interior of the new library is exceptionally dry, mold can still thrive on the moisture stored in the materials used to finish interior spaces. New materials can retain moisture for a surprisingly long time, and since everything in the building or addition will be new, it may be providing first-class accommodation for the all-too-common fungus. Thermal insulation is an especially likely host and may already be playing host to the enemy's legions.

The threat of mold should not be treated lightly. Not only can it irreparably damage the collection, but it poses a serious health hazard. Throughout your first year in the new building, check frequently for signs of mold even if it is not a common problem in your area. Purchase a high-quality humidity gauge to measure moisture levels and keep moving it from one area to another. Don't make assumptions about where dampness problems are greatest. Instead, keep track of the locations where you're getting the highest readings and do a little detective work to try to discover the source of the humidity. Make sure your contractor understands what a serious problem moisture poses for a library and report excessive levels while the building is still under warranty.

TIPS

Keep a careful record of maintenance after the building is completed. That way if you have to replace the automatic doors or heating system, that record can be used to get the construction company's insurance to pay for the replacement or, failing that, to disqualify that vendor from supplying the replacement item even if that vendor has the lowest bid.

Remember that some things won't work and may require replacements. One library got the architect's insurance to pay for the replacement of their entire HVAC system—they proved that it had been faulty from the start.

Be prepared for problems throughout the first year. Personnel problems are frequent as a result of the multitude of changes.

Your new space will be so wonderful and such an improvement over the old that you will eventually forget just how you suffered during its construction.

THE GRAND OPENING

After years of planning and daily crises, the actual dedication or grand opening may come as an anticlimax. If you are like most librarians, you are exhausted, having worked day and night to be ready for the festivities. Then you must sit through a ceremony in which everyone else is thanked and congratulated while you and your staff are almost an afterthought.

Anne Turner and Margaret Pelikan's humorous article in *American Libraries* really tells it like it is. They describe the excruciatingly correct behavior required of a library director during the sometimes painful proceedings. They recommend that you wear a "blank expression, varied occasionally by a polite smile" while "listening to the mayor explain how he/she has always loved libraries." They also caution against snarling "when you overhear the board chair telling local reporters how hard he/she personally worked to get the building built." A frosty smile is appropriate for the architect with whom you were "last on friendly terms eighteen months ago when the construction contract was signed."[2]

As you have already discerned, the dedication is unlikely to be the high point of your architectural odyssey. Don't get depressed; get some sleep. Tomorrow is another day, and the worst is over. Sure, you still have contractors in the building, supposedly attending to the myriad items on the punch list. More likely, they're deliberately hammering on drainpipes to hear the melodious notes ringing through the quiet study area, but so what? This, too, shall pass. The job is nearly done, and the time to begin enjoying your new, attractive, spacious, and highly functional library building is at hand.

Psychological Stress

Be prepared for an anticlimax. Will Manley, probably the funniest man in the library profession, has a wonderful column about the library director who has just completed a building project. She has been observed "sitting in her office

and crying for no apparent reason; complaining of numbness . . . reading Dr. Kevorkian's latest 'how-to' book; laughing hysterically . . . and wearing weird clothing." Will advises the concerned secretary that the director is merely experiencing post-building depression syndrome. He chronicles the lofty peaks and valleys of despair characteristic of building projects, like being gradually reduced to accepting a stucco-and-chicken-wire building half the size originally planned, with the nonfiction stack area eliminated. He cautions that the illness may last from two months to two years but promises complete recovery.[3]

It's time now to start putting aside all those frustrations and accusations and guilty qualms that have been a part of your life for the past few years. You did the best you could. You rescued the building from dozens of potential catastrophes and probably failed to prevent quite a few others. If only you knew three years ago what you know now! Well, you couldn't possibly have known. The mix of human, technical, and circumstantial ingredients in your building project was unique. Nostradamus himself couldn't have anticipated all the omissions and commissions and interactions that took place. They could not have all been included in this book, and no amount of burned midnight oil would have made much difference.

Librarians Are Amazing

Anyway, you were magnificent! Your skill at locating information paid off. Imagine how you would have been handicapped if you were not an information professional. However, just because you could locate gigabytes of information on lighting, heating, roofing, and all those other specialty areas, you were under no obligation to consume it all. You had neither the time nor the training to become an instant architect or fledgling electrician.

Speaking of architects and electricians, and all the other people who've been involved in your project, it's probably time to make peace, especially if they've at least made an effort to be somewhat responsive to the library's needs throughout the project. Their jobs have become increasingly complex in recent years, and they're probably finding it very difficult to remain up-to-date. Most never imagined when they entered the business that they would have to become computer experts, and they certainly didn't expect that much of their knowledge would become outdated every few years.

When you stop to think about it, they're really not so different from you. How could you possibly have predicted when you entered library school that you would someday need such sophisticated skills in such a wide variety of subjects? It never ceases to amaze me that we manage to pull off our building projects so successfully. Unfortunately, this is no time to rest on your laurels. Your new library will require a whole new approach to services and collections. You have a library that will serve your users well into the twenty-first century. Now it's time to develop a dynamic program that will do the same. Best of luck!

NOTES

1. Ted Ling, *Solid, Safe, Secure: Building Archives Repositories in Australia* (Canberra: National Archives of Australia, 1998).
2. Anne M. Turner and Margaret Pelikan, "The Proper Dedication Day: Two Directors Who Have Been There Review Excruciatingly Correct Behavior for the Uninitiated," *American Libraries* 21 (1990): 354–56.
3. Will Manley, "Facing the Public: Diary of a Library Building Project," *Wilson Library Bulletin* 63 (1988): 62–63.

LIBRARY MOVING RESOURCE ORGANIZATIONS

American Interfile and Library Relocations
55 Sweenydale Ave.
Bayshore, NY 11706
Toll-free: (800) 426-9901
Phone: (631) 231-3309
Fax: (631) 952-7521
Website: www.americaninterfile.com
E-mail: GHall@americaninterfile.com

Campbell Bros. Movers, Ltd.
55 Midpark Crescent
London, ON NGN 1A9
Ontario, Canada
Toll-free: (800) 265-6015
Phone: (519) 681-5710, ext. 257
Fax: (519) 681-7931
Website: www.campbellbros.com

Hallett and Sons Expert Movers, Inc.
7535 West 59th St.
Summit, IL 60501
Toll-free: (800) 645-6683
Phone: (708) 458-8600
Fax: (708) 458-7116
Website: www.hallettmovers.com

Library Design Systems, Inc.
P.O. Box 750757
Houston, TX 77275
Toll-free: (877) 234-1657
Phone: (713) 869-4075
Fax: (713) 869-4168
Website: www.ldssystems.com

McMurray Stern, Inc.
The Storage Solution Group
15511 Carmenita Rd.
Santa Fe Springs, CA 90670
Phone: (562) 623-3000
Website: www.mcmuraystern.com
E-mail: info@mcstern.com

National Library Relocations, Inc.
70 Bridge Rd.
Central Islip, NY 11749
Toll-free: (800) 486-6837
Phone: (631) 232-2233
Fax: (631) 232-2236
Website: www.nlrbookmovers.com
E-mail: info@nlrbookmovers.com

Office Movers, Inc.
Library Services Division
6500 Kane Way
Elkridge, MD 21075
Toll-free: (800) 331-4025
Phone: (410) 799-3200
Fax: (410) 799-3208
Website: www.omilibraryservices.com

William B. Meyer, Inc.
255 Long Beach Blvd.
Stratford, CT 06615
Toll-free: (800) 873-6393
Phone: (203) 383-6229
Fax: (203) 377-3838
Website: www.williambmeyer.com

Index

Note: In this index, page numbers followed by *t* indicate a Tips or Tales box.